UNDERSTA

POLICING

AND PROFESSIONAL

PRACTICE

UNDERSTANDING POLICING AND PROFESSIONAL PRACTICE

THE PROFESSIONAL POLICING CURRICULUM IN PRACTICE

BARRIE SHELDON AND PETER WILLIAMS
SERIES EDITOR: TONY BLOCKLEY

CRITICAL PUBLISHING

First published in 2022 by Critical Publishing Ltd

British Library Cataloguing in Publication Data
A CIP record for this book is available from the British Library

ISBN: 978-1-914171-95-6

This book is also available in the following ebook formats:
EPUB ISBN: 978-1-914171-96-3
Adobe ebook ISBN: 978-1-914171-97-0

Cover and text design by Out of House Limited
Project Management by Newgen Publishing UK
Printed and bound in Great Britain by 4edge, Essex

To order, or for details of our bulk discounts, please go to our website www.criticalpublishing.com or contact our distributor, Ingram Publisher Services (IPS UK), 10 Thornbury Road, Plymouth PL6 7PP, telephone 01752 202301 or email IPSUK.orders@ingramcontent.com.

Critical Publishing
3 Connaught Road
St Albans
AL3 5RX

www.criticalpublishing.com

Printed on FSC
accredited paper

CONTENTS

ABOUT THE SERIES EDITOR

TONY BLOCKLEY

Tony Blockley is the lead for policing at Leeds Trinity University, responsible for co-ordinating policing higher education, including developing programmes and enhancing the current provision in line with the Police Education Qualification Framework (PEQF) and supporting the College of Policing. He served within policing for over 30 years, including a role as Chief Superintendent and Head of Crime

ABOUT THE AUTHORS

BARRIE SHELDON

Barrie is a policing lecturer with Staffordshire University and has been connected with the Institute of Policing since its inception in 2019. He joined Staffordshire Police in 1972 as a cadet, leaving 32 years later as a senior investigating officer engaged in both operations and policy development, as well as having served as Deputy Police and Crime Commissioner for West Mercia Police.

PETER WILLIAMS

Peter is a senior lecturer within the Liverpool Centre for Advanced Policing Studies at Liverpool John Moores University and programme leader for online distance learning at both undergraduate and postgraduate level. He has also worked as a senior lecturer in policing with Teesside University and as an associate lecturer in criminology for the Open University in Wales. Prior to working in higher education, he was a police officer with Merseyside Police, retiring at the rank of inspector.

FOREWORD

Police professionalism has seen significant developments over recent years, including the implementation of the Vision 2025 and the establishment of the Police Education Qualification Framework (PEQF). There is no doubt that policing has become complex, and that complexity and associated challenges increase day by day with greater scrutiny, expectation and accountability. The educational component of police training and development therefore allows officers to gain a greater understanding and appreciation of the theories and activities associated with high-quality policing provision.

The scholastic element of the Vision 2025 provides an opportunity to engage in meaningful insight and debate around some of the most sensitive areas of policing while also taking the lessons of the past and utilising them to develop the service for the future. While there are many books and articles on numerous subjects associated with policing, this new series – The Professional Policing Curriculum in Practice – provides an insightful opportunity to start that journey. It distils the key concepts and topics within policing into an accessible format, combining theory and practice to provide you with a secure basis of knowledge and understanding.

Policing is now a degree-level entry profession, which has provided a unique opportunity to develop fully up-to-date books for student and trainee police officers that focus on the content of the PEQF curriculum, are tailored specifically to the new pre-join routes, and reflect the diversity and complexity of twenty-first-century society. Each book is stand-alone, but they also work together to layer information as you progress through your programme. The pedagogical features of the books have been carefully designed to improve your understanding and critical thinking skills within the context of policing. They include learning objectives, case studies, evidence-based practice examples, critical thinking and reflective activities, and summaries of key concepts. Each chapter also includes a guide to further reading, meaning you don't have to spend hours researching to find that piece of information you are looking for.

This book provides an underpinning of the role of the Police Constable and the profession of policing, providing an understanding of the foundations of policing, professionalism and its role within the Criminal Justice system. There is no doubt that decision making and the ethics of policing are under scrutiny; the information within this title provides a background and understanding for the reader on which to build.

The book identifies key topics of governance and accountability, professional standards and the changing landscape of policing in the twenty-first century. The book is intended to generate enquiry for the reader, that they will use this title as a foundation for further enquiry to develop their knowledge.

Having been involved in policing for over 40 years, the benefits of these books are obvious to me: I see them becoming the go-to guides for the PEQF curriculum across all the various programmes associated with the framework, while also having relevance for more experienced officers.

Tony Blockley
Discipline Head: Policing
Leeds Trinity University

ACKNOWLEDGEMENTS

Peter Williams would like to thank Moya Ward and Colin Davies OBE from the Liverpool Centre for Advanced Policing at LJMU for their shared knowledge and expertise in relation to the PEQF programme overall and their individual expertise in relation to the history of policing, the criminal justice system and key issues in relation to vulnerability. Their feedback has been invaluable and their freely-given time has been very much appreciated.

Barrie Sheldon would like to acknowledge the expertise, encouragement and support provided by Nick Howe, Phil Lee, and dedicated members of the Institute of Policing Team at Staffordshire University, including the valuable contributions made by Jane Sawyers, Martin Steventon and Sean Paley in providing chapters for this publication. Thanks also goes to Professor Ian Pepper, College of Policing, for the first chapter in this book, and an excellent mentor for me when entering the world of academia back in 2006 at Teesside University.

PART 1
THE CONTEXT OF PROFESSIONAL POLICING

CHAPTER 1
THE PROFESSION OF POLICING

IAN PEPPER

LEARNING OBJECTIVES

AFTER READING THIS CHAPTER YOU WILL BE ABLE TO:

- demonstrate a detailed knowledge of the history relating to police education and training;

- understand the components required for a profession of policing;

- understand the role of the College of Policing;

- describe and explain the initial entry routes to policing;

- critically discuss the move to change from a craft to a profession of policing.

INTRODUCTION

In the first half of the twentieth century, Vollmer (1933) discussed moves to professionalise the police service, along with associated opportunities to develop police training programmes which could be linked to college and university education. The concept of policing as a profession benefiting from links to higher education as opposed to being a craft has often been debated (Couper, 1994; Carlan and Lewis, 2009; Paterson, 2011; Green and Gates, 2014; Cordner, 2016). Greenwood (1957) suggests that any profession should have five distinct elements: a systematically developed and organised body of knowledge; authority to use professional judgement to advise a client; sanction by the community to use formal and informal powers; ethical codes of practice which ensure the provision of a service to whoever requests it; and finally a culture of professional practice. Green and Gates (2014) add self-regulation and accountability to an ever-evolving list of characteristics which could be required for a profession. Greenwood (1957) suggests examples of professions including architects, clergy, lawyers, professors, surgeons and teachers.

Neyroud (2012) adds to the debate of policing being either a craft or profession, concluding that in the twenty-first century, there is a need to recognise policing as a profession akin to that of the clergy, lawyers, teachers etc. He recommends the establishment of a single professional body for the police service which is outwardly focused; driven by the interests of the public; committed to ethical leadership, equality and human rights; develops the required professional standards, principles and values; and establishes the best qualifications for policing to help the police serve the public, along with the development of new knowledge and evidence to support policing (Neyroud, 2012). Across England and Wales, the police service has adopted degree-level study for new police constables and continues to embed evidence-based practice in order to advance the recognition of policing as a profession (Pepper et al, 2021).

This chapter describes and discusses the evolution of higher education qualifications for the police service, along with the linked requirement for development of new knowledge at the forefront of the discipline of policing, both of which are cornerstones required for establishing formal recognition of the profession of policing.

DISCUSSION

Vollmer (1933) discusses how the changing nature and new methods of policing adopted in the early twentieth century across the United States led to the requirement to move from either little or no formal training for new recruits to broader, formally recognised and co-ordinated policing-related training and education for both the new recruits and more specialist policing roles. Punch (2007) describes how historical documentation reveals how police constables in the UK were traditionally not well educated. Bitner (1970) highlights the important need for the development of further scholarship to support policing along with the co-ordination of the content for both training and educational programmes, as this would assist in enabling a move from a craft of policing to the provision of a professional status for those involved in policing. Moreover, Punch (2007) identifies the positive benefits for the police service and its culture of both recruiting those who have tertiary educational qualifications and encouraging those already serving to attend university. There is also recognition by the UK government (2019) that the evolving challenges faced by policing require a future workforce that can also evolve, learning on the way, solving problems, and not only use their experience gained from the craft of policing but also work with the evidence base.

The need to transform an existing culture of 'in-house' police training across England and Wales to embrace broader professional development and educational partnerships with both further and higher education is recommended by Neyroud (2012). Early twentieth-century approaches to developing formal educational curricula for a two-year college course for new or aspiring police recruits in the United States led to a diploma in police administration (Vollmer, 1933). The proposed programme content reflected the requirements for policing at that time in the United States and included core subjects such as English, psychology, political science and sociology along with electives such as typing, German language and commerce (Vollmer, 1933). Bitner (1970) suggests that professional schools focusing on policing should teach well-defined and justified fields of study, but it is less important that they learn specific facts than they learn more about transferrable techniques, methods and problem solving; he agreed though that those studying should achieve at least a two-year college degree. Couper (1994) goes further, suggesting that the recognition of the profession of policing will not happen until a baccalaureate degree is required for recruits. In addition, Sherman (1978) suggests that any undergraduate policing programmes should emphasise the importance, complexities and ethical dilemmas faced daily by police constables.

The College of Policing was established as the professional body for the police service across England and Wales in December 2012, with a remit to support all those who work in policing (College of Policing, 2020a). Building on a broad government agenda to recognise the profession of policing and a significant body of knowledge as to the constituents of a profession, the College of Policing (2020a) has three primary and complementary functions.

1. Establish and maintain the educational requirements for policing, ensuring quality and the recognition of professional expertise.

2. Build knowledge of what really works in policing so that in time evidence-based practice can replace custom.

3. Set the standards for policing and the service through, for example, the implementation of Authorised Professional Practice and a Code of Ethics to ensure standards of professional behaviour.

Neyroud (2012) details the importance of developing a defined professional qualifications framework to be used as a means of enhancing the specialist knowledge and skills required for those involved in neighbourhood or response policing and for investigators. Fleming and Rhodes (2018) highlight the importance of police constables possessing the ability to blend knowledge gained from the practical craft of policing with both political and evidence-based underpinning knowledge, while Greenwood (1957) discusses how the necessary acquisition of professional skills requires prior or simultaneous understanding and mastery of the underlying theory which applies to the particular skill in question. Pepper and McGrath (2019) also identify the importance of developing much broader employability skills within undergraduate policing programmes, which can be applied across a variety of workplaces. For example, employers indicate the ongoing demand for employees who have critical thinking skills such as being able to identify problems and opportunities, reflecting on professional practice, being open to adopting new perspectives and making decisions based on available information (Cottrell, 2017).

Pepper and McGrath (2019) describe how in 2016 the College of Policing proposed a range of initial entry routes to joining the police service as a constable, as a result establishing a coherent and standardised Policing Education Qualifications Framework (PEQF) which leads to degree-level study and qualifications. Establishing such a standardised and co-ordinated qualifications framework for policing is an important step linking higher education with the knowledge, understanding and practical skills required for contemporary policing (Wood, 2020b). It is clear that all those involved in policing must be consistently trained to the same high standards, equipped with the skills to deal with constantly evolving crime types, while adopting a problem-solving and evidence-based approach to their daily work (UK Government, 2019).

With the announcement by the UK government in October 2019 of an additional 20,000 police officers over three years of recruitment (which does not take account of similar numbers of new constables who are also required to replace those leaving or retiring from the service), the co-ordination and standardisation of education, training and qualifications is even more important to ensure that all the new police constables are equipped to police effectively well in to the twenty-first century and their professional status established and recognised.

The Quality Assurance Agency (QAA, 2014; UKSCQA & QAA, 2018) assure the quality and standardisation of requirements for the awarding of degrees across higher education; these are termed level 6 awards in the Framework for Higher Education Qualifications (FHEQ). All learners achieving the award of an honours degree must be able to demonstrate a systematic understanding and detailed knowledge of their chosen field of study (in this case policing). They must also demonstrate their ability to utilise specific techniques of inquiry within their discipline, along with the conceptual understanding to be able to critically discuss and solve problems; they must also adopt ideas which are at the leading edge of their study (QAA, 2014). They must also have an understanding of current research and know the limits of their own knowledge, as a result being able to manage their own learning and development (QAA, 2014). Paterson (2011) discusses how across many countries the adoption of higher education by the police service has been significant in developing among those serving a range of transferable skills, the ability to deal with the complexity of demands placed on policing and an ethos of lifelong learning.

As the professional body for policing, the College of Policing act as the custodian of both the National Policing Curriculum (NPC) and the PEQF, which in effect is an educationally levelled and professionally focused education, training and professional development framework. The PEQF programmes form part of the NPC and the College of Policing grant licences to quality-assured educational providers, and in some cases their police force partners, to deliver the programmes. The range of licensed programmes include those which are solely classroom-based knowledge and understanding for learners who aspire to join the police service and taught solely by providers of higher education. There are also those programmes which are a blend of knowledge and understanding along with work-based tutoring for those already employed by a police force; these are taught in partnerships established between a police force and a higher education provider.

The PEQF initial entry to policing programmes which lead to the award of an honours degree are:

1. Professional Policing Degree (PPD);

2. Police Constable Degree Apprenticeship (PCDA).

These degree-level programmes are complemented by other initial routes of entry to policing mapped to the PEQF, which include:

3. Degree Holder Entry Programme (DHEP);

4. Detective Degree Holder Entry Programme (DDHEP);

5. Police Community Support Officer (PCSO);

6. Special Constables Learning Programme (SCLP).

This chapter now explores each of these programmes in more detail.

1. PROFESSIONAL POLICING DEGREE (PPD)

Previously referred to as the 'Pre-join degree', the Professional Policing Degree (PPD) is a three-year full-time (or up to six-year part-time) traditional degree for those who aspire to join the police service but are not yet employed. This degree is funded by the individual learner for the duration of their studies. The degree is based within a higher education institution and is focused on developing within the classroom both the knowledge and understanding required for employment as a police constable. Subjects studied are informed by the NPC and include the role of the police constable, the criminal justice system, criminal law, criminology, criminal justice, roads policing, problem solving and research methods. The assessments are academically focused and include a research project.

Many higher education providers also encourage volunteering to assist with the development of employability skills; such volunteering is of course achievable within the policing environment as, for example, a special constable or police support volunteer. The benefits to an individual's employability are discussed further by Pepper and McGrath (2019).

It is notewothy that successful completion and the award of a BSc (Hons) or BA (Hons) in Professional Policing does not guarantee recruitment by a police force. Applications to join the police service should normally be made within five years of graduation. Those successful in their applications join their chosen force and complete any updates to their education along with their practical training, including independent patrol status (IPS) and then full operational competence (FOC). Once employed, graduates with a BSc (Hons) or BA (Hons) in Professional Policing serve a two-year probationary period in order to be confirmed in post as a substantive police constable.

2. POLICE CONSTABLE DEGREE APPRENTICESHIP (PCDA)

By the summer of 2022, the PCDA completely replaced its predecessor, the Initial Police Learning and Development Programme (IPLDP) which led to the award of a level 3 diploma (equivalent to an A level or BTEC level 3 National Qualification).

The PCDA initial route of entry to joining as a police constable is work based and primarily for those who have not already studied for and hold an honours degree. Learners are employed by a police force, attested (sworn in) and paid as a police constable from the start of their studies. The new police constables complete a fully funded, full-time (part-time options may be available) work-focused higher education and work-based apprenticeship programme. This includes both classroom academic study informed by the NPC and work-based learning on the frontline of policing, working shifts covering 24 hours a day, seven days a week. The academic learning includes study relating to response, community and roads policing, use of intelligence in policing, the conduct of investigations, evidence-based practice, research methods, problem solving and digital policing. The learning is applied in the practical work-place environment over the three years of the degree apprenticeship. Throughout, learners are supported by specially trained and experienced police frontline tutors to complete first independent patrol status (IPS) and then full operational competence (FOC) as multi-skilled and competent police constables working predominantly in either response policing or community policing.

On successful completion of FOC, academic assessments, an evidence-based research project and end point assessment (EPA), learners are awarded a BSc (Hons) or BA (Hons) in Professional Policing Practice and (having also served the required three years' probation during their degree-level study) become a substantive police constable.

3. DEGREE HOLDER ENTRY PROGRAMME (DHEP)

This initial route of entry to joining as a police constable is for those who already hold a degree in any subject and builds upon the knowledge, understanding and skills they have already developed as a graduate (such as research methods, the ability to critically analyse and solve problems). Employed by a police force from day one, attested and paid as a police constable, learners study a fully funded, part-time work-focused higher education and work-based educational programme.

The learners study in the classroom, informed by the NPC, and do work-based learning on the frontline of policing, working shifts covering 24 hours a day, seven days a week. The academic learning includes study relating to response, community and roads policing, the use of police intelligence, the conduct of investigations, evidence-based practice and digital policing. The learning is applied in the practical environment over the two years of the part-time graduate diploma. Throughout, learners are supported by specially trained and experienced police frontline tutors to complete first independent patrol status (IPS) and then full operational competence (FOC) as multi-skilled and competent police constables working predominantly in response policing or community policing.

On successful completion of FOC and the associated academic assessments, learners are awarded a Graduate Diploma in Professional Policing Practice and, after having served the required two years' probation during their study, are substantive police constables.

4. DETECTIVE DEGREE HOLDER ENTRY PROGRAMME (DDHEP)

In 2017, Her Majesty's Inspectorate of Constabulary and Fire & Rescue Service, the national body responsible for inspecting police forces, identified a nationwide shortage of in excess of 5000 detectives, leading to crimes not being investigated (HMICFRS, 2017). As a result, the National Police Chiefs' Council (NPCC) and the College of Policing were asked to explore options to address the shortage.

Part of the medium-term resolution of the shortage was to adapt the DHEP entry route to policing for graduates to focus on a qualified detective pathway from the start. This initial route of entry to joining as a detective constable is for those who already hold a degree in any subject and builds upon the knowledge, understanding and skills they already have as a graduate (such as research methods and problem solving). Employed by a police force, attested and paid as a constable from the start, learners study a fully funded, part-time work-focused higher education and work-based educational programme.

During the programme, learners' study includes response, community and roads policing, the use of police intelligence, investigations, evidence-based practice and digital policing, and they must also study and successfully complete the National Investigators Exam (NIE) and the Professionalising Investigation Programme (PIP) level 2. The learners study both in the classroom and do work-based learning on the frontline of policing working shifts covering 24 hours a day, seven days a week. The academic learning is applied in the practical environment over the two years of the part-time graduate diploma. Throughout, learners are supported by specially trained and experienced police frontline tutors to complete first independent patrol status (IPS) and then full operational competence (FOC) as detective constables working on investigations.

On successful completion of FOC and the associated academic assessments, learners are awarded a Graduate Diploma in Professional Policing Practice and (after having served the required two years' probation during their study) become substantive, competent and accredited detective constables.

5. POLICE COMMUNITY SUPPORT OFFICER (PCSO)

Police Community Support Officers (PCSOs) play a vital community-based public-facing uniformed role within policing. There are two entry routes for PCSOs: an apprenticeship or a standalone higher education certificate. Both routes of initial entry are the same in that the content of their programme of study is directed by the NPC; they are both completed over 12 months (College of Policing, 2020b). Having successfully completed the taught and workplace learning and assessment, the PCSO programmes culminate in a level 4 award. This award is either a certificate in community policing practice (if taught and accredited by a higher education institution in partnership with a force) or a diploma in community policing practice (if taught and accredited by an Ofqual-regulated awarding organisation) (College of Policing, 2020b).

If a PCSO chooses to join the regular police service, there is the opportunity to have their level 4 learning and subsequent experience recognised as prior learning within a new police constable role. It is therefore possible that, as new police constables, PCSOs with relevant awards may not have to re-study some elements of their learning.

6. SPECIAL CONSTABLES LEARNING PROGRAMME (SCLP)

Members of the special constabulary have a long history of supporting policing in a variety of situations, donating many hours in their voluntary roles. In 2019, the initial training for a special constable was migrated from its predecessor (Initial Learning for Special Constables) to the Special Constables Learning Programme (SCLP). This programme has been aligned to the first year of the PCDA at educational level 4 and volunteers study this part time as a work-based programme for approximately 18 to 30 months. This programme is assessed within the workplace across up to five phases (phase one learning, accompanied patrol status, directed patrol status, phase two learning and qualified special constable status) (College of Policing, 2020c). Although the special constables can opt to remain at the accompanied patrol status, the qualified special constable status provides evidence that the special constable can perform independent patrol in their own right within their chosen area of specialism.

Although not formally accredited as an academic award at level 4, those volunteers who study the various phases, and who choose to join the regular police service, can have their learning and subsequent experience recognised within their employed policing role so that they don't have to re-study elements of their learning (College of Policing, 2020c).

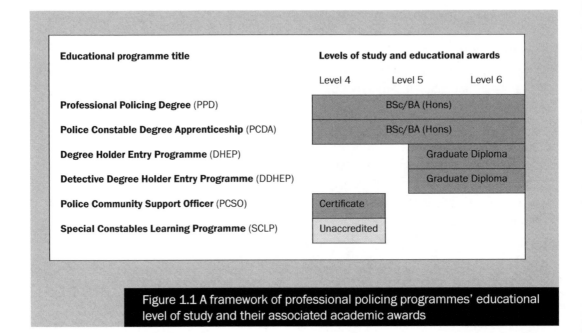

Educational programme title	Levels of study and educational awards		
	Level 4	Level 5	Level 6
Professional Policing Degree (PPD)	BSc/BA (Hons)		
Police Constable Degree Apprenticeship (PCDA)	BSc/BA (Hons)		
Degree Holder Entry Programme (DHEP)			Graduate Diploma
Detective Degree Holder Entry Programme (DDHEP)			Graduate Diploma
Police Community Support Officer (PCSO)	Certificate		
Special Constables Learning Programme (SCLP)	Unaccredited		

Figure 1.1 A framework of professional policing programmes' educational level of study and their associated academic awards

As the various initial entry routes describe, the opportunities to use the benefits of higher education as a catalyst to recognise the profession of policing have been extended to other roles beyond the police constable. The development of such nationally recognised qualifications for policing is highlighted by Green and Gates (2014) as one of a number of core components for establishing a profession. As an example, as well as new police constables achieving level 6 awards on the FHEQ, PCSOs also achieve a formal qualification at level 4. Such a qualification recognises the learner's limited knowledge of the underlying concepts of the discipline and an ability to solve problems in their subject area, accurately communicate and take some personal responsibility (QAA, 2014).

Once new police recruits have completed their education, workplace training and probation (of either two or three years' full time, or part-time equivalent), becoming substantive and competent constables, a large number of lateral career options are then available such as working as a specialist in response, community, firearms, intelligence, counter-terrorism or roads policing. There are also opportunities to progress vertically through national promotion processes to sergeant and above.

In 2021, the police workforce across England and Wales numbered slightly over 135,000 police officers across all ranks from police constable to chief constable, with just over 9200 PCSOs and 9100 special constables (Home Office, 2021a). All new recruits to these roles are exposed to the culture and profession of policing, and for many also through the educationally levelled initial entry routes described in this chapter. However, in order to further recognise and embed the profession of policing across the services culture, it is important that those already serving within these frontline and public-facing roles are also supported in their personal and professional development. To these ends, the College of Policing are making significant strides in the embedding of continuous professional development (CPD) within the police service, ranging from funded bursaries for studies within higher education, the creation of a professional development platform in collaboration with higher education to assist in the recognition of prior learning and experience, to the provision of online CPD events.

In addition to the police officers, PCSOs and special constables, in 2021 there were also just under 76,000 police staff and designated officers, along with 8000 police support volunteers within policing (Home Office, 2021a). These employees and volunteers are engaged in a variety of roles ranging from civilian investigators and coroners' officers to intelligence analysts and administrators, all integral to the day-to-day running and delivery of the service. It is also noteworthy that an additional 5000 people (both police officers and staff) work for the National Crime Agency (Home Office, 2021a). With a few exceptions where either police constables or police staff can perform the functions of the role (such as an investigator), to date the focus of the College of Policing and the PEQF has predominantly been the initial entry to the more public-facing frontline roles such as police constable and PCSO.

It seems clear that the broad profession of policing requires further attention (and can benefit significantly) from higher education (Cordner, 2016). However, one of the challenges faced by the College of Policing regarding wider police family developments across England and Wales, such as establishing standardised higher education initial entry routes for police staff roles, is that these roles are more local in their prerequisites for employment. Police staff roles sometimes require applicants to hold a professional qualification (such as in accountancy), while recruitment processes, selection, deployment and even job titles vary between forces (for example, recent jobs have been advertised in different forces for crime scene investigators, forensic investigators and scenes of crime officers; these are all the same roles). However, once recruited, both local and national CPD is made available and is encouraged.

REFLECTIVE PRACTICE 1.1

LEVEL 5

Consider the various initial entry routes to policing, and identify what additional police constable and police staff roles should be made to professional policing educational programmes within the PEQF and/or FHEQ. At what educational level should such programmes be studied?

The UK government (2019) are clear that the PEQF is essential in ensuring a consistent high-level approach to training for all new police constables, with a timely revision and alignment of other training products. Paterson (2011) discusses how across many countries the adoption of higher education by the police service has been significant in developing, among those serving in whatever capacity, a range of transferable skills, the flexibility to deal with the complexity of demands placed on policing and an ethos of lifelong learning. All of these abilities, along with others described by the QAA (2014) such as taking personal responsibility and making decisions in unpredictable situations, are easily aligned to those qualities possessed by a graduate police constable (or those studying other awards at level 6). In essence, the initial entry routes to policing across England and Wales for aspiring constables, new constables, detectives, PCSOs and special constables formally recognise the benefits to the service and the particular role relating to the evolution of the recognised profession of policing which can be achieved through the adoption of higher education.

The importance of building the evidence base of what works within policing is also an important component in the recognition of the police service as a profession. Creating new knowledge by embedding evidence-based policing (EBP) within the PEQF is described by Brown et al (2018), while Green and Gates (2014) identify the importance of involving police practitioners in the development and growth of a knowledge base. Sherman (1998) suggests that research should assist in guiding the practice of policing. This approach to building knowledge of what works concentrates on making the best use of straightforward approaches to research in controlled policing scenarios by practitioners, further supported by ongoing research into the results achieved by those making the best use of the more basic research in their professional practice. As such, the discipline of policing will always continue to move on, learning and applying something new (Sherman, 1998).

CRITICAL THINKING ACTIVITY 1.1

LEVEL 6

Refer to the following report: College of Policing (2020) *Policing in England and Wales: Future Operating Environment 2040*.

Looking at 'Part 1: Key trends and implications', critically consider the following.

- How would you rank the ten trends in order of importance for affecting police education and training?

- What police education and training would you add for new constables, staff and volunteers studying today's programme to meet the challenges presented by the ten future trends?

The College of Policing (2017a) also provides a broad definition of evidence-based policing (EBP), which focuses upon all those within policing reviewing and implementing the best available evidence to create, inform and challenge policies, practices and decisions. This definition acknowledges that EBP does not necessarily provide specific answers; instead, those working or volunteering within policing should use the available evidence to critically review and reflect on their practice, enabling an innovative approach to their work. The two honours degree routes of the PPD (Professional Policing Degree) and the PCDA contain the requirement for learners to both understand EBP and to complete undergraduate research projects. These research projects provide a unique opportunity for the service to co-ordinate research of value that should not be overlooked. They are often focused on resolving a specific policing problem completed by those studying the PCDA who are practitioners working within the profession. This is especially an opportunity to take into account the approach of Sherman (1998) of the production of hundreds of straightforward methodologically sound but basic research projects which are ethically approved; these projects can gather data and provide outcomes which can then be further explored and build the evidence base for the profession. Boulton et al (2020) suggest that in order for the service and higher education to make the best use of such research projects, the approach should use mixed methods for the research, the research should be transferrable and various types of opportunities should be used to disseminate the findings to different audiences of practitioners and academics. Pepper et al (2021) discuss a number of the opportunities and challenges presented by embedding EBP into the PCDA and professional practice.

Consider the following evidence-based policing feature which depicts how the evidence base might inform decision making.

EVIDENCE-BASED POLICING

Having recently completed Independent Patrol Status (IPS), a new police constable has commenced studying their second year of the PCDA. One afternoon during a work-based phase, the constable has been deployed on foot patrol in a local community.

On arrival, the constable noticed a small group of teenagers gathering immediately outside a local shop; the group of teenagers appear to be consuming alcohol and may be causing a nuisance to passers-by. The constable needs to consider, and make a decision, whether what they can see is contributing (or likely to contribute) to anti-social behaviour or is possibly even a crime.

National and local guidelines aim to tackle such anti-social behaviour, putting victims and communities first. Although there has not yet been a complaint, the constable decides that

$\longrightarrow$

this needs to be dealt with. Perhaps the solution is to issue dispersal orders to those teenagers in the group; failure to comply can result in imprisonment and/or a fine.

However, from their studies, the constable knows that when considering an appropriate response, the evidence base suggests that dispersal orders can alienate young people and even put them at risk (Cockcroft et al, 2016). Doss et al (2015) suggest that the effects of communicating with those involved at the right time on a professional level is likely to help reach a mutual understanding, in this case of the possible nuisance they are causing, enabling an appropriate resolution to be reached which is likely have a better outcome for all involved.

As a result of a professional discussion with the teenagers it is possible that they will not become alienated but are more likely to be positive towards the police, and will not be put at risk or become vulnerable. This may assist in enabling the development of the police constable's reputation within the community (and possibly the support of the shopkeeper). It is also possible for the police constable to reflect upon their use of discretion in relation to a dispersal order within their portfolio to evidence FOC.

Now consider the following policing spotlight, which presents you with a scenario and discussion point.

POLICING SPOTLIGHT

As a new substantive police constable having just completed a DHEP (achieving a Graduate Diploma in Professional Policing Practice) and two years of probation, you are asked to assist in policing a small-scale demonstration.

A small group of pro-fox hunters are demonstrating about what they feel was the injustice of a custodial sentence for animal cruelty relating to a particular hunt. The demonstration will walk from outside of the courts to the prison about 1000 metres away. In the briefing from the sergeant you are advised that intelligence suggests a group of anti-hunt lobbyists will gather on route to air their views. Your role is to escort the demonstration with colleagues in order to avoid any breach of the peace or social disorder.

As you set off walking near to the pro-hunt group you pass under a railway bridge in shadow where anti-hunt lobbyists are gathered on the pavement. You are between both groups when a person steps off the pavement, walking towards the group you are escorting.

- Discuss what, as the constable, you should do.

In the above policing spotlight, initially the constable needs to pause, look and think, and then apply the six elements of the National Decision Making Model (NDM) (College of Policing, 2014a).

1. Everything must be underpinned by the Code of Ethics and professional behaviour.

2. Gather the available information (what is known and what is happening).

3. Assess the threat and risk to the constable and others (do they need to act now? what could be the impact of actions?).

4. Consider police powers; policy and legislation are available.

5. What options and actions are available? (is a threat immediate? what time and resources are available?).

6. Take appropriate action and review (responding, recording and monitoring).

REFLECTIVE PRACTICE 1.2

LEVEL 6

Think about your area of specific interest in operational policing and what you are studying. Plan a policing topic or operational problem that you might focus on for your final research project.

CONCLUSION

There seems no doubt that the wholesale adoption of high-level qualifications for new recruits to policing will gradually have an impact within the service on the recognition of the profession. This will become even more evident as those who have completed the level 6 awards progress within their careers either laterally to specialist roles or vertically via promotion. In addition to the embedding of a code of ethics and expected standards of professional behaviour, the impact will be positive. Externally to the police service there is already a shift towards an expectation that policing is recruiting and retaining professionals able to operate with autonomy and accountability (APCC and NPCC, 2016).

Horizon scanning suggests that in 20 years, the police service will be operating in more complex environments where artificial intelligence, robotics and technology will transform workplaces (College of Policing, 2020d). As such the policing workforce of the future will need to operate flexibly and with agility, using not only traditional policing skills, but also developing a portfolio of technical skills to keep pace with emerging technologies. It will also be necessary to embrace interpersonal skills, such as creativity and the ability to network and lead collaborative partnerships (College of Policing, 2020d), all of which are expectations of those who hold level 6 awards.

However, there are also some challenges which may result in a state of inertia regarding the recognition of the profession of policing. As Tong and Hallenberg (2018) suggest, the adoption of technology may present hurdles (as well as opportunities) regarding consistency of approach across forces, the licensing and quality assurance of the educational programmes, changes to funding and visions of senior leaders, along with the training and education capacity of the service and educational providers to meet the demands of the workforce.

There is also no doubt that whichever higher education route to a policing career is chosen, transferring what has been learnt within the classroom to the operational context of professional policing practice will be challenging. However, within the initial routes where the learner is employed (such as PCDA and DHEP) there is also an opportunity for the learners to bring their operational experiences into the classroom for the benefit of all stakeholders involved in the educational process.

The PEQF will assist in the evolution of the policing profession if it continues to adapt to meet the needs of the service and is informed by wide-ranging and broad approaches to research and development of the evidence base (Brown et al, 2018). The implementation of the initial routes of entry are a good starting point to recognise the profession of policing, but in order to achieve success the PEQF must include opportunities for the whole police workforce to engage in professional development at the appropriate educational level. Pepper and McGrath (2019) suggest that the PEQF must be involved in ongoing consultations between the police service, higher education and the professional body. Such an approach will ensure the most appropriate education and training is made available to recognise the profession of policing and meet the requirements of contemporary and future policing.

SUMMARY OF KEY CONCEPTS

This chapter has explored some of the following key concepts:

- the history of police education and training;

- the components required to establish a profession of policing;

- the role of the professional body for the police service across England and Wales, the College of Policing;

- the range of initial entry routes to policing, with a focus on routes to joining as a police constable;

- the evolution of policing from a craft to the recognition as a profession.

CHECK YOUR KNOWLEDGE

1. What are two of the requirements for establishing a profession?

2. Who first discussed moves to professionalise the police service with links to higher education?

3. What are the three primary functions of the College of Policing?

4. Which initial entry routes to policing lead to the award of a full honours degree?

5. Which organisation is the custodian of the National Policing Curriculum (NPC)?

FURTHER READING

BOOKS

Pepper, I and McGrath, R (eds) (2020) *Introduction to Professional Policing: Examining the Evidence Base*. London: Routledge.
Written by both academics and policing practitioners, this textbook further explores a number of the core knowledge requirements which have been highlighted as key themes within both the Policing Education Qualifications Framework (PEQF) and the National Policing Curriculum (NPC).

Sherman, L (1978) *The Quality of Police Education: A Critical Review with Recommendations for Improving Programs in Higher Education*. Washington, DC: The Police Foundation.
This US text provides additional details of the historical context for the development of programmes for policing linked to higher education, discussing conflicting views on the benefits, quality and needs of the curriculum.

WEBSITES

QAA (2022) *Subject Benchmark Statement for Policing*. [online] Available at: www.qaa. ac.uk/quality-code/subject-benchmark-statements/policing (accessed 7 May 2022).
The Subject Benchmark Statement for Policing describes the type of study and the academic standards expected of graduates in policing. Like benchmarking statements for other academic disciplines, it details what graduates might reasonably be expected to know, do and understand on completion of their studies.

CHAPTER 2

THE FOUNDATION AND STRUCTURE OF THE BRITISH POLICE SERVICE

PETER WILLIAMS

LEARNING OBJECTIVES

AFTER READING THIS CHAPTER YOU WILL BE ABLE TO:

- critically evaluate the reasons for the establishment of the British police service;

- demonstrate knowledge of the 'Peelian' principles;

- assess their impact on British policing;

- understand the role of the constable and constabulary independence;

- describe the structures of the contemporary police service.

INTRODUCTION

Several competing theories exist within academia as to the justification for the establishment of the *New Police* in 1829. Within that debate, two key factors emerge on which there is consensus, the uniqueness of the British policing system and the role of Sir Robert Peel in its creation. That uniqueness is as influential now in contemporary Britain as it was in 1829 with the introduction of the Metropolitan Police.

Prior to the inception of the New Police, various models of policing had already existed from the *Watch* to the *Bow Street Runners* and some commentators argue that the New Police were merely a natural next step in the development of that model. However, while we will look at conflicting theories that surround the creation of the New Police, it is to Ireland and Sir Robert Peel's role as Chief Secretary to Ireland that provides a competing view and a key context for understanding the unique exceptional status of the British police service. This chapter focuses on the development of the British police and its unique status given the political concessions implemented by Robert Peel as Home Secretary. However, in order to establish the right context to fully appreciate the political maneuvring, it is necessary to critically review Peel's role into the development of policing in Ireland, starting with the Peace Preservation Force.

PEACE PRESERVATION FORCE

Modern police history begins not in Britain itself but in Ireland, with the passing of the Irish Peace Preservation Act in 1814, when Peel was Irish Secretary (Jeffries, 1952, p 53, cited in Newburn, 2005, p 69).

Robert Peel, still in his mid-twenties, became Chief Secretary to Ireland in 1812 and inherited a situation that threatened the peace and stability of Ireland, in addition to genuine concerns regarding challenges to British sovereignty across the island. He only had a notably inefficient policing system in which members were known as *barneys* to counter it. Furthermore, the Napoleonic Wars had taken their toll on military resources and many units had been withdrawn from Ireland (Williams, 2015).

Therefore, Peel created a new policing model and named it the Peace Preservation Force (PPF). It was deployed initially in Tipperary, but by 1822 had a strength of 2300, operational across sixteen of the most troublesome counties in Ireland (Emsley, 2001). Members of the PPF were nicknamed *Peelers*, a nickname that still exists in Northern Ireland in respect of police officers.

The structure of the PPF was one of a centralised semi-military policing organisation that eventually laid the foundations for the centralised, armed, gendarmerie-style Irish Constabulary (Emsley, 2001) that later became known as the Royal Irish Constabulary (RIC), controlled from Dublin Castle (Brogden, 2005). On the partition of Ireland in 1921, the police in the province of Northern Ireland dropped the name *Irish* and adopted the name *Ulster*, becoming known thereafter as the Royal Ulster Constabulary (RUC), a name that existed until the creation of the present-day force, the Police Service of Northern Ireland (PSNI) in 2001.The PSNI can therefore trace its roots directly to the inception of the PPF and it remains a force with centralised structures, as you will be asked to reflect upon in reflective activity 2.1 below. The structure of the PPF, and latterly the RIC, was a model replicated in some colonial police forces. There are two key features within this model: their links with the military and officers being located in barracks away from the civil population (Brogden, 2005), both of which were critical issues in the inception of the New Police by Robert Peel in 1829.

REFLECTIVE PRACTICE 2.1

LEVEL 4

Conduct an internet search with *PSNI our history* as keywords and look for the link 'A History of Policing in Ireland'. Read through the web page and consider the following questions:

a) For what reason do you feel Robert Peel established the Peace Preservation Force?

b) The structure of the PPF was replicated by the later Irish Constabulary. From what you have read in this chapter, from where do you think Robert Peel took the model of the PPF?

Sample answers are provided at the end of this book.

HOME SECRETARY

Robert Peel became Home Secretary in 1822 and immediately established a parliamentary committee to consider the feasibility of a publicly funded police force. However, Peel was aware that in 1785 a parliamentary bill forwarded by the government led by William Pitt the Younger was met with unyielding opposition, reflecting the power of the City of London in respect of their objections to the bill and the magistracy (Blair, 2009).

The 1822 Parliamentary Select Committee, no doubt to no surprise to Peel himself, effectively rejected the idea. Two extracts from that 1822 report are commonly cited: '*a system of police would make every servant a spy upon his master and all classes of society spies on each other*' (Blair, 2009, p 41).

And furthermore:

> **It is difficult to reconcile an effective system of police with that perfect freedom of action and exemption from interference, which are the great privileges and blessings of society in this country; and Your Committee think that the forfeiture or curtailments of such advantages would be too great a sacrifice for improvements in police, or facilities in detection of crime, however desirable in themselves if abstractly considered.**

(Blair, 2009, p 41)

Defeated, Peel turned his attention to reforms within the criminal law, although evidence indicates his enthusiasm for a professional police force was unabated.

After a brief interlude spent in opposition, Peel again became Home Secretary with the government on this occasion being led by the Duke of Wellington in January 1828, and he reinstated the Select Committee of Enquiry, inquiring into the state of the police in London. However Peel excluded the City of London from the scope of the inquiry, in order to usurp the expected opposition (Blair, 2009). He also avoided the replication of a centralised national force as in Ireland, particularly given the hostility to anything resembling the French model, such as a national gendarmerie and the so-called existence of spies, as reported by the 1822 Committee. The hostility across the country to anything French in the aftermath of the Napoleonic Wars had a significant influence on Peel's eventual plans for a preventative police force, and without doubt affected the development of the British police (Emsley, 2001). By this juncture, Peel was an experienced politician, and his eventual plans revealed some months later in the subsequent parliamentary bill validate the assertion that he was, by now at least, an astute politician and statesman and his bill a creation of political expediency.

The Select Committee was chaired by Peel's fellow member in the House of Commons for Oxford University, T G B Escourt (Emsley, 2003) and included others that were in general agreement with his overall ideas (Emsley, 2001). Not surprisingly, the committee reached conclusions that were conducive to Peel's assertions in respect of a preventative police organisation for London; in April 1829, he introduced the Metropolitan Police Bill, which was approved by Parliament in June 1829 (Emsley, 2003).

In his introductory speech to the House at the first reading stage, Peel referred to figures relating to committal proceedings in the courts, which indicated a rise in crime, broadly via changes to the criminal justice process that had made prosecutions easier. Ironically, these were reforms he had introduced (Emsley, 2003) in the interim period between the two select committees. He also stated the following, setting out his overall justification for the proposals in the bill:

> *I think – and it is useless to disguise the fact that the time has come, when, from the increase in its population, the enlargement of its resources and the multiplied development of its energies, we may fairly pronounce that the country has outgrown her police institutions and the cheapest and safest course will be found to be the introduction of a new mode of protection.*

(Brown, 2014, p xxiv)

Although the statistics in relation to crime began being collected in 1810 and the initial figures were retrospective to 1805, they only referred to committals for trial, which explains why Peel used them. By the mid-1830s they were divided into the following five main categories that have largely remained unchanged:

- *offences against the person;*

- *offences against property involving violence;*

- *offences against property not involving violence;*

- *offences against the currency;*

- *miscellaneous offences.*

Further categories were added as a result of the County and Borough Police Act 1856:

- *indictable offences notified to the police but necessarily resulting in an arrest or being solved;*

- *committals for trial on both indictment and before summary jurisdiction;*

- *the number of individuals convicted and imprisoned.*

(Emsley, 2007)

However, crime that was recorded by the police remained unpublished until 1876, the date when the first national crime statistics were officially made public (Muncie and McLaughlin, 2001). Therefore, Peel could only refer to committals for trial when presenting his proposals to Parliament.

The constables of the Metropolitan Police Force, the first of the New Police, began patrolling at 6pm on Tuesday 29 September 1829 (Blair, 2009, p 43). In doing so, they laid the foundations of a constabulary-style structure that subsequently developed throughout mainland Britain and remains a key feature of policing in Britain today, as do the so-called Peelian principles that accompanied the introduction of the New Police.

PEELIAN PRINCIPLES

Sir Robert Peel is frequently portrayed as a man of considerable foresight due to his steadfastness in finally securing a statutory professional policing service in the form of the Metropolitan Police. This was in addition to his acknowledged skill as a parliamentarian, as mentioned earlier. Accordingly, he is also accredited as the architect of the following set of nine principles of police, commonly referred to as the Peelian principles.

EVIDENCE-BASED POLICING

The nine Peelian principles are as follows.

1. *The basic mission for which the police exist is to prevent crime and disorder.*

2. *The ability of the police to perform their duties is dependent upon public approval of police actions.*

3. *Police must secure the willing co-operation of the public in voluntary observance of the law to be able to secure and maintain the respect of the public.*

4. *The degree of co-operation of the public that can be secured diminishes proportionately to the necessity of the use of physical force.*

5. *Police seek and preserve public favour not by pandering to public opinion but by constantly demonstrating absolute impartial service to the law.*

6. *Police use physical force to the extent necessary to secure observance of the law or to restore order only when the exercise of persuasion, advice and warning is found to be insufficient.*

7. *Police, at all times, should maintain a relationship with the public that gives reality to the historic tradition that the police are the public and the public are the police; the police being only members of the public who are paid to give full-time attention to duties which are incumbent on every citizen in the interests of community welfare and existence.*

8. *Police should always direct their action strictly towards their functions and never appear to usurp the powers of the judiciary.*

9. *The test of police efficiency is the absence of crime and disorder, and not the visible evidence of police action in dealing with it.*

(Police Success Blog, 2021)

While the principles carry the name of Robert Peel, the inference is that they were formulated by Peel during the inchoate phase of the Metropolitan Police Bill. However, Emsley (2014) reminds us that there is no evidence to support the assertion that they were written by Peel or indeed the first two Commissioners of the Metropolitan Police (Emsley, 2014). As Blair (2009) notes, Peel did issue instructions to his first two commissioners, Charles Rowan and Richard Mayne. However, 145 years later, in 1974 when Ian Blair joined the Metropolitan Police, he and the other recruits were required to learn by heart *the primary objects* of the police. The wording had hardly changed from that agreed between Peel and his two commissioners and an instruction that without doubt is derived from the Peelian principles.

> **The primary object of an efficient police is the prevention of crime: the next that of detection and punishment of offenders if crime is committed. To these ends all the efforts of the police must be directed. The protection of life and property, the preservation of public tranquility and the absence of crime, will alone prove whether those efforts have been successful and whether the objects for which the police were appointed have been attained.**

(Blair, 2009, p 42)

Similar wording to the above was found in *The Times* newspaper of 25 September 1829, four days before the first officers of the New Police began patrolling; the similarity of language will not be lost on us:

> **It should be understood from the outset, that the object to be attained is 'the prevention of crime.' To this great end every effort of the police is to be directed. The security**

of person and property, the preservation of the public tranquility, and all the other objects of the police establishment, will thus be better effected than by the detection and punishment of the offender after he has succeeded in committing the crime.

(Emsley, 2014, p 12)

The Peelian principles were attributed to him a hundred years later via the published work of Charles Reith, who stated that the principles were an extraction of both the initial foundations and subsequent development of the British police service. Reith published his work within the context that British policing was different to that of continental Europe (Emsley, 2014).

The perceived differences between continental policing and the police on the British mainland were a recurring theme from the period in which Peel presented his reformulated bill to Parliament, avoiding the centralised national police model, similar to the Peace Preservation Force, to the publication of Reith's work and the promulgation of the Peelian principles. Emsley (2014, p 15) asserts that Reith and others recognised the unique features of the English police as being non-military, unarmed and non-political, as opposed to the continental gendarmerie. There is certainly evidence to corroborate the notion that any form of centralisation was to be opposed. The debate on a police bill in 1856 which hinted at an enhanced role for central government included the following:

A stepping stone to that system of centralization which, however it might suit the Government of the Continent, was repugnant to the habits and feelings of Englishmen.

(Radzinowicz, 1981, p 75)

The government was further accused of '*an indecent lust for power*' and old arguments re-emerged, such as that '*England would soon be overrun by 20,000 armed policemen – perhaps Irishmen or foreigners, upon whom a bad Government could rely for the perpetration of acts of oppression*' (Radzinowicz, 1981, p 5).

CONTESTED REASONS FOR THE NEW POLICE

Reasons for the creation of the New Police based on Peel's 1829 Act of Parliament are far from straightforward. While there was an apparent rise in crime rates, as articulated by Peel in his address to Parliament, it is also clear that Peel had to be adroit in circumventing any opposition to his proposals, and there were many. The core issues among this opposition will now be explored, which will also provide a window into everyday life in Victorian Britain.

The New Police wore blue uniforms with top hats and swallow-tail coats, and their only evident protection was a wooden truncheon. Their appearance was not to appear in any way aligned to the military, particularly the infantry who wore short scarlet uniforms with colour facings and decorative piping (McLaughlin, 2007, p 3). As established earlier in the chapter, the overriding *raison d'etre* of the New Police was one of crime prevention. As McLaughlin (2007) emphasises, constables were provided with written instructions underlining the requirement to be civil and obliging to the public, irrespective of their background. This was no doubt an early attempt to gain acceptance among the public and adhere to the concept of policing by consent, which we will look at later. However, the opposition that Peel encountered in his initial attempts to implement a professional policing service manifested itself in the form of public protests against the robin redbreasts, crushers, bluebottles, bobbies, coppers, raw lobsters and peelers. The middle classes objected to paying for a public service that lowered the tone of their neighbourhoods and they had little faith in its success. Moreover, the working classes complained about the unjustified supervision of public areas and their leisure activities. The parishes of London were hostile to perceived central government control; trade unionists and other political radicals objected to imposition of *gendarmes* and the issue of *spies* monitoring their activities was heard once again (McLaughlin, 2007).

Notwithstanding this overt public hostility, there was some support for the creation of the New Police, as evidenced in Peel successfully steering his bill through Parliament to receive royal assent. It is important to examine where this support originated and, more importantly, the reasons for it.

CONSERVATIVE HISTORIES

Reiner (2010) and Brogden et al (1988) refer to the orthodox or conservative history concerning the reasons for the New Police. This view sees the requirement for a professional preventative police service as the logical response to the problems posed by urban and industrial revolution. Furthermore, the policing arrangements that the New Police replaced were seen as being grossly inefficient.

This was in a period in which the criminal justice system, directly influenced by the *classical* criminology of Cesare Beccaria (1764), was emerging from the period of the *bloody code* (Reiner, 2010, p 49), and adopted the principles as asserted by Beccaria. Those ideas were the *greatest happiness of the greatest number*; the certainty of punishment, proportionate to the crime that had been committed, and where deterrence, as opposed to retribution, was the primary objective (McLaughlin et al, 2003). Furthermore, it was a criminal justice system that now looked forward and not backwards, which is a principle that also exists today; the contemporary criminal justice system is modelled upon the theory put forward by Beccaria.

Therefore, there was a clear move towards efficiency. As Home Secretary, Peel had had instigated criminal justice changes that appeared to have produced meaningful results; accordingly, he quoted these recorded statistics in his opening speech in the House of Commons in 1829 when he presented the bill. In this context, given the clear shift away from the *bloody code* towards a reformed and modern criminal justice system, the enforcement element of the system, ie the police, also required reforming because as Reiner (2010, p 41) points out, '*the old system was said to be uncertain, uncoordinated, reliant on private and amateur effort and prone to corruption*'.

Brogden et al (1988) refer to three main factors in the justification for the New Police, and can be summarised as follows.

- *The importance of the* mob, *the fears by the respectable city dweller of a new urban working class which might come to rule the streets.*

- *Fear of crime, which dominated the official reports of the period.*

- Social disorganisation *resulting from the complex processes of urbanisation and migration.*

(Brogden et al, 1998, p 58)

Reiner (2010) concurs with these assertions and adds that the large and increasingly populous cities were believed to be breeding grounds for crime and disorder. The fear of ever-increasing crime was a key motivating factor for reform of the police, as were issues relating to public disorder referred to above by Brogden et al (1988) as *social disorganisation*. An irony that will resonate with many is that the prominent issues of almost 200 years ago, a fear of crime and public disorder, are the very same issues that police are consistently challenged for not addressing today, very often due to the apparent lack of visibility on the street. In the conservative or orthodox histories, this is what the New Police were mandated to combat and hopefully eradicate.

REVISIONIST HISTORIES

The central issue concerning revisionist histories is that the growth in cities and developing industrialisation ensued within a specific capitalist framework (Reiner, 2010). The speedy development of large urban areas precipitated enhanced segregation between the social classes. The least affluent areas were linked to greater crime and disorder, which reinforced the perception of the middle and upper classes that crime was a threat to the social order, originating from the *dangerous classes*, the rapidly increasing urban poor (Reiner, 2010).

In the revisionist histories, which link the emerging capitalist economy to both the justification for a new professional policing service and its implemented policing practices, which will be explored shortly, it should be remembered that capitalism itself creates inequality and, axiomatically, social class.

Brogden et al (1988) refer to professional police development within a crisis at the start of industrial capitalism. The new social relations created by the embryonic capitalism necessitated innovative methods for controlling social behaviour and restraining the lower social classes in their place, given that the traditional mechanisms of social control linked to feudalism had broken down with the growth of urban cities. Policing followed a similar process in terms of development to other means of social control such as prisons: the birth of the modern prison was aligned to the utilitarian Jeremy Bentham's *panopticon* design in 1778 and there was a fundamental philosophical shift towards reformation (Muncie and McLaughlin, 2001). There is certainly some support for this perspective and it appears that the first commissioners of the Metropolitan Police took the view that in order to protect the wealthy area of St James in London it was prudent to watch the slum of St Giles (Emsley, 2001, p 30). The phrase *we police St Giles to protect St James* is now often quoted in recognition of this particular perspective within the historical development of the British police.

Of course, this discourse referred to the so-called *dangerous classes* that occupied the central districts of the expanding urban areas, but it was not all confined to London; the work of Storch (1975) enlightens us about policing in working-class areas of northern England between 1840 and 1857 (Storch, 1975, cited in Fitzgerald et al, 1981). Storch notes that the police were referred to as *blue locusts* resented by the local working-class population. Their only apparent function was to walk as opposed to work and in doing so they devoured taxpayers' money, hence their description as *locusts* (Storch, 1975, cited in Fitzgerald et al, 1981). However, linked to the axiom of *policing St Giles to protect St James*, Storch asserts that a consensus manifested itself among the property-owning classes in northern England that it was imperative for a professional and bureaucratically organised lever of urban discipline to be introduced into working-class communities to enhance the moral and political authority of the state (Storch, 1975, cited in Fitzgerald et al, 1981, p 86).

The following gives an insight into the role of the police within these working-class communities in northern England, where the workforce for the emergent industries was drawn from the local community:

> *A great deal of the bitterness against the new police was a consequence of the fact that they were placed among the working classes to monitor all phases of working-class life – trade-union activity, drinking, gambling, sports as well as political activity. The overall mission of the police was to place working-class neighbourhoods under a constant and multifaceted surveillance.*

> (Storch, 1975, cited in Fitzgerald et al, 1981, p 90)

As mentioned earlier in the chapter, reasons for the creation of the New Police are both complex and contested. This chapter cannot provide the definitive answer but seeks to reference relevant academic material that is sufficient for an evaluation of the evidence. In critical thinking activity 2.1, you will have the opportunity to explore this issue further.

However, further reading is recommended into a fascinating period of British social history. Before leaving this section and the revisionist histories, the following from Brogden et al (1988, p 63) succinctly summarises the key issues of the argument:

> *It has been suggested that the primary duty of New Police was to confront the emergent working class whenever it threatened the bourgeois order – in industrial dispute, political protest and social unrest – bourgeois property, or, more generally, bourgeois notions of respectability and public propriety. From within this framework, the New Police were almost directly subordinate to local industrial and elite interests.*

CRITICAL THINKING ACTIVITY 2.1

LEVEL 5

Conduct an internet search for 'Policing Vision 2025'. In the document that emerges from the search results, go to section 4.1 on local policing. In that section it is claimed the British policing model '*is envied all over the world*'. In the context of this chapter and the conservative and revisionist histories explored earlier, consider critically the following questions.

a) Is that claim justified?

b) If yes, why? If no, why not? List your reasons, linking them to a referenced author in the chapter, for example: Reiner (2010).

Sample answers are provided at the end of this book.

POLICING BY CONSENT AND ACCOUNTABILITY

As mentioned earlier in the chapter, the police on the British mainland have some unique features to which can be added policing by consent, which is focused locally, and accordingly the police are accountable locally. Notwithstanding the policing by consent issue which is linked to several of the Peelian principles, it must be recognised that that consent has been severely tested and placed under great strain in the recent past. However, despite being established against a backdrop of opposition from across the spectrum of society, by the 1950s the police had become not only accepted but feted by a majority of public opinion (Reiner, 2010). By the 1950s, policing by consent had been accomplished in Britain to the degree that is realistically achievable (Reiner, 2010). This period in policing history is known as the 'golden age of policing'.

In respect of accountability, chief officers are considered to be *operationally independent* from formal political interference in operational matters, despite legislative change over the past few years, and police constables are law officers and not employees of the state (McLaughlin, 2007, p 80). Furthermore, and attributable to the unique organisational structure of the police service, those at the bottom who spend the most time on the street, unsupervised, enjoy the most discretion on how they carry out their job. In short, the police are independent of external interference operationally and have considerable discretion in exercising their operational responsibilities.

The year 1964 was a watershed for the police service with the eventual passing of the Police Act 1964, which introduced the *tripartite* arrangements for both the finance and governance of the police. The Act divided the governance of the police between three parties: the chief constable, commissioner in the case of the Metropolitan and City of London Police, the Home Secretary and the local police authority (Rowe, 2018). In respect of the accountability arrangements of the London forces, the Home Secretary acted as the police authority, while in the case of the City of London, the Court of Common Council for London assumed this role (Reiner, 2010). The legal position of the chief constable was later clarified by Lord Denning in 1968 (*Lord Denning, R v Commissioner of Police for the Metropolis, ex parte Blackburn*, 1968, 2, QB.118, p 136, cited in McLaughlin and Muncie, 2001, p 89). Lord Denning pronounced:

> *The chief constable is not the servant of anyone, save of the law itself. No Minister of the Crown can tell him that he must or must not prosecute this man or that one. Nor can any police authority tell him so. The responsibility for law enforcement lies on him. He is answerable to the law and the law alone.*

This wording reflects the situation at the time and the fact that there were no female chief officers but, as McLaughlin and Muncie (2001) assert, the operational independence of the chief constable was constitutionally guaranteed. This situation still pertains today, although with the comprehensive changes to accountability structures, the autonomy of the chief officers has been somewhat diminished compared to that enjoyed in 1964. The *tripartite* arrangements continued until the arrival of the Police and Crime Commissioners in 2012 (Rowe, 2017), which are discussed in more detail in Chapter 4.

CONTEMPORARY STRUCTURES

The constabulary-style structure of police forces on the British mainland are a direct legacy of Robert Peel and the political expediency exercised with the passing of the 1829 Act that created the New Police. Additionally, the structure of the police forces on the island of Ireland, as discussed earlier in the chapter, can trace their lineage from the Peace Preservation Force and Robert Peel. In the case of Scotland there have been some far-reaching changes in recent years, which will be explained shortly.

Apart from the City of London Police, all of the current police forces in England and Wales (often referred to as the Home Office forces) have witnessed their geographical boundaries being changed, or have been amalgamated with neighbouring forces. Some amalgamations occurred during the Second World War and this pattern continued following the Police Acts of 1946 and 1964. Legislation passed in 1972 abolished the remaining county borough forces and in April 1974 the Home Office created the 43 forces in England and Wales that we have today (Mawby and Wright, 2003). This involved several amalgamations of forces or parts of forces, creating what are referred to as the metropolitan forces in England and Wales, which in addition to the Metropolitan Police (London) are: West Midlands Police, Greater Manchester Police, West Yorkshire Police, and Merseyside Police. In addition to the 43 forces often referred to as the 'Home Office' forces there are three further police forces that have a national responsibility: the British Transport Police, the Civil Nuclear Constabulary, and the Ministry of Defence Police (Rogers, 2020). There are also police forces in Jersey, Guernsey and the Isle of Man; while their funding and accountability oversight differ, each one has arrangements in place for certain specific services, such as specialist criminal investigations, with mainland forces.

Created in Scotland at the same time were eight 'regional' forces (Rogers, 2020) but that recently changed following an announcement in the Scottish Parliament by the Justice Minister in 2011, faced with cuts in public spending. The announcement concerned the future structure of the police forces in Scotland and as from 1 April 2013 the existing structures were to be scrapped and replaced with a single national police force known as the Police Service of Scotland (PSS) (Fyfe, 2014), colloquially known as *Police Scotland*.

This is of course, centralisation, and a major shift away from the locally based constabulary structure that had existed since 1829. The legislation also introduced the Scottish Police Authority (SPA), with a membership of no more than 14 members and an independent chair appointed by ministers. There are no Police and Crime Commissioners in Scotland and functions expected of the SPA in respect of their strategic priorities resemble closely the responsibilities of the police authorities in England and Wales prior to being replaced by the Police and Crime Commissioners in 2012.

England and Wales have retained the constabulary structure which is compatible with the facilitation of local policing, as opposed to a centralised structure; this assertion excludes the objections to any centralised model, although they are still relevant today. This is covered in critical thinking activity 2.2 at the end of this chapter, which challenges you to reflect on this issue further.

However, the bedrock of the local policing structure is the Basic Command Unit (BCU) (Rogers, 2020), which equates to a geographical area within a police force. Until the intro-duction of the BCU model across police forces in England and Wales in the 1990s, these geographical areas were referred to as *divisions*. Across most police areas in England and Wales there are at least three BCUs and many of them share coterminous geographical boundaries with local authorities, designed to expedite partnership working, under the auspices of bodies such as the Crime and Disorder Reduction Partnerships, also known as Community Safety Partnerships.

The National Crime Agency was created in 2013 from both the Serious and Organised Crime Agency and the Child Exploitation and Online Protection Centre. This also absorbed some of the responsibilities from the former UK Border Agency and is often referred to as the *British FBI*. Its role is to investigate organised crime that transcends both regional and international borders, working closely with regional organised crime units (ROCU) and the Serious Fraud Office, in addition to local police forces. It also acts as the UK point of contact for international police agencies, notably Interpol and Europol.

CRITICAL THINKING ACTIVITY 2.2

LEVEL 4

Given the decision by the Scottish Parliament to centralise the police service in Scotland, and the traditional opposition to that structure as outlined in this chapter, consider the issues for and against centralisation. List your responses.

A sample answer is provided at the end of this book.

SUMMARY OF KEY CONCEPTS

This chapter has explored the following key concepts.

- Robert Peel founded the Peace Preservation Force in Ireland, a centralised military-style structure some 15 years before the introduction of the New Police.

- As Home Secretary in 1822, Peel established a parliamentary committee to explore the feasibility of a publicly funded police service, which was rejected.

- He then turned his attention to reform of the criminal law and justice system.

- Peel used these reforms to bolster his argument for a publicly funded police service in 1829.

- He astutely restricted his scope of the bill to the Metropolitan Police area only, aware of the opposition to a national centralised service.

- Reasons for the introduction of the New Police vary from conservative to revisionist histories.

- Further police forces based on boroughs/counties followed the pattern of the Metropolitan Police.

- Peelian principles retain their significance and influence today and provide the model for policing by consent.

- Chief officers retain independence in relation to operational matters.

- There has been some movement towards centralisation with Police Scotland and the National Crime Agency but policing in England and Wales retains its constabulary-style structure, which is a legacy of the opposition to a centralised *gendarmerie*-style policing structure.

CHECK YOUR KNOWLEDGE

1. What was Robert Peel trying to achieve by introducing the Peace Preservation Force?

2. Why did his attempts to introduce a police service in England and Wales fail?

3. What measures did he introduce that facilitated success with the inception of the New Police in 1829?

4. What are the key elements of the conservative histories in relation to the New Police?

5. What role does capitalism play in the assertions of the revisionist histories?

6. What is the uniqueness of the British police?

7. Why is policing by consent such an important concept?

8. Is it correct that chief officers are independent in policing operations?

9. What year were the metropolitan forces created in England and Wales?

10. What is a BCU?

FURTHER READING

BOOKS

Clements, P (2008) *Policing a Diverse Society*. Oxford: Oxford University Press.
This text explores police training, multiculturalism, community policing, community–police relations, discrimination in law enforcement, communication and police administration.

Donnelly, D and Scott, K (2011) *Policing Scotland*. 2nd ed. Abingdon: Routledge.
This was published just prior to Police Scotland coming into being (2013) but covers all historical aspects of Scottish police development and the variances with England and Wales in respect of prosecution relationships and processes.

Grieve, J, Harfield, C and MacVean, A (2007) *Policing*. London: Sage.
This book covers the emergence, history, function and role of the police, governance and accountability, comparative policing, transnational policing, public order, investigation, organised crime, terrorism, cyberspace, ethics and human rights.

Loader, I and Mulcahy, A (2003) *Policing and the Condition of England: Memory, Politics and Culture*. Oxford: Oxford University Press
This title focuses on English policing since 1945, the sociology of policing, the fracturing of police authority, police governance and English policing in a contemporary culture.

Wright, A (2002) *Policing: An Introduction to Concepts and Practice*. Cullopmton: Willan.
This book focuses on early twenty-first-century policing issues, policing protest, crime prevention and community safety, and problem-solving policing.

WEBSITES

Crime and Courts Act 2013 [online] Available at: www.legislation.gov.uk/ukpga/2013/22/contents (accessed 12 June 2022).

Police Reform and Social Responsibility Act 2011 [online] Available at: www.legislation.gov.uk/ukpga/2011/13/section/3/enacted (accessed 12 June 2022).

CHAPTER 3

POLICING AND THE CRIMINAL JUSTICE SYSTEM

PETER WILLIAMS

LEARNING OBJECTIVES

AFTER READING THIS CHAPTER YOU WILL BE ABLE TO:

- understand the role and function of the criminal justice system (CJS);

- critically evaluate the role of the police service within it;

- understand key criminal justice principles and terms;

- analyse the role of key partners within the CJS;

- describe key elements and concepts of legislation relevant to the CJS;

- evaluate critically the Covid-19 challenge and if the CJS is fit for purpose.

INTRODUCTION

The criminal justice system (CJS) in England and Wales shares a uniqueness with the British police service in that it has developed differently from the rest of Europe. Policing, as we covered in Chapter 2, rejected a national structure common to most of Europe, ie the *gendarmerie national* in the case of France. In criminal justice, its structure and mode of delivery is different from the rest of Europe, underpinned by its legal foundation, which is often referred to as the 'Anglo-Saxon' or 'Anglo-American' procedure (Hodgson, 2005).

There is tacit acceptance in society that *criminal justice* is the primary means by which the nation state takes responsibility for constructing criminal laws and, in doing so, trying, prosecuting and ultimately sanctioning those that transgress those laws. *Civil justice* is concerned with seeking resolution of contractual disputes, normally brought by a private individual for the harm caused; this is not the case with the criminal law as the action is brought by the state (Drake et al, 2010). A fundamental difference however is the standard of proof; in the criminal justice system it is *beyond reasonable doubt*, while in the civil court it is *on the balance of probabilities*, which is a lower threshold.

Britain and France, for example, do share one common theme in relation to the foundations for their modern criminal justice systems, which is constitutional reform. In the case of Britain, this followed the Glorious Revolution of 1688, and in the case of France it was after the French Revolution (1789–99).

In England and Wales, a contribution to the *Gentleman's Magazine* in 1777 reads as follows.

> *There is none which shines more eminently conspicuous than trial by jury. This invaluable prerogative is the birthright of every Englishman and distinguishes the laws of this happy country from the arbitrary decisions of other states.*

> (Beattie, 1986, p 314)

Certainly, *state law*, which is defined as law supported by central government (Sharpe, 2001), was being extended. Over the seventeenth and eighteenth centuries, criminal law was added to via statute, thus becoming a key element in the wider context of social control (Sharpe, 2001, p 110).

So, while both jurisdictions can point to watershed events, in the case of England and Wales, there are several credible academic debates as to the reasons for this development and which classes within society benefitted. This has similarities with the implementation of the New Police. Notwithstanding that, it is clear that the early foundations to the modern criminal justice system (CJS) were being constructed during this period. However, in the case of England and Wales, the system developed differently from the rest of Europe, and it is to that CJS that we now turn.

ADVERSARIAL AND INQUISITORIAL SYSTEMS OF CRIMINAL JUSTICE

The Anglo-Saxon or Anglo-American model as mentioned earlier (Hodgson, 2005) is also known as the *adversarial system*, which is the model of criminal justice specific to common law systems of justice, such as Australia, Canada, the United States, as well as England and Wales. The other prominent model underpinned by civil law, the *inquisitorial system*, is utilised across nations in continental Europe and major European countries, such as Germany and France.

Scotland is a separate jurisdiction from England and Wales and has key structural elements of the *inquisitorial system* within it, such as the Procurator Fiscal, an independent lawyer who directs police investigations, with strong similarities to the model applied in France. The other remaining nation in the United Kingdom, Northern Ireland, although a separate jurisdiction from England and Wales, applies an *adversarial model* and, given the political history of Northern Ireland, is unambiguously derived from the English and Welsh system.

THE ADVERSARIAL SYSTEM

The *adversarial* system of criminal justice is the model that is applied to all criminal courts in England and Wales: the magistrates' courts and the Crown Court when sitting to hear criminal trials. The principle of the *adversarial* model is that the prosecution brings the case to court and presents their evidence. The role of the defence is to challenge or refute the evidence presented, rendering criminal trials in English and Welsh criminal courts to the prosecution-v-defence model, hence the term *adversarial*. However, there is far more to the system than is implied by that simplification and providing a context is required to fully appreciate the mechanisms at play.

Under the *adversarial* system, the responsibility for preparing the case rests with the parties involved themselves. In the case of the prosecution, it is the Crown that performs that function. The role of the judge, who normally sits with a jury in a criminal trial, is to act as an independent umpire (Welsh et al, 2021). Their primary role during the trial is to ensure that it is conducted in accordance with the laws of evidence, in addition to ruling on matters of law that are raised by prosecution and defence counsel during the trial. The judge, however, does not decide on guilt or innocence as that is a matter for the jury; however, in the case of a guilty verdict, it is the role of the judge to pronounce the sentence. The theory surrounding the *adversarial* system is that truth is best uncovered by powerful arguments on both sides, prosecution and defence, and in turn analysed and evaluated by an independent adjudicator (Welsh et al, 2021).

The same structure applies in a magistrates' court, although there is no jury present and magistrates hear the case. In these hearings, referred to as summary trials, matters of law are dealt with by the clerk of the court, who in turn advises the sitting magistrates, which normally number three and are collectively referred to as a *bench*. They are likely to be *lay magistrates* who are ordinary members of the public who volunteer for the post which they perform in a part-time mode. There are also full-time magistrates, now called *district judges*, previously *stipendiary magistrates* until the 1999 Access to Justice Act introduced the title of district judges. These are already professional lawyers and tend to hear the more serious cases that come before a magistrates' court (Joyce, 2017).

The *adversarial* model also requires that prosecution evidence is gathered appropriately and in accordance with the rules of evidence. The system is trial centred and preparation of a case for trial is a primary purpose of the investigation and the evidence that is gathered. Defence lawyers are meant to play an active part in the investigative stage of a criminal case by representing the suspect and advising them accordingly. The importance attached to the credibility of the practices implemented in collecting evidence can be assessed by the amount of additional regulations concerning the rules of evidence that have been introduced in recent years, necessary to ensure fairness and propriety in the investigative function (Welsh et al, 2021).

The *adversarial* model is often summarised as being a *search for the proof* as opposed to the inquisitorial system of justice to which we now turn.

THE INQUISITORIAL SYSTEM

The inquisitorial system is often referred to as the *search for the truth*, and although elements from both systems can be found in both the adversarial model and the inquisitorial model, the overall approach is different.

The French inquisitorial model, which is probably the pick of the continental models to illustrate the differences from the adversarial model, dates from the thirteenth century and is a creation of a longstanding and centralised state role, which is not dependent upon equality between the parties (Hodgson, 2005). Originally, the initial inquiry was conducted by a representative of the state, who was not involved with the case and accordingly took on the role of investigator, prosecutor and, if justified, implemented coercive measures to determine if the case should proceed to trial or not. Unlike the adversarial system, the defence played no part in the pre-trial process. This procedure highlights that one of the key differences between the two systems is that the inquisitorial model has a longer pre-trial phase, while the adversarial system has a longer trial period (Hodgson, 2005).

Therefore, in an inquisitorial system the primary role in a criminal inquiry is undertaken by the court. A file is prepared to enable the judge taking the case to fully understand the key issues involved. The judge then decides which witnesses to call and examines them in person (Welsh et al, 2021); this also includes the defendant of course.

In some inquisitorial systems the case file is prepared by an examining magistrate, in the French example the *juge d'instruction*; in the less serious cases, this is done by the prosecutor and police. However, in France, to separate the function of the investigation and prosecution, legal changes in 1958 established the independence of the *juge d'instruction* from that of the prosecutor, the *procureur* (Hodgson, 2005). In practice, today it is only the more serious cases that would attract the attention of the *juge d'instruction*; nevertheless, police investigations, unlike in England and Wales, are supervised by the *procureur*, who is a qualified lawyer.

The Royal Commission on Criminal Justice (RCCJ) 1993 investigated the feasibility of the inquisitorial model being adopted in England and Wales; the recommendation was against this model and to remain with the adversarial model.

CRITICAL THINKING ACTIVITY 3.1

LEVEL 6

Access the report of the Royal Commission on Criminal Justice (1993). Read the section named 'Adversarial or Inquisitorial' and answer the following questions.

a) What does the '*force of criticisms*' refer to?

b) Why do they believe that a system where '*critical roles are kept separate*' is beneficial, and to whom?

c) What do the references to Italy and France refer to?

d) Consider which system you feel better protects the legal rights of the defendant. Make a list of your reasons to justify your answer.

Sample answers are provided at the end of this book.

DUE PROCESS AND CRIME CONTROL

In addition to debates about the structure of the CJS, the primary one we have just considered, there are other controversies in relation to various models within the CJS and how it delivers justice daily. One of the key issues concerns *due process-v-crime control*, which was first examined by Herbert Packer in an article published in the *University of Pennsylvania Law Review* in 1964 (Drake et al, 2010).

Crime control identifies criminality as a major threat to social order and that the suppression of it is the *raison d'etre* of the CJS. To attain this goal, the police need to achieve high arrest rates, which in turn result in convictions, in doing so highlighting efficiency and timeliness in reaching the predestined outcome. While wrongful convictions are regretted, along with the discretion of the police they are acceptable providing they do not bring the overall CJS into disrepute. Packer called this *assembly line justice* (Drake et al, 2010).

However, at variance with this model is due process, which has at its heart the protection of the individual from the unjust acts of the state. To achieve this, it places procedural safeguards, such as the presumption of innocence, rigorous adherence by the police and judicial authorities to proceedings, and an effective appeals procedure. The overall objective is to ensure the moral authority of the CJS, where stringent compliance to the law, equality within it and the upholding of individual rights is of more significance than sanctioning offenders. Packer referred to this as *obstacle course justice*. In the crime control model, the main function of the CJS is to adhere to law and order; in the due process model, the primary aim is to protect civil liberties (Drake et al, 2010).

THE ROLE OF THE POLICE WITHIN THE CRIMINAL JUSTICE SYSTEM

The role of the police service within the CJS is extremely wide-ranging. While there are other key agencies that undertake prominent functions that are both significant and influential in the everyday operations of the CJS, it is self-evident that the police are the gatekeepers of the CJS. Although we have outlined some of the structural features of the CJS and the role of the police in that, it is not possible to capture the entire roles and responsibilities within this chapter; therefore, the focus will be on some critical tasks that perhaps reflect that gatekeeper status.

However, first, let us consider some of the basic core tasks that incorporate the role of a police officer (Lodge, 2020):

- maintaining order;

- law enforcement;

- protecting the public;

- investigating crime;

- dealing with witnesses and victims.

One of the key roles of the police service is to record both incidents and crimes that are reported to them. In the case of the latter specifically, this is crucial not only for the wider CJS, but for society as a whole to fully understand what the crime problem actually is, in order that the problem of crime can be addressed properly. There is far more to this task than merely providing a police reference number to a victim in order to facilitate a claim to an insurance company and retaining statistics to furnish them later to the Home Office. It is a role that needs to be completed professionally, ethically and in accordance with the processes connected to the National Crime Recording Standards (NCRS), which will be referred to shortly.

Unfortunately, this has not always been the case; for example, a report in *The Guardian* newspaper on 18 March 1999 revealed how a number of police forces were involved in malpractice concerning the recording of crimes and in some cases, perhaps more signifi-cantly, not recording them in order to present a picture that was more favourable in respect of police performance, particularly in the area of *detected* criminal offences (Davies, *The Guardian*, 18 March 1999, cited in Muncie and McLaughlin, 2001).

EVIDENCE-BASED POLICING

Crime statistics have been a consistent area for debate, and the following from Quinney and Wildeman (1977) (Muncie and McLaughlin, 2001) may pro-vide some alternative perceptions in relation to what crime statistics tell us.

- The *orthodox* approach to the measurement of statistics asserts that the data reflect a continuing intent by certain individuals who make rational choices to commit crime. The apparent over-representation of minority ethnic groups and the propensity of the lower social classes to commit crime reflect their tenuous commitment towards social order.

→

- The *interactionist* approach, however, interprets the data differently and does so by contending that the figures only represent what and where police forces choose to target and deploy their resources accordingly.

- The *structural conflict* approach maintains an alternative perspective, linked to power in society, and insists that the official statistics do not reflect crime as such, but do indicate how dominant groups maintain their governing status through acquiescence or coercion of the powerless. Increasing crime rates are therefore a tangible illustration of a failure to achieve consensus, of ever-increasing social division and inequality and the determination of the state to retain dominance via criminalisation, coercion and persecution.

(Muncie and McLaughlin, 2001, p 25)

Without debating the issues in detail set out above, it is sufficient to summarise here that the issues surrounding crime statistics are complicated. From 1982 onwards, the British Crime Survey was introduced and repeatedly exposed that only about 50 per cent of crime was reported (Muncie and McLaughlin, 2001). Therefore, given that the reported statistics are the main indicator of the crime problem, solutions were sought to address the issues involved.

This led to the introduction in 2002 of the National Crime Recording Standard (NCRS) (Maguire and McVie, 2017). The overall idea was an attempt to introduce a standardised and consistent approach across the country for crime recording, which is now based on the *prima facie* notion that allegations and reports of crime should be accepted at face value and recorded as such, at least until a supervisor authorises that they could be re-classified as *no crime* and only then where evidence exists to justify that (Maguire and McVie, 2017). The *prima facie* threshold is important because until the NCRS was introduced, police forces were working to different thresholds; some were using the *prima facie* system and others the *evidential* threshold which required some evidential corroboration to support the allegation of crime before it was officially recorded. Hence, this led to a distorted and false picture across England and Wales and one which the NCRS was designed to ameliorate.

KEY PARTNER AGENCIES WITH THE CRIMINAL JUSTICE SYSTEM

There are several partner agencies that the police service works alongside within the CJS and it is necessary to understand who they are and what they do. The first agencies that will be highlighted are those that make up community safety partnerships.

COMMUNITY SAFETY PARTNERSHIPS

Community safety partnerships (CSPs) were originally called *crime and disorder reduction partnerships* and were introduced on a statutory footing by the flagship legislation of the incoming Labour government in 1997, specifically the Crime and Disorder Act 1998; how the Act was introduced is worthy of further exploration.

Following the report by Lord Justice Scarman into the inner-city disturbances in 1981, predominantly in Brixton and Toxteth, he made several recommendations in respect of police and community relations, aimed at enhancing that relationship. One was the introduction of lay visitors to police stations, now called *custody visitors*, and another was the introduction of police and community forums, held quarterly and *de facto* consultation meetings involving the community on everyday police matters (McLaughlin and Muncie, 2001). The change in emphasis from police to the community was symbolic and unobtrusive in the context of what subsequently developed.

The publication of the Home Office Circular 8/84 encouraged a multi-agency methodology towards crime prevention (McLaughlin and Muncie, 2001, p 305) and laid the groundwork for major change; there was now an official recognition that police could not deal with crime unilaterally. To control the problem of crime, in preference to responding to its aftermath, crime prevention, now called *crime reduction*, emerged as a key issue (Blake et al, 2010). This was attributable to two key factors: the effect of the British Crime Survey and in 1983 the formation of the Home Office Crime Prevention Unit, influenced by the right realism school within criminological theory.

EVIDENCE-BASED POLICING

Following Circular 8/84, the Home Office introduced the *Five Towns Project* in 1986, based on the contents of the circular and as a result crime prevention measures were implemented. Based on the apparent success of the project in 1988, the *Safer Cities Programme* was launched which involved 16 cities, administered by the Home Office, and introduced watchwords such as *Safer Salford* for example, a practice that became routine following the eventual implementation of the Crime and Disorder Act 1998 (Blake et al, 2010).

The government, still apparently frustrated by the gradual adoption of crime reduction partnerships and Circular 8/84 in general, established an inquiry into this specific area under James Morgan which reported in 1991, referred to as the Morgan Report. When Morgan reported he made 19 recommendations, including the introduction of a statutory responsibility on local authorities (with the police) for the '*stimulation of community safety and crime prevention programmes, and for progressing at a local level a multi-agency approach to community safety*' (Blake et al, 2010, p 131).

Rather surprisingly, given the context of the Morgan Report, the then Conservative government, which had been proactive with crime reduction initiatives, did not implement the contents of the report and effectively shelved it. However, it formed the basis of the content of the Crime and Disorder Act 1998 by legislating the partnership approach to crime prevention and making it a statutory requirement for local authorities and the police to create community safety partnerships (Muncie and McLaughlin, 2001). This brought not just local authorities as partners of the police operating within the CJS, but other agencies as well that, given their core role, may not be readily associated as having any relationship with the CJS. Reflective practice 3.1 provides an opportunity to develop your knowledge further in this specific area.

REFLECTIVE PRACTICE 3.1

LEVEL 4

The Crime and Disorder Act 1998 placed a statutory duty on local authorities and police to form community safety partnerships. Section 5 of that act designated five 'responsible authorities': find out who they are and what community safety is. Explore the provision in your area and examine one initiative that they are currently involved with. Then reflect on the initiative and consider its effectiveness as a multi-agency approach.

The Act required that local authorities were responsible for reducing crime in their areas. Subsequent evidence gathered suggested that once bedded in, much was achieved in creating effective partnerships (Loveday, 2013). One of the requirements was for local police to work closely alongside local councils as *responsible partners* in reducing crime and disorder, including the fear of crime. This measure appeared to justify police claims that they alone could not address the problem of crime, borne out later by research. One of the reasons put forward to explain this was that environmental factors, which the police had no control or influence over, were significant in the local crime problem, but that the local authority did have some powers and influence to intervene (Loveday, 2013). One of the criticisms of CSPs was that they were overly bureaucratic; however, there was a general acceptance that the partnerships were highly positive and a considerable improvement on what had come before the 1998 Act (Loveday, 2013).

The partnerships offered a multi-agency response to addressing community problems such as anti-social behaviour and drugs and, being locally based, the structures facilitated the success of *neighbourhood policing*; a policing model that unfortunately in some forces has not survived the cutbacks in policing brought about by austerity measures.

CSPs have also had their influence reduced with the introduction of Police and Crime Commissioners (PCCs), who have had the community safety budget incorporated into a general police and community safety budget (Loveday, 2013), which has been subject to austerity cuts since 2010 and indicates a declining model. While it is also difficult to envisage that a governing party that effectively scrapped the initial idea as set out by the Morgan Report is to reinvigorate the sector, it is recognised that the landscape has moved on from merely addressing acquisitive crime and anti-social behaviour, as identified in a Local Government Association (LGA) report (LGA, 2018).

The LGA report highlighted the pressure on local authorities, both in the enhanced demand for services and the centrally imposed decreasing financial circumstances created by austerity measures. In addition to the introduction of PCCs, the LGA pointed to increasing responsibilities in areas such as modern slavery, child sexual exploitation, extremism, and statutory obligations under the *Prevent* strategy, all having coalesced to impinge on resourcing for the CSPs. However, a government policy paper released on 27 July 2021, the *Beating Crime Plan*, is effectively the strategy document for policing and criminal justice. It contains references to partnership working and under the Police, Crime, Sentencing and Courts Act 2002, statutory obligations will be placed on partners in respect of key issues such as serious violence. Although, despite the cuts to resources and alterations to oversight and management as identified by Loveday (2013) and the increasing and diverse responsibilities as referred to by the LGA, it is possible that the CSP may be able once again to make an effective contribution to reducing crime and disorder (Home Office, 2021b).

POLICING SPOTLIGHT

In your role as an operational police officer, you are asked to read and familiarise yourself with the key components that will directly affect how you undertake your professional practice in the short and medium term. You will find that the 'Beating Crime Plan', as indicated above, is effectively the strategy document for police and the criminal justice system in the future and certainly post-Covid-19.

The document contains an executive summary and five individual chapters detailing what the proposed changes are. For example, there is a commitment to extend the use of the Nightingale courts, in order to assist with reducing the waiting time for criminal cases to proceed to court. The document is important and provides a signpost as to proposed changes to policing and criminal justice in the future.

The 'Beating Crime Plan' (Gov.uk, 2021a) is a detailed document setting out this strategy for how the government intends to meet the challenges presented by the problem of crime. This will impinge on all disciplines within policing when being responded to. The policy sits alongside the government proposals in relation to drugs strategy.

CRITICAL THINKING ACTIVITY 3.2

LEVEL 6

In December 2021, the government announced their ten-year drugs strategy that included enforcement and enhanced resources for treatment services. The Minister for Crime and Policing formally announced the strategy in Parliament:

> *Local partners working together on our long-term ambitions will be key to the strategy's success and we will develop a new set of local and national measures of progress against our key strategic aims, with clear account-ability at national and local levels.*
>
> *(UK Parliament, 2021a)*

a) Search for and browse through the drugs strategy online ('From Harm to Hope'). Then consider how CSPs can effectively address some of the issues highlighted by the minister to meet the outcomes the government hope to achieve through delivery of the strategy, specifically in relation to:

– the overall approach to drug enforcement;

– addressing issues concerning *county lines*;

– supporting initiatives in respect of drugs treatment;

– focusing on the education proposals;

– contributing towards the Advisory Council review.

Sample answers are provided at the end of this book.

CROWN PROSECUTION SERVICE

The Crown Prosecution Service (CPS) was established in April 1986 as a result of the Prosecution of Offences Act 1985, as recommended by the Royal Commission on Criminal Procedure (RCCP), 1981 (the Phillips Commission). This was one of several key recommendations, in addition to laying the foundations for the Police and Criminal Evidence

Act (PACE) 1984, introduced on 1 January 1986. Therefore, the CJS in England and Wales underwent major change at this time and in the years that followed.

The justification for the RCCP merits some further analysis and initially focused on the lack of separation of powers between the investigation and the prosecution processes; proponents of the *inquisitorial* system would claim that to be a structural flaw in the *adversarial* system of justice.

The RCCP was established in the aftermath of the findings and recommendations contained in the Fisher Report 1977 concerning the murder of Maxwell Confait in 1972, and the subsequent convictions of three youths charged with a variety of offences, including murder. They were convicted at the trial, but the convictions were later overturned by the Court of Appeal.

Fisher made several recommendations, one being that somebody legally qualified should be involved in the case at an early stage. This is a recurring theme in respect of English criminal justice and additionally there was a case for a separate independent prosecution system to clearly define the functions of investigation and prosecution (House of Commons, 1977, 2.44 and 45).

The RCCP published its report for a '*fair, open, workable and efficient system*' (Sanders and Young, 1994, p 1) and the legislation that followed introduced both the CPS and PACE 1984, together with accompanying codes of practice, heralding massive change in the CJS. Due to expediency our focus is restricted to the most salient issues, and they will be developed further.

Prior to the inception of the CPS, the metropolitan county areas such as Merseyside, Greater Manchester and the West Midlands had their own county prosecuting solicitor's departments which were part of the metropolitan county structures for work in the magistrates' courts, although for some minor matters such as road traffic collision (RTC) offences, police took on the role of prosecutor. For matters in the Crown Court, barristers were instructed. This relationship operated under the traditional solicitor–client relationship and under this model, the police had the final say on whether a prosecution should proceed or not. Many prosecutors did not favour this arrangement, which became apparent in their submissions to the RCCP (Sanders and Young, 1994). This presented problems and there was clear evidence of police overcharging in certain cases where evidence was lacking and, as the solicitors were instructed by the police, there was little they could do apart from acquiesce, despite having advised to the contrary. This was the very issue that the Confait case highlighted, where the prosecutor was unable, or unwilling, to act independently (Welsh et al, 2021). The RCCP therefore recommended an independent prosecution service which would prosecute in cases where the police had charged a suspect.

This is worth reflecting upon as the police still had the duty to charge, but the proposed prosecution body would pursue the charge in court. In a total reversal of the previous relationship, if they did not agree with the police, they could decide to drop the charges, amend them or request the investigators to seek further evidence. That independent body recommended by the RCCP was the CPS and while the decision to charge/prosecute may seem to be an anomaly, the CPS did introduce a threshold test concerning new cases from the *prima facie* test applied by the police to a requirement for '*a realistic prospect of a conviction*' (Alderson, 1992, p 27), thereby enhancing the level of proof required before proceeding to trial.

The RCCP recommended a local arrangement for the new prosecution service and pronounced: '*[a] centrally directed national prosecution system for England and Wales is neither desirable nor necessary and we do not recommend its establishment*' (Alderson, 1992, p 29).

The government disregarded the advice and opted for a national centralised structure, unlike the constabulary structure of the police and the local focus of the magistrates' courts. While the CPS is 'independent' of the police and possesses decision-making powers independent of the investigation, it is important to remember that in a criminal process that leads to trial, under the *adversarial* structure, both the police and the CPS are on the same side. Furthermore, it is axiomatic that implementing a system that involves qualified lawyers having a mandatory function introduces a degree of professionalism that was hitherto lacking.

It is fully appreciated that there was conflict between the CPS and the police as new working practices developed, but this should have been foreseen. Senior police officers, familiar with and committed to a crime control model, who traditionally had their instructions followed without question, were being overruled. Given that both PACE 1984 and the CPS injected a major dose of due process into the system, this was hardly surprising.

The head of the CPS is the Director of Public Prosecutions (DPP), an office that was created in 1879 to advise the police in matters connected with crime and deal with specific important cases (Sanders and Young, 1994). At the time of the inception of the CPS, the DPP had a staff of about 70 lawyers, who dealt with murders, other serious offences and advised in prosecutions involving police officers. With the inauguration of the CPS, despite a sudden expansion to over 1500 lawyers, it was obvious that the organisation was understaffed (Sanders and Young, 1994). Manifestly, in the interim period to the contemporary one, the organisation has evolved and is clearly a thoroughly professional and specialist criminal justice agency and despite having the national structure it has a local focus.

REFLECTIVE PRACTICE 3.2

LEVEL 4

Access the CPS website and answer the following questions.

a) How many CPS areas are there in England and Wales?

b) In which CPS area is your local police force located?

c) What must prosecutors follow when deciding whether to prosecute a case or not?

d) The Full Code Test has two stages; what are they?

e) List one factor from each stage that Crown Prosecutors need to consider and reflect on the independence of the role.

Sample answers are provided at the end of this book.

In an attempt to further separate the powers of investigation and prosecution, PACE 1984 introduced the role of the police 'custody' officer, normally a sergeant. The idea was that the custody officer would remain independent of any investigation and would unilaterally be responsible for decisions in respect of charging suspects and the associated issues linked to disposal, such as the consideration for bail after charge.

However, research into the decision making of custody officers (Welsh et al, 2021) revealed that they routinely acquiesced with the wishes of the investigating officer.

In 2001, the Right Honourable Lord Justice Auld was asked to carry out a review of the criminal courts in England and Wales, and in the subsequent report he recommended that the CPS should be involved in the initial decision to charge (Auld, 2001, p 12).

This recommendation was implemented with the statutory charging scheme in 2006 (Joyce, 2017), having been incorporated into the Criminal Justice Act 2003, and introduced the system where the CPS would decide the charge, unless for minor matters such as RTC offences. However, the scheme was refined by the Coalition Government in 2012 and the police now decide the charge once again, in about 70 per cent of criminal cases, with the CPS deciding in the more serious and complex crimes (Joyce, 2017).

COURTS IN ENGLAND AND WALES

As discussed earlier in the chapter, there are two tiers of criminal courts in England and Wales: the magistrates' court, which hears summary trials, and the Crown Court, which deal with indicatable and *either-way* offences. A person charged with an indictable offence can only be tried in the Crown Court. An either-way or *hybrid* offence can be heard in either court, where the magistrates can determine which court deals with the case or the defendant can elect for trial before a judge and jury.

Historically, magistrates' courts were designated by the geographical jurisdiction of the court and referred to as *petty sessional areas*, which meant in practice that most areas had local magistrates' courts. However, that has now changed; the Courts Act 2003 altered that arrangement, introducing one *commission of the peace* for England and Wales, divided into about 100 local justice areas (Joyce, 2017). The legislation also introduced Her Majesty's Courts Service (Blake et al, 2010), which became effective in 2005 (Joyce, 2017). Following legislation passed in 2013, the responsibility to appoint magistrates now rests with the Lord Chief Justice, who in practice delegates the task to the senior presiding judge for England and Wales (Joyce, 2017).

Due to austerity measures the Coalition Government, which formed an administration between the Conservative Party and the Liberal Democrats between May 2010 and May 2015, closed many local magistrates' courts (Donoghue, 2014) via the Ministry of Justice; the reformed structure following the 2003 legislation made it straightforward to do that. However, in many areas now it is difficult to see how magistrates' courts in England and Wales serve *local* justice, given their geographical remoteness, a key principle within criminal justice in England and Wales historically.

Crown Courts are located throughout England and Wales and are geographically divided into seven regions, previously known as *circuits*, six for England and one for Wales (Joyce, 2017). They are divided into three tiers, depending on the seriousness of the offence, tier 3 being the lowest where circuit judges normally sit.

Appeals from the Crown Court are heard by the Court of Appeal and are heard by the Lord Justices of Appeal. The highest court in the country is the Supreme Court, which was created by the Constitutional Reform Act 2005; previously the highest court of appeal in the land was the House of Lords. The Supreme Court consists of 12 Justices who deal with a limited number of criminal cases in a court normally consisting of five justices.

THE CRIMINAL JUSTICE SYSTEM POST-COVID-19: IS IT FIT FOR PURPOSE?

The Covid-19 pandemic presented major challenges to the police service in the management of hastily formulated Covid-19 regulations contained in the Coronavirus Act 2020. The legislation was passed by Parliament in four days and effectively bypassed the committee stages, where traditionally potential problems with the proposed legislation are identified and rectified. This occurred due to expediency, leaving a situation that presented the police service and the public with deficient legislation, and with implications for the CJS. While the legislation was intended to be public-health led, the intention was that police would operate in a joined-up approach and they were issued with guidance to apply the four 'E's principles of *engage, encourage, explain* and *enforcement*. For the latter element, fixed penalty notices (FPN) were to be issued and the matter disposed of outside of a magistrates' court hearing.

Evidence provided to the Justice Committee in Parliament revealed that by 25 August 2020, 17,864 FPNs were issued in England and Wales and 50 per cent had not been paid within the 28-day period, which had implications for the wider CJS, most notably the CPS as they sought to prosecute the alleged breaches (Parliament UK, 2021).

Additionally, waiting times for trial had drastically increased, by so much that the then Justice Secretary Robert Buckland proposed that jury trials be cut to seven jury members instead of twelve and for less serious cases to proceed without a jury (McConville and Marsh, 2020).

It was a policy of the 2010–15 Coalition Government to close magistrates' courts (Donoghue, 2014); there were 900 in 1970, compared with only 156 left open in August 2020 (McConville and Marsh, 2020). The figure of outstanding cases stood at 364,122 on 30 June 2021 (Gov.UK, 2021b).

A report published by the National Audit Office in October 2021 identified that the backlog of cases in the Crown Court increased by 48 per cent between March 2020 and June 2021, including serious cases such as rape. At the current rate the backlog may have ramifications for the system for the next three years and afterwards post-November 2024 (National Audit Office, 2021).

The actions of the 2010–15 Coalition Government could now be described as myopic given the current state of the CJS and while there is no criticism to be levelled at personnel that work within the CJS, political expediency has under-valued the role of criminal justice within UK society.

SUMMARY OF KEY CONCEPTS

This chapter has explored the following key concepts.

⚙ The standard of proof in a criminal court is to prove an offence beyond all reasonable doubt.

⚙ Within the UK (except for Scotland) an adversarial as opposed to an inquisitorial approach is adopted by the CJS.

⚙ Police are gatekeepers of the CJS.

⚙ The introduction of the Crown Prosecution Service has separated the functions of investigation from prosecution.

⚙ Police now partner with several agencies while dealing with crime and disorder.

⚙ The statutory charging system was introduced to transfer the decision to charge from the police to the CPS; this has now been refined and the CPS charge in the more serious cases.

⚙ Austerity measures and Covid-19 have placed the CJS under stress.

CHECK YOUR KNOWLEDGE

1. What is the key principle of the adversarial system?

2. The Fisher Report (1977) was as a result of what murder case?

3. Which independent body recommended the introduction of the Crown Prosecution Service?

4. Who recommended that the Crown Prosecution Service be involved in recommending the initial charge?

5. Who has the overall responsibility to appoint magistrates in England and Wales?

   Sample answers are provided at the end of the book.

FURTHER READING

Fox, C, Albertson, K and Wong, K (2013) *Justice Reinvestment: Can the Criminal Justice System Deliver More for Less?* London: Routledge.
This is a US publication primarily, but provides a useful introduction to the concept of 'justice reinvestment' and delivery of the CJS in economic uncertainty.

Hucklesby, A (2014) *Criminal Justice*. Oxford: Oxford University Press.
This provides a good overview of the CJS, including the police service.

Pearson, G and Rowe, M (2020) *Police Street Powers and Criminal Justice: Regulation and Discretion in a Time of Change*. London: Bloomsbury.
This book discusses police culture, discretion within the CJS, arrest and detention and technical changes.

Smart, U (2006) *Criminal Justice*. London: Sage.
This book contains good coverage of the criminal justice system but also includes chapters on the Probation Service and prisons, both key agencies within the CJS.

Travis, L F and Edwards, B D (2015) *Introduction to Criminal Justice*. Boston, MA: Elsevier.
This is a US publication but includes some useful UK material and covers the CJS, crime and crime control; policing and law enforcement; criminal courts and imprisonment.

PART 2
THE CORE CONCEPTS OF POLICING

CHAPTER 4

POLICE GOVERNANCE AND ACCOUNTABILITY

BARRIE SHELDON

LEARNING OBJECTIVES

AFTER READING THIS CHAPTER YOU SHOULD BE ABLE TO:

- understand how the police service is governed and how the police are held to account;

- understand how legislation has shaped police governance today;

- describe and explain the role of the Police and Crime Commissioner;

- understand the role of Her Majesty's Inspectorate of Constabulary and Fire & Rescue Service and how they contribute to holding the police to account;

- critically discuss the effectiveness of police governance.

INTRODUCTION

This chapter explores the role of those who manage the police at the highest level, the responsibility that is given to them and how the police service is held to account both nationally and at a local level.

The modern police service was founded in 1829 by Sir Robert Peel, the then Home Secretary, who introduced the concept of '*Policing by consent*' that remains the premise for policing today.

Peel introduced nine principles of policing, the second being:

> *To recognise always that the powers of the police to fulfil their functions and duties is dependent on public approval of their existence, actions, and behaviour, and the ability to secure and maintain public respect.*

(Emsley, 2014, p 11)

It is critical that the police have the trust and confidence of the public, and policing governance plays a pivotal role in assuring this (Hough and Roberts, 2004).

This chapter starts by exploring some definitions of governance and provides a historical perspective, describing the Watch Committee, the Police Authority, and going to where we are today with the introduction of the Police and Crime Commissioner (PCC) in 2012, whose role it is to hold the police to account on behalf of the public. Since 1829, legislation has played a key role in changing the face of police governance and the chapter provides a brief overview of relevant legislation.

The chapter concludes by exploring other bodies that hold the police to account. Nationally, Her Majesty's Inspectorate of Constabulary and the Fire & Rescue Service (HMICFRS) can scrutinise police activity and make recommendations for change. At a local level many groups have the ability to hold the police to account, including independent custody visitors (ICV), independent advisory groups (IAG) and various ethics groups.

DEFINITIONS AND HISTORICAL PERSPECTIVE

The police are an integral part of society and play a critical role in keeping our communities safe. To do this they are granted a wide range of powers that enable them to meet the challenges of emergency response, protecting the vulnerable, carrying out investigations and bringing people to justice.

These powers are aligned with certain safeguards and direction provided through legislation, guidance and policy. Legislative examples include: the Police and Criminal Evidence Act (PACE) 1984, providing powers of arrest, search, detention, and questioning; the Human Rights Act 1998, controlling interference with a range of human rights; and the Regulation of Investigatory Powers Act (RIPA) 2000, which provides safeguards for directed and intrusive surveillance.

Decimus Junius Juvenalis, born in the first century, was a Roman satirical poet who posed the question 'Quis custodiet ipsos custodes', which translates as 'who will guard the guards themselves?' (Highet, 2021). How do we know that the police use their powers lawfully, responsibly and ethically, and who guards the police to ensure that they do this? Effective governance provides the solution.

The police service is publicly funded through central government and more locally through a precept (council tax). Currently, PCCs are given significant sums of money for policing, and the budget allocated for the financial year 2021/22 was £15.8 billion (Home Office, 2020b). When control of a substantial budget is involved, the public need to be reassured that their money is spent wisely, providing value for money, and that the policing provided is both efficient and effective.

It is equally important that powers granted to the police are used ethically, responsibly and are not abused. Policing has undergone a significant change since 2010 with decreasing budgets during a prolonged period of austerity. Demand for policing services has increased exponentially with an increased focus on harm reduction, with managers being challenged to maximise limited resources. Taylor-Griffiths et al (2014) suggest that there is now an expectation that police resources are deployed to maximise both effectiveness and efficiency, and that empirical research must provide the evidence base for any increase in budget.

EVIDENCE-BASED POLICING

Let us consider the cost and use of body-worn cameras in policing. The Metropolitan Police spent £3.4 million on purchasing 22,000 camera licences that included docking stations, online storage and access to a management portal, provided by Axon (Metropolitan Police, 2018). This was only a three-year contract that would need to be sustained. The cost was significant and those responsible for making financial decisions needed to find the necessary funding within the police budget or seek an increase to it, while being assured of its viability and cost effectiveness.

$\longrightarrow$

The College of Policing provide a crime reduction toolkit based on empirical research that tells us that the use of body-worn cameras does not have a significant impact on crime-related outcomes but does recognise the benefits of positive changes in behaviour by both police officers and members of the public (College of Policing, 2021a).

More recently, an American study following a cost–benefit analysis on the use of body-worn cameras suggested that an investment of $1 billion could be turned into $5 billion, in relation to reduced cost of investigations, use of force and compensation claims (Williams et al, 2021).

GOVERNANCE

In overseeing the use of police powers and ensuring effectiveness and efficiency, there needs to be a form of governance, but what exactly does the term '*governance*' mean? Two definitions are provided below:

> *The way in which an organisation is managed at the highest level, and the systems for doing this.*

> (Cambridge Dictionary, 2020)

> *The activity of governing a country or controlling a company or an organization; the way in which a country is governed, or a company or institution is controlled.*

> (Oxford Learner's Dictionary, 2020)

The first definition highlights management at the highest level and you need to consider what is meant by this. What is the highest level? Is it central government, a local authority, a PCC or a chief constable? Who does police the police and how do the public hold the police to account?

The second definition brings in the issue of *control*. What is the extent of this control and how effective is it? Reiner (2010, p 223) considers control of the controllers in relation to keeping police practice within a broad framework in line with '*democratically decided communal values*'. Jones (2008, p 694) suggests that the framework of police governance and accountability link to processes and institutions depending on relationships with other mechanisms at individual, organisational and wider societal levels.

History shows that since the inception of the modern police service in 1829 the police have not always got things right, at times significantly impacting public confidence and trust. In June 1991, the Queen commissioned a team to examine the effectiveness of the criminal justice system (CJS) in England and Wales. The team was chaired by Viscount Runciman of Doxford, who published his report in 1993. Within the first chapter of the report reference is made to a series of miscarriages of justice relating to high-profile Irish republican terrorism and murder convictions (Runciman, 1993).

Those convicted of the crimes spent many years in prison, later being released by the Court of Appeal. There were allegations of forced confessions, police torture including sleep deprivation and beatings, expert evidence being discredited, and police officers being accused of lying. Following the release of the Broadwater Farm Three (convicted of the murder of PC Keith Blakelock during a riot in Tottenham in 1985), a cartoon appeared in *The Guardian* newspaper depicting a man late for a date, providing the excuse that he had asked a police officer for the time and that he had lied (Reiner, 2010, p 85).

POLICING SPOTLIGHT

MISCARRIAGE OF JUSTICE

Stefan Kiszco was sent to prison in 1976 for the murder of schoolgirl Lesley Molseed, a crime he did not commit. As a result of information received, the police held Kiszco as a suspect. He was a vulnerable intellectually disabled suspect, and while in custody he was not informed of his right to have a solicitor, his request for his mother to be present during interview was refused, and he was not cautioned until some time after his detention. He made a confession that he quickly retracted, explaining that he had only confessed because the police had told him he could go home to his mother if he confessed (Burnside, nd).

Some years later, forensic evidence cleared Kiszco because semen deposited by the perpetrator on the victim's clothing could not have been his. He had a health condition at the time where he could not produce sperm and this evidence was not made available to his defence team. He was released 16 years after his conviction and died one year later. In 2007, Ronald Castree was convicted of the murder after his DNA was matched with the semen on the victim's clothing (Wallace, 2006).

CRITICAL THINKING ACTIVITY 4.1

LEVEL 4

Find out more about miscarriages of justice through internet research and consider whether the unethical actions of investigators and others could happen today. What is different today to prevent similar miscarriages of justice? When considering this, think about governance and accountability, and how both legislation and technology may have provided a range of safeguards.

A sample answer is provided at the end of this book.

The same year that Runciman produced his report, there was further controversy following the racist murder of Stephen Lawrence, where the Metropolitan Police were accused of institutional racism. The public inquiry report commissioned following the murder stated: '*The investigation was marred by a combination of professional incompetence, institutional racism, and a failure of leadership by senior officers*' (Macpherson, 1999, 46.1).

More recently, we have seen civil rights organisations challenging alleged misuse of power by the police granted by the Coronavirus Act 2020 (Liberty, 2020).

History shows that significant legislative changes have been made and today legislation plays a key role in controlling the use of police powers. Earlier within this chapter three key pieces of legislation were highlighted (PACE 1984, HRA 1998 and RIPA 2000) that significantly curtailed police malpractice and maintained confidence in policing critical for maintaining police legitimacy.

Research has suggested that the use of technology produces positive outcomes, improves policing practice, and enhances trust and legitimacy within communities (Strom, 2017, pp 2–3). The use of body-worn video cameras by police officers today provides a good example of this.

GOVERNANCE BODIES

At the time Sir Robert Peel founded the Metropolitan Police, early governance was provided by one of His Majesty's Secretaries for State who was tasked with the more efficient administration of the police (section 1, Metropolitan Police Act 1829). However, Morris (2004, cited in Emsley, 2014, p 18) states that policing in London was ultimately under the control and supervision of the Home Secretary, who generally left policing to the Police Commissioner.

Elsewhere, as police forces were established throughout the country, watch committees and standing joint committees provided early governance, holding the police to account on service delivery. They were later replaced by police authorities following the Police Act 1964, which governed the police service until they were replaced by the PCC in 2012.

Her Majesty's Inspectorate of Constabulary (HMIC) was introduced in 1856 with a remit to inspect forces for efficiency, and this role continues today. In 2014, Sir Tom Winsor (Her Majesty's Chief Inspector of Constabulary) announced a new regime of 'PEEL' inspections, highlighting the fact that substantial funds are provided for policing, and that the public are entitled to know through accountability how that money is being spent and how well they are being served (HMICFRS, 2016). The role of HMIC, how it developed and PEEL inspections are explored later in the chapter.

KEY GOVERNANCE LEGISLATION

It was not until 1964 that significant changes were made to police governance with a tri-partite approach where central government, police committees and the police were given distinct roles and responsibilities. This was followed two decades later with a raft of new legislation that altered the landscape of police governance and accountability, culminating in the introduction of the PCC.

Below is a list of some of the key governance legislation:

- Police and Criminal Evidence Act 1984;

- Police and Magistrates' Courts Act 1994;

- Police Act 1996;

- Crime and Disorder Act 1998;

- Police Reform Act 2002;

- Police and Justice Act 2006.

To find out more about this legislation and how it shaped policing governance, see the further reading section at the end of this chapter.

POLICE AND CRIME COMMISSIONER (PCC)

In their 2010 election manifesto, the Conservative Party made a pledge to voters that they would replace what they described as *'invisible and unaccountable police authorities'* with an elected individual who would set police priorities in conjunction with local communities (Cameron, 2010, p 57).

Following a successful election, they delivered on their manifesto pledge and police authorities were replaced by PCCs in November 2012. At the time of writing in 2022, 39 of the 43 territorial police forces within England and Wales are governed by a PCC. The exceptions are the Metropolitan Police, who are governed by a deputy mayor based within the Mayoral Office for Policing and Crime (MOPAC). In 2017, the Greater Manchester PCC was replaced by the Mayor of Greater Manchester, Andy Burnham, while in May 2021 the West Yorkshire PCC was replaced by the Mayor of West Yorkshire, Tracy Brabin. These changes did not apply to the City of London Police, who remained governed by a common council defined as a *'Police authority'* (Section 6, AZA Police Act 1996).

The Policing and Crime Act 2017 provided PCCs with the opportunity to take on governance of the Fire and Rescue Service, and as of 2022 there are four Police, Fire and Crime Commissioners (Essex, Northamptonshire, North Yorkshire, and Staffordshire). The Local Government Association (2020), responding to a review of PCCs, made it clear they did not support forced mergers of police and fire governance, which should only take place where there is local agreement.

The role required of the PCC is set out in the Police Reform and Social Responsibility Act (PRSR) 2011. The PCC is required to maintain the police force for the area that they are responsible for and ensure that it is efficient and effective. They are required to hold the chief constable to account for a range of issues set out in the Act, including having regard to the police and crime plan (see below), providing value for money, engagement with local people, equality, diversity and safeguarding (section 1 of PRSR 2011 provides a full list).

They have full control of the police budget referred to as the *police fund* (s 21 PRSR 2011), which is made up from a police grant provided by central government, and a precept element that is collected by local authorities through council tax. Other grants are provided for capital expenditure and the safeguarding of national security.

VICTIMS

PCCs have a responsibility to provide financial support to victim services and in November 2013 were awarded £20.8 million by the Ministry of Justice to set up the local commissioning of victim services, including restorative justice (Fuller, 2014, p 2). In 2019/20, almost

£70 million was provided to PCCs for victim services (HM Government, 2019). MOPAC receive separate funding for victim services and for the financial year 2020/21 they were allocated just under £12 million (Mayor of London, 2020).

Most PCCs have set up additional funding to support both victim services and those concerned with tackling problems of crime, disorder and reducing harm in the communities they serve. Prior to the introduction of PCCs, many organisations involved in the provision of these services struggled for funding, a fact that was recognised by the All Party Parliamentary Group for Domestic and Sexual Violence (2015) who reported that the provision of domestic and sexual abuse services was not fit for purpose with many services under financial pressure and struggling to survive, with some having been lost and more expected to follow.

DISMISSAL OF CHIEF CONSTABLE

The PCC has significant powers that include the appointment and dismissal of the chief constable. This attracted controversy from the outset when the Avon and Somerset PCC, Sue Mount-Stevens, upon taking office in November 2012 required the chief constable Colin Port to reapply for his job, which he refused to do, and he quit. She courted further controversy in 2017 when she dismissed a further chief constable, Nick Gargan, whom she had appointed to replace Colin Port.

These are momentous decisions made by an individual that have the potential to erode public trust without appropriate safeguards in place, and it is appropriate to ask the question of who governs or controls a PCC? Chief Constable Port challenged the PCC's decision and went to court to seek a judicial review, but his application was dismissed by the High Court judge, Mr Justice Edwards-Stuart (BBC News, 2013). During a parliamentary debate in October 2015 about the dismissal of chief constables, the Security Minister John Hayes stated that he remained confident that the interests of people and communities are properly served by the processes in place (Hayes, 2015). Later within this chapter we will discuss the role of the *Police and Crime Panel* who oversee the work of the PCC and provide some accountability, although limited.

POLICE AND CRIME PLAN

Sections 5–10 of the PRSR 2011 refer specifically to *community safety and crime prevention*, setting an agenda for PCCs to focus on reducing harm within communities and tackling the problem of crime through effective preventative measures. A PCC when elected is required to produce a police and crime plan that sets out a series of objectives relating to a strategy for policing the area and how crime and disorder reduction will be tackled.

The plan contains information about the policing area, the financial resources that are available, how performance will be measured, and grants available to reduce crime and disorder. The chief constable is held to account by the PCC to deliver this plan on behalf of the people, having been elected through a democratic process.

Before issuing a police and crime plan the PCC will consult widely and is required by the Act (PRSR 2011, s 6) to consult with the chief constable, send a draft plan to the police and crime panel, have regard to any recommendations made by the panel, provide them with a response and make any response available to the public.

Section 10(2) of the PRSR 2011 states that a PCC and a community safety partnership (CSP) must 'act in cooperation with each other'. Funding for the CSP was initially provided by central government but was transferred to PCCs, providing them with control over how the funding is allocated and used. It provided an opportunity to ensure that the partnerships effectively met their statutory requirements and enabled alignment with the police and crime plan.

A similar provision was made within the Act (PRSR 2011, s 10(3)) to ensure that criminal justice agencies worked effectively with the PCC to 'make arrangements... to provide an efficient and effective criminal justice system for the police area'.

The following is an example of how a newly elected PCC developed his police and crime plan.

POLICING SPOTLIGHT

POLICE AND CRIME PLAN

On 1 April 2013, Bill Longmore, the PCC for West Mercia Police, published his police and crime plan. Prior to producing the plan, he had spent four months walking the three counties of West Mercia, talking to local people and meeting with leaders and key people concerned with criminal justice, victim support, local government, business and other organisations concerned with policing.

This provided a basis for the plan, but there were many other considerations to be made when putting the plan together. This included a strategic intelligence analysis, current policing performance, consultation with victim organisations, and among other considerations being cognisant of the priorities of other key organisations such as community safety partnerships, the Criminal Justice Board and safeguarding boards. Consideration was also given to assessment and inspection reports provided by Her Majesty's Inspectorate of Constabulary and Fire & Rescue Service.

The plan contained 11 objectives that reflected the consultations made and to which the chief constable was held to account (Longmore, 2012, pp 10–29). These objectives were:

1. to provide effective policing;

2. to reduce violent crime with a focus on addressing harms caused by alcohol;

3. to reduce harm caused by drugs with a focus on treatment;

4. to reduce the volume of anti-social behaviour incidents;

5. to reduce re-offending, bringing offenders to account;

6. to develop and implement a business crime strategy;

7. to work in partnership to protect the most vulnerable in society;

8. to deliver a supportive and effective response to victims and witnesses;

9. to reduce the number of casualties on roads;

10. to meet the requirements of the strategic policing requirement;

11. to develop and implement a community engagement strategy.

Search online for *strategic policing requirement* to find out more about it.

REFLECTIVE PRACTICE 4.1

LEVEL 4

Using the internet, find a copy of the police and crime plan for your police force area. Identify what your PCC priorities are and how the force is held to account. Once you understand the relevance of the priorities, consider whether they reflect the needs of your community.

THE POLICE AND CRIME PANEL

The panel is made up of councillors from each local authority within the police area supported by two or more co-opted members. They have limited powers of holding a PCC to account, and section 28(2) of the PRSR 2011 specifically states that they are required to effectively support the PCC in carrying out their functions. Section 28(6) of the PRSR 2011 provides the panel with the power to review or scrutinise decisions made, or other action taken by the PCC, and they can veto decisions relating to the council tax precept and the appointment of a chief constable. When the panel reviews or scrutinises a decision and makes recommendations, the PCC may not agree with the recommendations made, and may decide not to comply with them. This can be a cause of some frustration to panel members and highlights the limitations of the panel in holding a PCC to account.

The panel is required to review the draft police and crime plan, or any variations to it, and to provide a report with recommendations if appropriate. The PCC is required to publish an annual report and the panel can instruct the PCC to attend a meeting to discuss the report and answer questions. If the PCC or their deputy is charged with a criminal offence where the maximum term of imprisonment for the offence is more than two years, the panel have the power to suspend the PCC or deputy (PRSR 2011, s 30). In respect of misconduct by the PCC or the deputy, the panel have limited powers and can deal with complaints via informal resolution; however, where criminal conduct is alleged, the matter is referred to the Independent Office for Police Conduct (IOPC) for investigation. Figure 4.1 provides a recap of the functions and relationship between the chief constable, PCC, and the Police and Crime Panel.

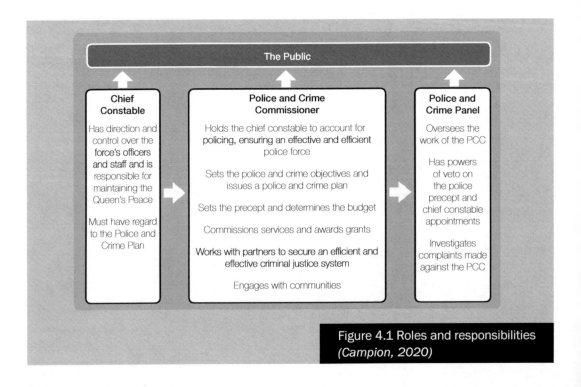

Figure 4.1 Roles and responsibilities (Campion, 2020)

In July 2020, the Home Secretary Priti Patel announced a review of the role of PCCs and referred to the need for British people to know that the police will uphold the law and be held to account. She explained that the review would '*improve accountability, scrutiny and transparency*', putting people at the centre of the PCCs' decision making (Home Office, 2020c). An early response to the review from the Local Government Association (LGA) highlighted that local politicians continue to have mixed views about the merits and value of PCCs. They recognise that the panels do have a wide remit of scrutiny, but concerns remain about not having the right tools to effectively hold the PCC to account (LGA, 2020, p 2).

POLICING SPOTLIGHT

PCC VOTE OF NO CONFIDENCE

On 1 October 2021 the PCC for North Yorkshire, Philip Allott, was interviewed on BBC Radio York following the conviction of Wayne Couzens for the kidnap, rape and murder of Sarah Everard in March 2021. His comments included the need for women to become '*street-wise*' and resulted in public outrage. An online petition signed by thousands of people demanded that the PCC should resign, and the Police, Fire and Crime Panel received over 90 complaints from the public.

No criminal offence had been committed and as this was a non-criminal complaint the only powers available to the panel were through an informal resolution procedure. They could not impose any sanctions but had the power to require the PCC to attend a meeting, answer questions, publish a report and make recommendations (North Yorkshire Police, Fire and Crime Panel, 2021).

The day prior to the panel meeting with the PCC on 14 October 2021, most of his staff signed a letter to state that they had no confidence in him and that they had received over 900 letters of complaint following the radio interview. The panel unanimously stated that they too had '*no confidence*' in him, and following this the PCC announced his resignation (Easteal, 2021).

REFLECTIVE PRACTICE 4.2

LEVEL 5

Consider the powers invested in a PCC who holds the chief constable and their police force to account on behalf of the people, and answer the following question.

a) How effectively is the PCC held to account and how does the current governance arrangements compare with that of the police authority they replaced in 2012?

A sample answer is provided at the end of this book.

HER MAJESTY'S INSPECTORATE OF CONSTABULARY AND FIRE & RESCUE SERVICES (HMICFRS)

For the past 150 years, Her Majesty's Inspectorate of Constabulary has cast a watchful eye over the work of the Police Service and has helped to assure its integrity, efficiency, and effectiveness.

(Cowley and Todd, 2006, p 8)

The County and Borough Police Act 1856 saw the creation of Her Majesty's Inspectorate of Constabulary (HMIC). Every county and borough were required to maintain a police force that was '*efficient*' and to be inspected each year by the inspectorate. If assessed as efficient, the government would contribute to one quarter of the running costs of the police force with the rest being raised from local rates. The Act did not apply to the Metropolitan Police or City of London Police, which had separate but similar arrangements (Cowley and Todd, 2006, p 11).

HMIC have a long and distinguished history, playing a key role through their inspectorate function of holding forces to account in relation to effectiveness and efficiency. Significant funding and resources are provided to the police service, and communities need to be reassured that this investment is being used wisely to meet their needs, such as effectively tackling and reducing the problems of crime, disorder and vulnerability. There are trust, confidence and integrity issues that need to be considered from a public perspective and HMIC play a valuable part in providing the checks and balances necessary and contributing to public reassurance.

The Policing and Crime Act 2017 extended the Inspectorate's role to include the Fire and Rescue Service and became known as HMICFRS.

The Inspectorate is independent of the chief constable, appointed by the Crown, and can be called to Parliament to give evidence to various parliamentary committees. The Police Act 1996 requires the setting of an annual inspection programme to be approved by the Home Secretary, who has the power to make additions to the programme (HMICFRS, 2018).

The Inspectorate are not regulators with powers to intervene, direct and enforce action following inspections, but they do have powers to secure information. They do not have the powers to order change, but they will make recommendations that the chief constable will be expected to take notice of and action accordingly. The PCC is required to respond to the recommendations made within 56 days of receipt of the inspection report (HMICFRS, 2018).

HMICFRS provide a range of inspections that include the annual PEEL assessments (see below), thematic inspections, and carry out joint inspections with others such as the Prisons and Probation Inspectorates. In addition to the 43 police forces in England and Wales, they have a wider inspection remit that includes the British Transport Police, Ministry of Defence, National Crime Agency, Police Service of Northern Ireland, and others.

PEEL INSPECTIONS

In December 2013, the Minister for Policing, Criminal Justice and Victims announced an uplift in funding of £9.4 million for the HMIC to fund a new programme of all-force PEEL inspections. The purpose was to *'enable the public to see how well their force is performing when it comes to cutting crime and providing value for money'* (Green, 2013).

PEEL is a mnemonic for *Police Effectiveness, Efficiency and Legitimacy* and it was in 2014 when HMIC produced their first set of PEEL inspection reports for all 43 police forces in England and Wales. Following an inspection, forces were provided with a grading, which saw five forces assessed as *'Outstanding'*, thirty-five as *'Good'* and three as *'Requires improvement'* (Winsor, 2014).

Effectiveness explores whether the force is providing the right policing services and how well the services are working. It can cover a wide range of force responsibilities from the prevention of crime, investigating crime and protecting vulnerable people through to tackling serious organised crime. Efficiency is concerned with providing value for money and considering how effectively a force matches its resources to policing demand, while legitimacy focuses on how a force operates fairly and ethically within the law (HMICFRS, 2020a, p 59).

Initially the elements of PEEL were inspected separately but in 2018/19 they were integrated, providing a single inspection and adopting a risk-based approach where forces previously assessed as performing well would be inspected in fewer areas. In 2020, the process evolved further with the adoption of an intelligence-led and continuous assessment model (HMICFRS, 2020a, p 63).

Another product of the PEEL assessments are *spotlight* reports that bring out themes identified during the inspection process. One example of this is a report published by HMICFRS in February 2021, *A Spotlight on Stop and Search and the Use of Force* (HMICFRS, 2021a).

CRITICAL THINKING ACTIVITY 4.2

LEVEL 5

Find the above-mentioned report (*A Spotlight on Stop and Search and the Use of Force*) on the internet, analyse the content and consider the following questions.

a) What is the problem that HMICFRS is attempting to resolve?

b) Do the recommendations have the potential to resolve the problem and if not, why not?

c) How will police legitimacy be enhanced?

Sample answers are provided at the end of this book.

LOCAL ACCOUNTABILITY

Exploring police accountability at a local level finds many initiatives and schemes that are in place to scrutinise policing actions and decisions. Many of these are driven by PCCs and some are long established such as independent custody visitors.

INDEPENDENT CUSTODY VISITORS (ICVs)

The idea of custody visitors was first suggested by Michael Meacher MP at a Home Affairs Committee in 1980, following two recent deaths in custody. He proposed that visits should be made by members of the public or lawyers, who would turn up unannounced at police stations to check on the welfare of detainees (Kendall, 2020, p 3).

In 1981, following the Brixton riots, Lord Scarman conducted a public inquiry making a recommendation that communities be invited to inspect the way police detain people in their custody. Initially the government failed to act on the recommendations but later introduced a 'lay visitors' scheme. In July 1984, the Home Secretary Leon Brittan announced in Parliament that in conjunction with the Metropolitan Police Commissioner, he had set up a lay visiting scheme for police stations in the borough of Lambeth (Hansard, 1984).

The year 1984 also saw the introduction of PACE, accompanied by codes of practice with code C setting out procedures for the lawful detention, treatment and questioning of people. However, it was not until 2002 that the scheme became a statutory obligation through section 51 of the Police Reform Act 2002.

PCCs now have a statutory responsibility to run and fund ICV schemes and employ local volunteers who make unannounced visits to police custody centres to check on the rights, entitlements, wellbeing and dignity of detainees held in police custody.

INDEPENDENT ADVISORY GROUPS (IAGs)

The roots of IAGs lie in the tragic murder of Stephen Lawrence, killed following a racist attack in Plumstead, London in April 1983. Sir William Macpherson was asked to conduct a public inquiry into the investigation of the murder and the failings of the Metropolitan Police. Within the report he stated: '*The need to re-establish trust between minority ethnic communities and the police is paramount*' (Macpherson, 1999, 46.31).

From 1999, groups in various guises started to appear across the police service encouraging the development of policing partnerships involving people from diverse groups. The Metropolitan Police set up the first IAG in January 1999 to represent *visible minority groups*, and later in February 2000 a *lesbian, gay, bisexual and transgender* advisory group was formed following the bombings in Soho targeting the gay community (Dixon, 2018, p 687).

In 2011, national advice and guidance on the role, function and governance of IAGs was provided by the Association of Chief Police Officers (ACPO), providing a framework to maximise the value of IAGs within the police service (Leppard, 2011, p 5).

IAGs are now well established and assist with strategic planning, policy development and scrutiny of police activity, and can provide invaluable assistance in relation to investigations involving diverse communities.

Dixon (2018, p 695), exploring the role of IAGs in the age of the PCC, suggests that the need for IAGs is as great now as it was when Macpherson reported in 1999. PCCs have been proactive in setting up a wider range of scrutiny measures to hold the police to account, but Dixon highlights a potential problem of an overlap with other groups, the voice of the IAG becoming diminished and a need for greater partnership working.

OTHER METHODS OF ACCOUNTABILITY

There are many other ways in which the police service is held to account by other organisations and members of the public. PCCs take different approaches, but provide opportunities for public scrutiny around decisions, for example the cautioning of people for offences or use of out-of-court disposals. There are various iterations of value, integrity, trust and ethics groups which scrutinise issues that cause people concern, for example the ethical recording of crime, the use of stop and search, how police complaints are dealt with, and the use of force.

The police have a key statutory duty to secure value for money in the use of public funds. Section 17 of the PRSR 2011 provides the Secretary of State with a power to provide a financial code of practice to give clarity around the governance arrangements for policing within England and Wales (Home Office, 2018a, p 7).

SUMMARY OF KEY CONCEPTS

This chapter has discussed the following key concepts.

- It is critical that the police have the trust and confidence of the public and policing governance plays a pivotal role in ensuring that trust and confidence.

- Governance has been shaped by legislation and there remains a tripartite approach of government (Home Secretary), PCC and the chief constable.

- Government provides a strategic direction and measures police performance.

- The PCC is elected through a democratic process and is a representative of the people, who can hold the chief constable to account on their behalf.

- The chief constable enjoys operational independence.

- HMICFRS provide an inspectorate function and hold forces to account in relation to their efficiency, effectiveness and legitimacy.

- Local accountability plays a key role in holding police forces to account.

CHECK YOUR KNOWLEDGE

1. Describe the tripartite governance system introduced by the Police Act 1964.

2. What are the PCCs' statutory responsibilities?

3. What accountability does the PCC have to the Police and Crime Panel?

4. Describe the elements of a police and crime plan.

5. What do the PEEL assessments introduced by HMIC in 2014 assess?

FURTHER READING

BOOKS

Joyce, P (2011) The Control and Accountability of the Police Service. In *Policing Development and Contemporary Practice* (pp 117–49). London: Sage.
Chapter 6 in this book provides an excellent historical overview of key governance legislation.

WEBSITES

Association of Police and Crime Commissioners. [online] Available at: www.apccs.police.uk (accessed 12 June 2022).
Explore the website and its links and get to know more about the role of the PCC and the range of their work.

Her Majesty's Inspectorate of Constabulary (HMIC) (2006) *A History of Her Majesty's Inspectorate of Constabulary*. [online] Available at: www.justiceinspectorates.gov.uk/hmic frs/media/the-history-of-hmic-the-first-150-years.pdf (accessed 10 June 2022).
Provides a historical account of the HMIC and the important role it plays to assure people about the efficiency, effectiveness and integrity of the police service.

CHAPTER 5
PROFESSIONAL STANDARDS

JANE SAWYERS

LEARNING OBJECTIVES

AFTER READING THIS CHAPTER YOU SHOULD BE ABLE TO:

- ⚙ understand the code of ethics and the standards of professional behaviour, together with the necessity to maintain professional standards in policing in both professional and personal lives;

- ⚙ discuss why people in positions of respect and authority may fail to comply with policy, guidance and legislation and commit criminal offences;

- ⚙ explain the difference between complaints and misconduct and how the police have developed policies and procedures to reduce the possibility of professional malpractice;

- ⚙ describe the role of professional standards departments (PSDs) and the Independent Office for Police Conduct (IOPC);

- ⚙ analyse how the independent bodies, Her Majesty's Inspectorate of Constabulary and Fire & Rescue Services (HMICFRS) and IOPC hold the police to account on behalf of the public;

- ⚙ demonstrate knowledge of the importance of appropriate professional relationships with individuals who are, or may be, vulnerable.

INTRODUCTION

POLICING SPOTLIGHT

In December 2021, PC Paul Chadwick, a former Gwent police officer, was jailed for 18 months after being convicted of two counts of misconduct in a public office. The convictions related to two women he had taken witness statements from in the course of his duties. Chadwick was investigated by the Independent Office for Police Conduct (IOPC) for abuse of his position for a sexual purpose (IOPC, 2021).

The way police officers behave can have a huge impact on how the public feels about the police and therefore it can be argued that how complaints about police actions are dealt with can either damage or restore public trust in policing. In the previous chapter, Peel's second policing principle was highlighted, and it is appropriate to revisit this in the context of professional standards:

> *To recognise always that the power of the police to fulfil their functions and duties is dependent on public approval of their existence, actions, and behaviour, and on their ability to secure and maintain public respect.*

> (Mayhall, 1985, pp 425–6)

A police complaints system should aim to put things right which have gone wrong, improve service and restore public confidence (IOPC, 2020).

The term *professional standards* is used in many ways, including to refer to the practice of individuals in a professional group. It can also be used to refer to documents that set out the standards expected of people in an organisation (Hughes, 2012). In policing and for the purpose of this chapter, professional standards is a combination of the two and is the conduct and behaviour expected from those serving with the police.

This chapter describes and discusses the necessity for maintaining professional standards in the police service, and the standards of professional behaviour and code of ethics that police officers are expected to uphold. It will explain the roles of force PSDs, the IOPC, and describe the processes for dealing with complaints from members of the public and internal misconduct allegations. It discusses the role of HMICFRS in holding the police to account. The chapter also examines why police officers may become involved in poor behaviour and misconduct and in particular the abuse of position for a sexual purpose.

LEGISLATION AND THE CODE OF ETHICS

The police have a significant amount of power given in law to them to enable the protection of members of the public. They can stop, detain and arrest people, fingerprint and photograph them, and search their person and property. For the police to do these things and maintain the support of the public, they must be seen to be using the law fairly, treating people properly and have accountability when questioned (Lewis, 1999). Police officers are also able to exercise discretion when enforcing the law, for instance in deciding whether to make an arrest or not, and therefore it is particularly important that there are structures and mechanisms in place to hold the police to account for these decisions.

The following is the legal framework in place covering professional standards in policing.

* Police Reform Act 2002 – this act introduced the Independent Police Complaints Commission (IPCC), now the IOPC.

* The Police (Conduct) Regulations 2020 – these regulations detail disciplinary proceedings which apply only to police officers (including former officers).

* The Police (Complaints and Misconduct) Regulations 2020 – applies to all persons serving with the police including police officers (and former officers), civilian police staff and designated police volunteers.

* The Police (Performance) Regulations 2020 – police officers up to the rank of chief superintendent but excludes police officers on probation.

There is also guidance that should be considered alongside the legislation.

* Home Office Guidance, Conduct, Efficiency and Effectiveness: Statutory guidance on professional standards and integrity in policing.

* IOPC statutory guidance.

* College of Policing code of ethics.

* College of Policing guidance on outcomes in police misconduct proceedings.

For some considerable time, police conduct focused on a *discipline code* and a *code of conduct* which identified what police officers were not allowed to do. In 2006, the Home Office announced the development of a new code of professional standards which was focused on a statement of expectations of how every officer should behave and every officer understanding the high standards of behaviour expected of them rather than what they should not do (MacVean, 2012). This led to the introduction of the ten standards of professional behaviour which are set out in Schedule 2 of The Police (Conduct) Regulations 2020.

1. *Honesty and Integrity* – police officers are honest, act with integrity and do not compromise or abuse their position.

2. *Authority, Respect and Courtesy* – police officers act with self-control and tolerance, treating members of the public and colleagues with respect and courtesy. Police officers do not abuse their powers or authority and respect the rights of all individuals.

3. *Equality and Diversity* – police officers act with fairness and impartiality. They do not discriminate unlawfully or unfairly.

4. *Use of Force* – police officers only use force to the extent that it is necessary, proportionate and reasonable in all the circumstances.

5. *Orders and Instructions* – police officers only give and carry out lawful orders and instructions. Police officers abide by police regulations, force policies and lawful orders.

6. *Duties and Responsibilities* – police officers are diligent in the exercise of their duties and responsibilities. Police officers have a responsibility to give appropriate cooperation during investigations, inquiries and formal proceedings, participating openly and professionally in line with the expectations of a police officer when identified as a witness.

7. *Confidentiality* – police officers treat information with respect and access or disclose it only in the proper course of police duties.

8. *Fitness for Duty* – police officers when on duty or presenting themselves for duty are fit to carry out their responsibilities.

9. *Discreditable Conduct* – police officers behave in a manner which does not discredit the police service or undermine public confidence in it, whether on or off duty. Police officers report any action taken against them for a criminal offence, any conditions imposed on them by a court or the receipt of any penalty notice.

10. *Challenging and Reporting Improper Conduct* – police officers report, challenge or take action against the conduct of colleagues which has fallen below the standards of professional behaviour.

In 2010, the newly formed Coalition Government asked Peter Neyroud, the former chief executive officer of the National Policing Improvement Agency (NPIA) and chief constable of Thames Valley Police, to undertake a review of police leadership and training. The subsequent report contained several recommendations, including the creation of a new professional body to set standards for policing (Neyroud, 2011). Neyroud argued that policing 'needs to move from being a service that acts professionally to becoming a professional service' (Neyroud, 2011, p 11). This led to the introduction, in 2013, of the College of Policing as the professional body for policing in England and Wales. The College has responsibility for setting standards and promoting ethical behaviour in policing and some of its initial work was to develop a code of ethics for policing. Professional bodies often publish codes of ethics and Holdaway (2017) suggests that it was important for the College of Policing to do the same. In 2014, the College of Policing produced a code of ethics which provides more detail about the behaviours expected by the standards of professional behaviour. It lays out nine policing principles that not only underpin the standards of professional behaviour but are also at the heart of decisions taken in policing every day (see reflective practice 5.1). The code of ethics (set out below) applies to police officers and police staff, including those working on permanent or temporary contracts and a casual or voluntary basis (College of Policing, 2014b).

- *Accountability* – you are answerable for your decisions, actions and omissions.

- *Fairness* – you treat people fairly.

- *Honesty* – you are truthful and trustworthy.

- *Integrity* – you always do the right thing.

- *Leadership* – you lead by good example.

- *Objectivity* – you make choices on evidence and your best professional judgement.

- *Openness* – you are open and transparent in your actions and decisions.

- *Respect* – you treat everyone with respect.

- *Selflessness* – you act in the public interest.

(College of Policing, 2014b)

REFLECTIVE PRACTICE 5.1

LEVEL 4

Consider the ten standards of professional behaviour and think about what kind of behaviour by a police officer might lead to a complaint or internal misconduct investigation.

A sample answer is provided at the end of this book.

WHY PEOPLE IN POSITIONS OF AUTHORITY ACT UNPROFESSIONALLY OR CRIMINALLY

A rapid evidence assessment carried out by McDowall et al (2015) for the College of Policing examined studies of policing and other professions which looked at actions to improve ethical behaviour and prevent misconduct. The evidence from the studies suggested that factors that influence wrongdoing fell into three broad areas: organisational factors, situational factors and individual characteristics. In relation to organisational factors, the presence of strong ethical leadership, where standards and expectations were clearly defined, was found to have an impact. The results of a study by Resick et al (2013) showed that employees who believed their leader to be ethical were more likely to have a positive attitude towards their organisation and act appropriately. Conversely, actions by senior leaders which were felt not to be ethical could have a negative effect on behaviour (Umphress et al, 2009). Policing finds itself under constant scrutiny from both politicians and the media and Punch (2009) argues that a lack of ethical leadership in a climate of political and media pressure to produce results can result in police wrongdoing. Situational factors include the behaviour of others, for example, where a suspect is resisting or drunk, police officers were more likely to use excessive force. Also covered by situational factors is what is termed the '*blue code of silence*' where officers are reluctant to report their colleagues (McDowall et al, 2015, p 33). Several studies in the College of Policing research conducted by McDowall et al (2015) pointed to individual characteristics of officers and staff which impacted on wrongdoing. Gender was one example of this, with studies indicating that male officers were more likely to engage in wrongdoing than female officers (Harris, 2009). It is suggested that these individual characteristics are much more difficult to address through policy and guidance and therefore ethical leadership and standard setting become more important.

There is research evidence that shows that police officers are reluctant to report colleagues who engage in misconduct or unethical behaviour (Westmarland, 2005). This was recognised as early as the 1960s when Banton (1964) wrote that police officers are reluctant to report other officers who break the rules. Reasons for this reluctance include police culture, uncertainty about the rules and a belief that certain behaviour was not serious enough to report. An international study carried out by Klockars et al (2004, p 17) found that *the most dramatic finding that emerges from the contours of integrity concerns the worldwide prevalence of the code of silence*.

EVIDENCE-BASED POLICING

REPORTING COLLEAGUES

In a study by Westmarland and Rowe (2016), officers from three UK police forces were given 11 different scenarios of potentially corrupt colleagues and asked how seriously they viewed the behaviour of these officers. The respondents were also asked about whether they would report the behaviour and the responses between seriousness and reporting were then compared. Some of the scenarios outlined activities that could be viewed as minor, while others amounted to serious behaviour including criminal offences committed by police officers. As could be expected, the study found that the more serious the conduct, the greater likelihood of it being reported. It did also find, however, that some officers would not report conduct even though they considered it to be serious.

The code of ethics aims to address such non-reporting by not only promoting the standards of behaviour and principles which are expected but also requiring all those in policing to prevent unprofessional behaviour by questioning it and where necessary reporting it (College of Policing, 2014b). The code is explicit in saying that *all staff have a duty to act if they believe the Code may be breached* (see policing spotlight examples below). The code does still allow for discretion but is intended to get police professionals to make ethical decisions and do the right thing by combining principles and standards of professional behaviour.

CRITICAL THINKING ACTIVITY 5.1

LEVEL 5

a) You are told by a colleague on your neighbourhood policing team that she accepts small gifts such as chocolate and books from members of the community she serves. Consider what questions you would ask your colleague and whether she can justify accepting these gifts.

b) You and another officer are crewed together and come across a vehicle at the side of the road with a driver who is clearly intoxicated. Your colleague knows the driver, who is a police officer at another station, and he insists that the two of you do not breathalyse the driver but instead take him home. Reflect on what you would say and what action you would take.

Sample answers are provided at the end of this book.

COMPLAINTS AND MISCONDUCT

For the public to have confidence in the police complaints system, that system needs to be easily understood and accessible and not put off members of the public from making a complaint (IOPC, 2020). The public must have the confidence to report on inappropriate behaviour and confidence that the organisation will deal with it. Prenzler (2009, p 79) reasons that '*a robust and fair complaints and discipline system is essential to control misconduct, encourage public confidence in police integrity, and ensure the loyalty and confidence of honest police*'. The IOPC produce statutory guidance which details how forces are expected to promote the complaints system and explains the different ways forces should endeavour to help understanding of how to make a complaint (IPOC, 2020). This includes online, using social media and in-person at police stations and in custody suites. Forces are also expected to have information about making a complaint on their websites which is easy to understand and explains the procedure for making a complaint. All police forces have a department responsible for the recording and investigation of complaints and conduct matters, usually called the Professional Standards Department (PSD), and members of the public are encouraged to report complaints to the force concerned to be logged by the PSD (IOPC, 2020).

There are two routes that can lead to an investigation into the conduct of a person serving with the police: a complaint or a conduct matter. A complaint is defined as: '*Any expression of dissatisfaction with a police force that is expressed by or on behalf of a member of the public*' (Police Reform Act 2002). A complaint can be made about the conduct of any person serving with the police or against the organisation. The person making the complaint is termed a *complainant*. If a complaint is about an individual then the complainant can be the person to whom the conduct occurred, a person affected by the conduct or who witnessed it, or someone who is acting on behalf of any of these people. In some circumstances, complaints can also be made about the conduct of an officer who is off duty, for example, a complaint made about an off-duty officer using racist language would be likely to result in an investigation. A 'conduct matter' is defined as:

> **Any matter which is not and has not been the subject of a complaint, where there is an indication (whether from the circumstances or otherwise) that a person serving with the police may have committed a criminal offence or behaved in a manner which would justify disciplinary proceedings.**

> (Police Reform Act 2002)

Conduct matters are usually identified by intelligence gathering or reported using internal reporting mechanisms.

The IOPC (2020) statutory guidance details the process for the handling of complaints and conduct matters and the general principle is that complaints should be handled in accordance with the wishes of the complainant. This means that some complaints fall outside schedule 3 of the Police Reform Act 2002 and can be dealt with promptly rather than being formally recorded. Examples of such complaints include where the complainant is satisfied after being provided with an explanation or receives an apology for poor service. The guidance also covers the handling of complaint and conduct matters and lists matters which must be recorded. The majority of complaints and conduct matters are recorded and investigated by the PSD. There are however certain complaints and conduct matters which must be recorded and referred to the IOPC under the mandatory referral criteria. These include allegations of conduct which amount to:

- a serious assault;

- a serious sexual offence;

- serious corruption, including abuse of position for a sexual purpose or for the purpose of pursuing an improper emotional relationship;

- a criminal offence or behaviour which is liable to lead to disciplinary proceedings and which, in either case, is aggravated by discriminatory behaviour on the grounds of a person's race, sex or religion;

- any offence for which the sentence is fixed by law or any offence for which a person of 18 years or over (not previously convicted) may be sentenced to imprisonment for seven years or more;

- complaints or conduct matters arising from the same incident as one where conduct falling within the above criteria is alleged;

- any conduct matter relating to a chief officer (or the Deputy Commissioner of the Metropolitan Police Service) and any complaint relating to a chief officer (or the Deputy Commissioner of the Metropolitan Police Service) where the appropriate authority is unable to satisfy itself, from the complaint alone, that the conduct complained of, if it were proved, would not justify the bringing of criminal or disciplinary proceedings.

An appropriate authority must also refer complaints which arise from the same incident about which there is a complaint alleging that the conduct complained of resulted in death or serious injury (Regulations 4 and 7, The Police (Complaints and Misconduct) Regulations 2020).

Voluntary referral of complaints and conduct matters can also be made to the IOPC where it is considered appropriate due to the seriousness of the matter or other exceptional circumstances (IOPC, 2020).

CRITICAL THINKING ACTIVITY 5.2

LEVEL 4   MANDATORY REFERRALS

a) An officer has been communicating privately with a victim of domestic abuse, whom he met in the course of his duties. He has been communicating with the woman with the aim of establishing a relationship with her, using his personal email address. Eventually, the woman reported his behaviour to the police. Does this meet the IOPC mandatory referral criteria (IPCC, 2016a)?

b) An officer reported his colleague when he felt he had used unnecessary force on a member of the public during an arrest. The officer's statement gave a false rationale both for the arrest and for the use of force, justifying them when there was no basis for either the arrest or for the level of force used. Does this meet the IOPC mandatory referral criteria (IPCC, 2016a)?

Sample answers are provided at the end of this book.

INDEPENDENT BODIES

The first oversight body for complaints against the police was the Police Complaints Board (PCB) introduced by the Police Act in 1976. The PCB did not have any ability to investigate complaints but rather it looked at completed investigations already carried out by police forces. This changed with the Police and Criminal Evidence Act in 1984, which introduced the Police Complaints Authority (PCA) to replace the PCB, and this new body had the power to supervise complaint investigations carried out by the police (Smith, 2005). The PCA was followed, in 2004, by the Independent Police Complaints Commission (IPCC), which became the first independent body to have the power and resource to investigate complaints against the police.

Calls for an independent body to investigate complaints against the police had occurred over many years with both Scarman's inquiry into the Brixton Riots and Macpherson's inquiry into the death of Stephen Lawrence highlighting the need for such an independent body (Scarman, 1981; Macpherson, 1999). This resulted in the Home Office appointing KPMG to look into the feasibility of more independence in investigations of complaints against the police. KPMG (2000) carried out a study involving the views of stakeholders from both inside and outside the criminal justice system and recommended that two models introducing more independence should be further explored. The two models were:

1. cases investigated independently without any direct involvement of police officers;

2. teams which consisted of police officers who were seconded to an independent body working with non-police investigators; the team would be led by a non-police investigator.

The resulting consultation led to the Police Reform Act 2002, and the establishment of the IPCC following the second recommended model. The IPCC became operational in 2004 and had far greater powers than its predecessors to not only monitor the way forces dealt with complaints and misconduct but to also initiate, carry out and oversee investigations (Hardwick, 2006). Initially, the IPCC followed the second model and many of its investigators and senior staff were seconded or former police officers. This led to concerns and criticisms about its independence and, in 2012, the newly appointed chairperson of the IPCC, Dame Anne Owers, announced a move to get a better balance by developing a programme specifically aimed at recruiting and training investigators from a non-police background (Owers, 2012). Subsequent growth saw the IPCC taking on more and more investigations and between 2013 and 2018 they doubled in size. This led to a change of name and structure and in 2018 the IPCC became the Independent Office for Police Conduct (IOPC, 2018). The IOPC is led by a director general and is independent of both the police and the government. The legislation which changed the IPCC to the IOPC was the Policing and Crime Act 2017 and this also gave the IOPC additional powers. This included the power for the IOPC to begin investigations without a referral from the police and the power to present cases at misconduct hearings (Policing and Crime Act 2017).

Investigations that are carried out by the IOPC or the police force PSD have three broad outcomes:

- *an officer has no case to answer in relation to their conduct;*

- *the police force should launch disciplinary proceedings;*

- *evidence is passed to the Crown Prosecution Service for criminal charges to be considered.*

(IOPC, 2018)

If a decision is taken to launch disciplinary proceedings, those proceedings can either be for misconduct, which would result in a misconduct meeting unless there are already live sanctions against the officer, or gross misconduct which would result in a misconduct hearing (Home Office, 2020a).

Table 5.1 Definitions for the purpose of bringing disciplinary proceedings

Type of allegation	Definition (as defined by the Conduct Regulations)	How to be dealt with
Gross misconduct	A breach of the standards of professional behaviour that is so serious as to justify dismissal	Formal investigation Misconduct hearing IOPC/PSD
Misconduct	A breach of the Standards of Professional Behaviour	Formal investigation Misconduct meeting IOPC/PSD

At a misconduct hearing where there is a finding of *misconduct*, the following sanctions are available (Home Office, 2020a):

- written warning;

- final written warning;

- reduction in rank;

- dismissal without notice.

At a misconduct hearing where there is a finding of *gross misconduct*, the following sanctions are available (Home Office, 2020a):

- final written warning;

- reduction in rank;

- dismissal without notice.

HER MAJESTY'S INSPECTORATE OF CONSTABULARY AND FIRE & RESCUE SERVICES

The role of HMICFRS was highlighted within the previous chapter as an inspectorate body responsible for holding the police to account. Within a professional standards context they have a very different role to the IOPC as an inspection body rather than a regulator, making recommendations rather than giving direction. They can be commissioned, by the Home Secretary, to carry out inspections of police forces and these often follow high-profile events where police actions have been questioned. One such inspection followed the August 2011 disorders which started in London and spread to other parts of the country (HMIC, 2011). A more recent example was the inspection of how the Metropolitan Police Service policed the vigil in memory of Sarah Everard on 13 March 2021 (HMICFRS, 2021b). Both commissions followed significant media criticism of the actions of the police and, it is suggested, allowed for more transparency of those actions and met the HMICFRS remit of reporting on policing in the public interest.

REFLECTIVE PRACTICE 5.2

LEVEL 5

a) Identify other policing examples where HMICFRS may have been commissioned by the Home Secretary.

b) Consider the relationship between the role of HMICFRS and the IOPC in the context of professional standards.

Sample answers are provided at the end of this book.

VULNERABILITY AND ABUSE OF POSITION FOR A SEXUAL PURPOSE

This chapter began with a policing spotlight on the actions of a Gwent police officer in Staffordshire who was jailed for 18 months after being convicted of two counts of misconduct in a public office relating to contact he had with females he met in the course of his duties. There is a public expectation that police officers and staff have a role to help and protect and therefore allegations that they not only fail to protect but carry out abuse of someone who is vulnerable are particularly serious. In 2011, former Northumbria police officer Stephen Mitchell was sentenced to life imprisonment following conviction for two rapes, three indecent assaults and six counts of misconduct in a public office. The court was told he targeted women he met while on duty (Carter, 2011). This case and Mitchell's subsequent conviction led to the IPCC and Association of Chief Police Officers (ACPO) separately examining this type of behaviour and its prevalence in policing. A joint report was produced to raise the profile of cases of police officers and staff abusing their powers to carry out sexual abuse (IPCC, 2012). The report draws parallels with similar professions where individuals have a lot of power and trust placed in them, such as doctors and religious leaders. It makes clear that in the police service this type of behaviour must be treated as corruption and is, therefore, a mandatory referral to the IOPC. The report provides details of six case studies of officers who either resigned or were convicted and dismissed following allegations of abusing their powers for a sexual purpose. One of the cases involved other officers receiving misconduct sanctions because the officer concerned admitted to them that sexual acts had taken place and none of them reported it. Policing students are encouraged to read this report and the detail of the case studies to recognise some of the indicators of this type of behaviour and the actions necessary to both prevent it from happening and report it when they have any concerns (see link in reference list entry for IPCC, 2012).

The Mitchell case prompted significant action and subsequent reviews by several bodies associated with policing, including a change to police regulations requiring forces to publish results of misconduct hearings (Sweeting et al, 2021). The National Police Chiefs' Council (NPCC) provided a definition of abuse of position for a sexual purpose:

> *Any behaviour by a police officer or police staff member, whether on or off duty, that takes advantage of their position as a member of the police service to misuse their position, authority, or powers in order to pursue a sexual or improper emotional relationship with any member of the public.*

(NPCC, 2017)

In 2016, as part of its inspection of the legitimacy of police forces, HMIC identified abuse of position for sexual gain as a serious corruption offence and asked forces specific questions about how they were dealing with it. The national overview report highlighted how the victims were often some of the most vulnerable people in society, such as those who had suffered domestic abuse (HMIC, 2016). The report found evidence that, overall, the police service had failed to learn the lessons from the other reviews and inspections when it came to tackling abuse of position for a sexual purpose. The focus on this area of serious corruption has continued with further inspections and College of Policing guidance.

VETTING

An effective vetting process is essential in identifying individuals who are unsuitable to work within the police service. In 2006, all forces agreed national standards for vetting to ensure consistency across the police service in England and Wales. The College of Police also produce a vetting code of practice and authorised professional practice to support the application of the national standards. Despite this, in 2019, HMICFRS carried out inspections to see how forces were tackling abuse of position for a sexual purpose and still identified some serious concerns in vetting procedures in individual forces (HMICFRS, 2019). The inspection report found that some forces were not proactive enough in looking for corruption and needed to employ more officers in counter-corruption units, invest in appropriate monitoring software and form better partnerships with agencies supporting vulnerable people. Given the serious impact on victims and public confidence in policing of this type of corruption (see policing spotlight example below), the focus by oversight bodies will no doubt continue.

POLICING SPOTLIGHT

VETTING CASE STUDY

A court described a PC as someone who had joined the police 'to gain the keys to a sweetshop'. He met a 13-year-old girl after answering a call to a domestic incident. He contacted her on social media, exchanging sexual messages and photos, returning to her home three days later. He drove her to a country lane, where he filmed himself raping her. The applicant had passed the vetting process in October 2016. Before he was appointed as a police officer, a complaint of rape had been made against him in 2017 in another force area. His recruitment was put on hold. When no further action was taken against him, the force resumed his recruitment application but didn't revisit his vetting. Unknown to the force, two further complaints of sexual offences against children had been reported against him to neighbouring forces. Further vetting checks would have revealed this. Six months after joining the police, he met his victim. He was jailed for a total of 25 years, for 37 different offences.

(HMICFRS, 2019, p 16)

In September 2021, Wayne Couzens was handed a whole life sentence for the kidnap, rape and murder of Sarah Everard (Dodd and Siddique, 2021). Couzens, who was a serving police officer at the time, abused his position as a police officer to falsely arrest Miss Everard while she was walking home in south London in March 2021. The public reaction to the murder was far reaching and understandably highly damaging to the credibility and legitimacy of policing in the United Kingdom (Harfield, 2021). The case raised serious concerns about vetting and in October 2021 the Home Secretary launched an inquiry to investigate issues raised by the conviction of Couzens, including vetting. She also commissioned HMICFRS to undertake a thematic inspection to provide an assessment of the capability and capacity of policing in relation to vetting and corruption.

The murder of Sarah Everard highlights, in the most appalling circumstances, the importance of professional standards in policing and how the rigorous and continuous vetting of persons serving with the police is essential to identify such individuals and prevent them being recruited or continuing to serve.

CRITICAL THINKING ACTIVITY 5.3

LEVEL 5

The IOPC have launched a number of investigations following the murder of Sarah Everard. These investigations involve at least four different police forces, and several are connected to the use of social media by police officers. Familiarise yourself with those investigations by visiting the IOPC website. Critically analyse the use of social media by police officers and consider the need for forces to impose restrictions on officers regarding its use.

A sample answer is provided at the end of this book.

SUMMARY OF KEY CONCEPTS

This chapter has discussed the following key concepts.

- The behaviour of police officers can have an impact on public confidence in policing.

- The College of Policing has played a key role in professionalising the police service and developed the code of ethics.

- There is a difference between complaints against the police and internal misconduct investigations, and the most serious matters are referred to the IOPC.

- Both the IOPC and HMICFRS have a key oversight role in relation to the behaviour of persons serving with the police.

- Abuse of or using position for a sexual purpose severely damages public confidence in policing.

CHECK YOUR KNOWLEDGE

1. Which piece of legislation introduced the IPCC (now the IOPC)?

2. Who does the code of ethics apply to?

3. According to research, which three broad areas influence wrongdoing?

4. What term of imprisonment makes an offence relevant for mandatory referral criteria?

5. What three sanctions are available at a misconduct hearing following a finding of gross misconduct?

FURTHER READING

BOOKS

MacVean, A (2012) *Handbook of Policing, Ethics, and Professional Standards.* London: Routledge.
The book includes different perspectives on how ethics and professional standards have been developed in policing and the following two chapters are recommended:
- Part II, Chapter 8 – Robins, R (2012) Police Deviance: Child Sexual Abuse
- Part III, Chapter 17 – Grieve, J (2012) Navigating the Moral Minefield

JOURNALS

Holdaway, S (2017) The Re-professionalization of the Police in England and Wales. *Criminology and Criminal Justice*, 17(5): 588–604.
This article will assist in understanding the reasons for the introduction of the College of Policing and the move to professionalise the police service.

WEBSITES

The IOPC circulate a newsletter (*Focus*) to police forces that contains case studies and aims to give advice to PSDs on complaint and conduct matters – search the internet using the keywords '*IOPC Focus*'.

CHAPTER 6
DECISION MAKING AND ETHICS

BARRIE SHELDON

LEARNING OBJECTIVES

AFTER READING THIS CHAPTER YOU SHOULD BE ABLE TO:

- understand the police code of ethics and the police national decision model;

- understand risks associated with decision making and the use of discretion;

- understand and analyse the potential impact of bias when making policing decisions;

- apply professional approaches to policing, demonstrating ethics, fairness and integrity;

- critically evaluate the impact upon policing of differing values, ethics and norms within a diverse community.

INTRODUCTION

Ethical behaviour comes from the values, beliefs, attitudes, and knowledge that guide the judgements of each individual. Everyone in policing has to make difficult decisions and complex choices every day of the week.

(Pearce, 2014, foreword)

A key skill for a police officer is decision making. Some decisions will be straightforward, while others will be challenging, complex and require professional judgement. Initially, it is natural for a police recruit to question whether they have the ability to make good decisions. Lack of experience may be a factor, together with a worry about making wrong decisions.

Decisions made by police officers impact on people, including victims, witnesses and suspects. Decisions relating to use of policing powers, dealing with incidents and vulnerability require care, personal integrity and appropriate use of discretion. Good decision making engenders confidence and trust within a community and contributes significantly to public trust and confidence in the police, ie police legitimacy.

Consequently, ethical behaviour is a key requirement for all police officers and can be directly linked to decision making. The chapter briefly highlights some of the theories related to ethics and revisits the *code of ethics* introduced by the College of Policing in 2014. The *national decision model* framed within the code of ethics is explored, together with the risks related to police decision making.

Following this, the use of police discretion is considered – a topic that continues to attract much public debate. For example, as a result of the Covid-19 pandemic new legislation was introduced with a government expectation that the police would apply common sense and discretion while enforcing the law. Turner and Rowe (2020), when considering how the new rules were put into practise, suggest that one police officer's idea of common sense could be another person's idea of a police state.

Next follows an examination of the impact of stereotyping, prejudice and bias on decision making. Decisions made tainted by stereotyping, prejudice and bias can have severe implications for all parties involved and bring the police service into disrepute.

Finally, the chapter concludes by exploring one specific aspect of policing, namely the use of force. Ethical considerations can be applied to many areas of policing and there is not the scope within this chapter to visit other key areas such as covert policing, policing of public disorder, intelligence, community policing and so forth. More information can be found on these topics in the further reading section at the end of the chapter.

ETHICS THEORY

Decision making is an everyday occurrence for a police officer, who will on occasion be faced with ethical dilemmas. A police officer is directly accountable for any decisions made and may be required to provide to a court, inquest, tribunal or other inquiry a justifiable rationale for a decision made. For example, what options were considered at the time? Why was the chosen option taken? Why were the other options rejected?

Decisions can be viewed through a number of different, and sometimes competing, ethical perspectives. Within a policing context, you may feel that certain ethical theories are more relevant than others. Table 6.1 provides a brief and basic overview of some of the key academic theories related to ethics.

Table 6.1 Ethical theories

Ethical theory	Brief overview
Utilitarianism	Teleological and consequential theories are primarily concerned with the consequence of the act being moral or not. It is the end result that counts, with the means of getting there being a secondary consideration.
Deontology	The end result is not of primary importance but determining the moral intent of the decision or action is.
Virtue ethics	If you are a good person, you will do good things, and to be good you must do good.
Ethics of care	Simply described as caring for others.
Egoism	An action that is self-serving, bringing happiness or benefit to self.
Religion or divine command theory	Will differ depending on the religion, but for example 'God' will be the source for all principles and provides direction.
Natural law	God enables humans to reason in a natural way to make ethical choices.
Social contract theory	Unwritten social contract with society that we will not break laws or moral codes.
Rawls' theory of justice	A society in which the principles of justice are found in a social contract.
Moral relativism	Differences in morality from culture to culture.

Adapted from McCartney and Parent (2015)

To find out more about these theories and how they can relate to law enforcement, see the further reading at the end of the chapter.

To highlight the relevance of the theory of ethics and how it can relate to policing practice, consider the three incidents set out in the following policing spotlight, with a focus on saving life where people have got into difficulty in water.

POLICING SPOTLIGHT

INCIDENT 1

In May 2007, Jordan Lyon, ten years old, drowned in a pond while it was alleged two Police Community Support Officers (PCSOs) stood by and watched, making no attempt to rescue him while waiting for police officers to arrive. A senior police officer later stated that *'It would have been inappropriate for PCSOs who are not trained in water safety to enter the pond'* (*The Guardian*, 2007).

INCIDENT 2

In July 2015, the body of teenager Jack Susianta was pulled out of the River Lea in Walthamstow. He was being pursued by police officers and entered the river of his own accord and was later seen to disappear underwater. Members of the public criticised the police for their lack of action and urgency to save the boy; however, this was refuted by the police who said that it could have placed officers' lives at risk if they had entered the water immediately. A senior police officer stated that a *'dynamic assessment'* of potential risks was required. PC Wilson later entered the water having asked permission to do so on his radio and being told that it was his decision to make. Having entered the water attempting to find the teenager, he did get into difficulty and had to be helped (Walker, 2016).

INCIDENT 3

In February 2018, a police officer from Bury, Lancashire who could not swim dived into a freezing river to save a man. A senior police officer later stated that this was *'a prime example of why people join the force – to protect people and make sure they are away from harm'* (BBC News, 2018).

CRITICAL THINKING ACTIVITY 6.1

LEVEL 6

- Consider how you as a police officer would have acted in any of the situations above. What decision would you make in those circumstances and what is the motivation behind your decision?

- Consider the ethical theories set out above and decide which may be relevant to you, and how it may impact on your decision making.

These are difficult decisions for a police officer to make and in life and death situations the way forward may not always be clear. Legislation, guidance and policy will need to be considered; however, the individual decision maker may choose a different course of action based on ethical reasoning that is contrary to the legislation, guidance and policy, depending on the circumstances presented. It is important to ask yourself what really matters. Is it the end result, the moral obligation (duty) to save life, the caring for others, doing good to be good, bringing happiness for the benefit of yourself or the need to comply with the law?

In the above policing spotlight we see police officers making different decisions dependent on the situation they are facing at the time, based on what could be argued as sound ethical decision making, despite criticisms voiced by others. Wood (2020a, p 118) suggests that if a police officer's decisions are predetermined by others, 'the police role becomes subservient such that ethical considerations become redundant'.

Later in this chapter elements of the national decision model will be explored, together with the risks associated with decision making that can be applied to the three case studies and compared with your thoughts from the exercise above.

CODE OF ETHICS

In the previous chapter, the code of ethics was explored and discussed in the context of professional standards. The code lies at the heart of policing decisions and should be applied consistently with the principles and standards of behaviour contained within the code (College of Policing, 2014b).

The principles set out within the code of ethics originate from the *Principles of Public Life* published in 1995 by the Parliamentary Committee on Standards in Public Life. They apply to anyone who works as a public office holder, which includes the police. There are seven principles forming the basis of the code of ethics: selflessness, integrity, objectivity, accountability, openness, honesty and leadership (Nolan, 1995, p 14). Research has shown that ethical behaviour contributes to improved confidence and trust in the police.

EVIDENCE-BASED POLICING

In a report, *Promoting Ethical Behaviour and Preventing Wrongdoing in Organisations* (McDowall et al, 2015), based on 57 studies completed across a range of professions including policing, evidence was provided of interventions, mechanisms and levers with the potential to promote and encourage ethical behaviour, and prevent wrongdoing.

It was found that interventions that embraced the principles of procedural justice (for example, fair decision making and treating people with respect) improved trust and confidence, and perceptions of the police (McDowall et al, 2015, p 14)

NATIONAL DECISION MODEL

In 2012, the Association of Chief Police Officers (ACPO) introduced a national decision model (NDM), a tool based on values and designed to provide an easy, logical and evidence-based approach when making policing decisions (ACPO, 2012, p 1). At the heart of this decision-making model was the statement of mission and values provided by ACPO a year earlier, and later replaced by the code of ethics in 2014. The model has five logical stages that provide a framework to assist police officers in making decisions, shown in Figure 6.1.

To assist with remembering the elements of the model, the College of Policing (2014a) provide a mnemonic that is easy to understand and one that you may find useful when making decisions: CIAPOAR

Code of ethics

Information

Assessment

Powers and policy

Options

Action and **R**eview

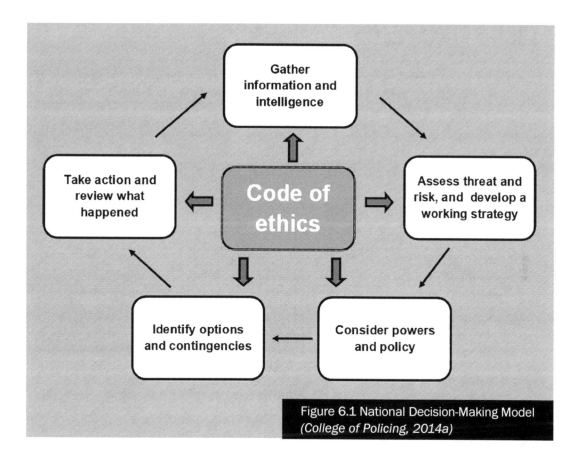

Figure 6.1 National Decision-Making Model
(College of Policing, 2014a)

So how does this work in practice? The following critical thinking activity provides you with a fictitious scenario to consider and an opportunity for you to apply the national decision model. Use the mnemonic to structure your answer.

CRITICAL THINKING ACTIVITY 6.2

LEVEL 4

Imagine that you are a police officer on patrol, and you come across a person collapsed in the street who appears to have had too much to drink. How are you going to deal with this person?

While considering your answer, work though and apply the elements of the NDM.

A sample answer is provided at the end of the book.

RISK PRINCIPLES

Policing is a risky business: fact! Having to make tough and dynamic decisions, to do the right thing, in ambiguity and uncertainty is all part of everyday policing.

(EMPAC, 2018)

To support the NDM the College of Policing provided ten risk principles (set out below) to encourage a more positive approach to risk, to support decision makers and build confidence in taking risks.

Principle 1: *The willingness to make decisions in conditions of uncertainty (ie risk taking) is a core professional requirement of all members of the police service.*

Principle 2: *Maintaining or achieving the safety, security and wellbeing of individuals and communities is a primary consideration in risk decision making.*

Principle 3: *Risk taking involves judgement and balance. Decision makers are required to consider the value and likelihood of the possible benefits of a particular decision against the seriousness and likelihood of the possible harms.*

Principle 4: *Harm can never be totally prevented. Risk decisions should, therefore, be judged by the quality of the decision making, not by the outcome.*

Principle 5: *Making risk decisions, and reviewing others' risk decision making, is difficult.*

Principle 6: *The standard expected and required of members of the police service is that their risk decisions should be consistent with those a body of officers of similar rank, specialism or experience would have taken in the same circumstances.*

Principle 7: *Whether to record a decision is a risk decision in itself, which should be left to professional judgement.*

Principle 8: *To reduce risk aversion and improve decision making, policing needs a culture that learns from successes as well as failures. Good risk taking should be identified, recognised and shared.*

Principle 9: *Since good risk taking depends on quality information, the police service will work with partner agencies and others to share relevant information about those who pose risk or those who are vulnerable to the risk of harm.*

Principle 10: *Members of the police service who make decisions consistent with these principles should receive the encouragement, approval and support of their organisation.*

(College of Policing, 2018a)

To find out more about these risk principles it is strongly recommended that you visit the College of Policing authorised professional practice (APP) and work through the additional information provided for each of the principles (see further reading at the end of the chapter).

Risk assessment is an inherent and key element of policing that must be considered when making policing decisions, as reflective practice 6.1 encourages you to explore.

REFLECTIVE PRACTICE 6.1

LEVEL 4

Reflect on your understanding of the risk principles, the application of the NDM and their use in policing practice. How confident would you be using the model supported by the risk principles? Would they provide you with the confidence to make good decisions? Do you feel that you would be supported by the policing organisation for decisions made? How do they contribute to public reassurance for police decision making?

USE OF DISCRETION

Discretion is the bedrock of policing; it allows reasoned and fair decisions based on experience to be taken by police officers without the need to take a course of action merely to satisfy targets.

(Police Federation, 2018, p 4)

A police officer making decisions has a power of discretion when carrying out their duties, but consider how the power is deployed, how an officer is held to account when using discretion, and potential impact on policing confidence.

Following initial training a police officer will soon be given operational duties, working in communities and dealing with numerous incidents daily, a proportion of which will relate to the commission of criminal offences, breach of traffic regulations or local bye laws. Officers have powers to stop and search people, use force and seize property.

The low visibility of police work is recognised, with potential little monitoring or direct supervision, giving officers considerable discretion in relation to how they use their powers in any given situation (McLaughlin, 2007). Common law provides a duty on police officers to use their powers with discretion, and it is interesting to note that legislation is often drafted stating that '*a constable may, rather than a constable must*' when referring to a policing power (Waddington, 2013, p 14). Importantly the code of ethics recognises the necessity of discretion within policing, but that it should be used wisely. It provides practitioners with the following advice for use of discretion:

- *use your training, skills and knowledge about policing;*

- *consider what you are trying to achieve and the potential effects of your decisions;*

- *take any relevant policing codes, guidance, policies, and procedures into consideration; and*

- *ensure you are acting consistently with the principles and standards in this Code.*

(College of Policing, 2014b, p 9)

Discretion is necessary, otherwise the criminal justice system would grind to a halt should every misdemeanour result in an arrest or prosecution. Consider the responsibility of a police officer when making a discretionary decision such as to arrest or not to arrest. It is suggested that a police officer is a gatekeeper to the criminal justice system (McLaughlin, 2007) and once a decision is made to arrest, the implications for the person concerned can be severe. However, this needs to be balanced with issues such as risk, public safety, community and victim expectations, and the seriousness of the offence, which may assist with decision making. There are certain occasions when the use of discretion would not be appropriate, for example, a vulnerable victim at risk of harm, an offence committed as a series within a community, a prolific or priority offender, and any person who is being managed under multi-agency public protection arrangements (MAPPA).

In critical thinking activity 6.2 you considered how to deal with a person collapsed in a street. If a criminal offence had been committed there were several options highlighted in relation to how you might deal with the person concerned, from making an arrest to taking no action at all. As a policing practitioner your decision would be based on the NDM with appropriate risk considerations, supported by the code of ethics, providing you with a rationale for the decision made and placing you in a position to account for that decision if required to do so.

Discretion is at the heart of the ten risk principles, and members of the police service who make decisions consistent with the principles should receive the encouragement, approval and support of their organisation (see principle 10 in the previous section).

REFLECTIVE PRACTICE 6.2

LEVEL 5

In 2020, the Covid-19 pandemic resulted in the government producing emergency legislation to provide the police with additional powers to restrict freedom of movement and gatherings during national lockdown. This was controversial and unpopular with large numbers of people and potentially had implications for 'policing by consent'. Find out more about the legislation concerned, police actions reported in the media, and reflect on the police response, considering how discretion could feature in legislation compliance.

Some of the media reports related to heavy-handed or over-zealous policing, for example on 4 September 2020, the *Independent* newspaper headline read: *Majority concerned about 'heavy handed' policing of lockdown restrictions, finds survey.* This referred to a civil liberties survey by *Liberty* that found 58 per cent of voters were concerned about heavy-handed policing of lockdown measures (Woodcock, 2020).

To put this in some context, in April 2021 HMICFRS produced a report *Policing in the Pandemic* (HMICFRS, 2021c) following a review of how ten police forces had responded to the pandemic. Introducing the report, HMI Parr commented on how quickly the legislation had been introduced, resulting in significant interest in police actions by both the public and the media. He suggested that on rare occasions some police decisions were seen as heavy handed and recognised that when this did happen the police service were quick to reflect and learn from their actions (HMICFRS, 2021c, p 1).

At the time when the legislation was enacted, rather than leave to individual officer discretion the National Police Chiefs' Council (NPCC) provided guidance to assist officers with decision making. They introduced a four-phase approach of engage, explain, encourage and, as a last resort, to enforce the law (Turner and Rowe, 2020). To sum up, discretion is a key policing attribute and if used wisely will engender confidence in policing.

IMPACT OF BIAS ON DECISION MAKING

There are certain obstacles that can impact on making good decisions, for example:

- conscious bias;

- unconscious bias;

- stereotyping, prejudice and discrimination.

Bias is defined by the *Cambridge Dictionary* (2021) as: *'The action of supporting or opposing a particular person or thing in an unfair way, because of allowing personal opinions to influence your judgement'*.

Conscious bias refers to the attitudes and beliefs you may have about a person or group on a conscious level and is something that you will be aware of. In contrast, when implicit or unconscious bias occurs the mind makes rapid judgements and assessments of people and situations, without you realising that any sort of bias has occurred. This has been influenced by various individual factors, including background, cultural environment and personal experiences. Importantly, it is possible that you may not be aware of these views and opinions or be aware of their potential impact and implications (Advance HE, 2020).

REFLECTIVE PRACTICE 6.3

LEVEL 4

Reflect on your life experiences to date and ask yourself the question whether it is possible that you may have a certain bias against any person or group, and if so, how you would tackle this when making policing decisions.

It is likely that an individual may be unaware of any unconscious bias. Harvard University provide an *'Implicit Association Test'* (search the internet for: 'Harvard implicit bias test') that you may find useful to discover any unconscious bias. Complete one or more of the tests and reflect on the results provided.

Any form of bias, stereotyping, prejudice and discrimination is not acceptable when making policing decisions, and will impact significantly on victims, witnesses, suspects, confidence of policing in communities, and ultimately police legitimacy. Uncontrolled discretion can also provide a platform for bias in policing where without adequate training and supervision, decisions based on stereotyping, prejudice, or even discrimination, can go unchallenged. The police power of stop and search provides a good example of this and Sanders and Young (2008) highlighted the problem of people being stopped for reasons such as age, social class, gender and race.

POLICING SPOTLIGHT

Section 4 of the Vagrancy Act 1824 provided police officers with a discretionary power to arrest anyone they suspected of loitering with intent to commit an arrestable offence, colloquially known as the 'sus' law. The discretion was mainly uncontrolled and came to a head in 1981 in Brixton, London, where a disenchanted and oppressed black community rioted in protest of police misuse of the sus law during operation 'SWAMP 81' where plain-clothed officers took to the streets to stop and search mainly young black men, in an attempt to tackle a burglary and street robbery problem.

In this case and others, control of police powers was becoming a major public issue. Following recommendations made by Lord Scarman following the riots in 1981, together with recommendations made by the Royal Commission on Criminal Procedure 1981, new legislation was introduced to provide more control over the powers enjoyed by the police: the Police and Criminal Evidence Act 1984 (PACE).

Section 1 of the Act provided the police with the power to stop and search people in a public place, provided that the officer has *reasonable grounds* to suspect that a person is carrying stolen or prohibited articles. This was a shift away from people being stopped because of a nebulous suspicion, or gut feeling, at the discretion of a police officer, to one where the legal requirement was to justify the reasonable grounds with the added potential of strengthening individual accountability.

Although PACE provided more clarity and accountability for the use of police powers, stop and search remained controversial. Joyce (2011) highlights the issue of stereotyping raising criticisms about the way stop and search powers were being used against black youths, with the implication that members of the black community were problematic, resulting in lack of co-operation with the police and eroding police legitimacy in the communities concerned.

Following the murder of Stephen Lawrence in London 1993, a public inquiry found the Metropolitan Police '*institutionally racist*', and the treatment of a significant witness Dwayne Brookes was criticised, with an assessment that he was '*stereotyped as a young black man exhibiting unpleasant hostility and agitation, who could not be expected to help, and whose condition and status simply did not need further examination or understanding*' (Macpherson, 1999, p 36).

Brooke's colour and stereotyping was highlighted as a collective failure of those officers to treat him properly and meet his needs. The inquiry produced 70 recommendations, including the requirement for all police staff to be trained in racism awareness and valuing cultural diversity (Macpherson, 1999 – recommendation 49).

In 2021, Her Majesty's Inspectorate of Constabulary and Fire & Rescue Services (HMICFRS) looked once again at use of stop and search powers and suggested that no force fully understood the impact of the use of police powers, finding that disproportionality persisted within the police service without anyone being able to explain why. In 2019/20, Asian and minority ethnic people were four times more likely to be stopped and searched by the police than white people, and in the case of black people this was nine times more likely, and in some forces the likelihood was even higher (HMICFRS, 2021a).

A further inquiry was conducted 22 years later, following disquiet from Baroness Lawrence (mother of Stephen), to assess the progress of the recommendations made by Macpherson; it was presented to Parliament in July 2021. It was restated that individual bias and prejudice have no place in policing and should be strongly challenged. Police forces have a responsibility to be vigilant and proactive in shaping organisational culture, and need to have management systems and training in place to address conscious and unconscious bias and prejudice. The inquiry reiterated that training for addressing racism and valuing cultural diversity remains as important as ever (UK Parliament, 2021b, pp 146–7).

ETHICS AND THE USE OF FORCE

This section concludes the chapter and briefly explores some ethical aspects and issues arising from the police use of force. For police officers, the power of being able to use force comes with a great responsibility and a need to ensure that it is carefully and ethically applied.

It has already been stated that policing by consent and ultimately police legitimacy is founded on the trust and confidence that communities have in policing. It relies on strong community relationships, based on transparency and ethical practice in respect of the authority and application of powers given to the police. Lack of transparency and poor ethical practices may result in corruption or perceived corruption by the community (Stewart, 2013).

The use of force is necessary for effective policing and is supported by a legal frame-work, for example section 1 of the Criminal Law Act 1967, which allows any person to use reasonable force for the prevention of crime, effecting or assisting with the arrest of an offender, and persons unlawfully at large. The Human Rights Act 1998 protects a person's right to life (article 2), right to prohibition from torture, inhumane or degrading treatment (article 3), and right to liberty and security (article 5). Decisions made in relation to the use of force should be proportionate, legal, reasonable, accountable and necessary (College of Policing, 2018b).

British police are relatively lightly armed compared with other police services worldwide, but considerable change has taken place since the turn of the twenty-first century with patrol-ling officers wearing body armour as a matter of routine and carrying more sophisticated weaponry (Waddington and Wright, 2008). Today officers have wide access to incapacitant sprays, electrical stun devices (taser) and firearms that can be quickly deployed to incidents. When carrying out certain operational raids, police can be seen wearing balaclavas, military-style clothing, using chain saws to effect entry to a building, and in some key areas openly carrying firearms.

Police officers joining the service today are provided with comprehensive personal safety training where legislation, regulations and powers are discussed, together with the range of options available when dealing with conflict situations. Options start with low-level interventions such as effective communication, then use of actual force, which may include simply taking hold of a person to make an arrest, bodily restraint or applying handcuffs, escalating to use of a truncheon, incapacitant spray or taser, to the ultimate lethal option, which is the deployment and use of firearms.

Waddington (2013) highlights that use of force by the police can on occasions be among the most controversial and damaging behaviour to attract widespread public criticism. Deaths in police custody or during arrest following restraint or following a police shooting naturally attract widespread media attention and public concern. The examples are many, such as the shooting of Jean Charles de Menezes at a tube station in London in July 2005 after being mistaken for a terrorist, and Mark Duggan in London in August 2011, during an attempted arrest for serious crime. Dalian Atkinson was killed in August 2016 when a taser was deployed during an incident in Telford, Shropshire, which later resulted in a police officer being convicted of his manslaughter in June 2021.

In March 2016, the Independent Police Complaints Commission (IPCC), now known as the Independent Office for Police Conduct, published a report, in which it suggests that the public broadly support the use of force by the police, but this confidence is less enjoyed by young people and those from black and minority ethnic (BME) communities. Trust across the population surveyed about the police use of force was 83 per cent, but this dropped to 76 per cent for BME groups, 71 per cent for young people, and 69 per cent for those living in London (IPCC, 2016a).

One of the recommendations from the IPCC report was that police use of force should be formally recorded and it was in April 2017 that the Home Office required all police forces to start recording the use of force by police officers, with an aim to improve transparency and accountability, and help inform police practices. In the year ending 31 March 2020, there were 492,000 incidents recorded where the police had used force (Home Office, 2021c). This figure is likely to be a lot lower than the actual number of incidents that occurred but provides a basis for analysis and policy development.

In February 2021, HMICFRS published a report about the disproportionate use of police powers. They provided a range of statistics that included the fact that black people were about 5.7 more times likely to have force used on them rather than white people, and that officers were 9 times more likely to have drawn tasers (not discharged them) on black people compared to white people. They recommended that by July 2021 the police service should have external scrutiny processes in place and keep the community informed about any action taken (HMICFRS, 2021a). Shortly after the publication of the report, the London Mayor Sadiq Khan launched a project to involve communities in the oversight of use of force. Bedfordshire, Cambridgeshire and Hertfordshire police forces set up an independent scrutiny panel drawn from the communities in each county. They are provided with an understanding of the rules and policies relating to the use of force, and then scrutinise use of force by reviewing police officer accounts, body-worn video and other records to highlight areas of concern and good practice (Nuefville, 2021).

To sum up, the use of force is a serious consideration for a police officer that can have implications for the recipient and confidence in policing. Decisions will sometimes need to be made quickly, and it can be quite challenging to assess risk and deal with factors such as mental health, drugs and alcohol. It is the code of ethics at the centre of the national decision model that provides the basis of sound decision making regarding the use of force.

SUMMARY OF KEY CONCEPTS

This chapter has explored the following key concepts.

- Police officers often find themselves having to make difficult decisions and complex choices.

- Decisions made by police officers impact on people, including victims, witnesses and suspects.

- The code of ethics lies at the heart of policing decisions and should be applied consistently.

- Risk assessment is an inherent and key element of policing that must be considered when making decisions.

- Discretion is a key policing attribute and if used wisely engenders confidence in policing.

- Any form of bias, stereotyping, prejudice or discrimination is not acceptable when making policing decisions.

- Police legitimacy relies on strong community relationships, based on transparency and ethical practice in respect of the authority and application of powers given to the police.

CHECK YOUR KNOWLEDGE

1. What are the six elements of the national decision model?

2. Where do the principles set out within the code of ethics originate from?

3. Where does the power come from to use discretion as a police officer?

4. When should a police officer not use discretion?

5. What was the police training issue highlighted in the parliamentary report assessing the progress of the recommendations made in the Macpherson inquiry?

6. What is the legal framework for the police use of force?

FURTHER READING

BOOKS

McCartney, S and Parent, R (2015) *Ethics in Law Enforcement*. Victoria, BC: BCcampus. [online] Available at: https://opentextbc.ca/ethicsinlawenforcement/ (accessed 11 June 2022).
Chapter 2 explores major ethical systems, making links to law enforcement and providing several moral dilemmas to consider.

Waddington, P A J, Kleinig, J and Wright, M (2013) *Professional Police Practice: Scenarios and Dilemmas*. Oxford: Oxford University Press.
This book provides policing scenarios, covering a wide range of issues related to ethical policing, with good opportunities for personal reflection and to develop decision-making skills.

WEBSITES

College of Policing APP (authorised professional practice). [online] Available at: www.coll ege.police.uk/app (accessed 11 June 2022).
The College of Policing APP provides key guidance for the national decision model and the risk principles that support decision makers. It is recommended that the sections 'Risk' and 'National decision model' are worked through to supplement the content of this chapter.

Her Majesty's Inspectorate of Constabulary and Fire & Rescue Services (HMICFRS) Reports – Rolling Programme of Crime Data Integrity Inspections. [online] Available at: www.justiceinspectorates.gov.uk/hmicfrs/our-work/article/crime-data-integrity/reports-rolling-programme-crime-data-integrity (accessed 12 June 2022).

This relates to the ethical recording of crime and provides a series of reports relating to the rolling programme of crime data integrity inspections. It is an opportunity to find a report relating to your policing area.

PART 3
PROFESSIONAL POLICING IN PRACTICE

CHAPTER 7
POLICING IN PRACTICE

MARTIN STEVENTON

LEARNING OBJECTIVES

AFTER READING THIS CHAPTER YOU WILL BE ABLE TO:

- understand the developing complexities facing policing in the twenty-first century;

- discuss how core elements of the National Policing Curriculum (NPC) support continuous professional development and create a competent workforce;

- explain the roles and responsibility of key UK law enforcement agencies;

- identify and analyse current threats facing the UK;

- critically evaluate the future challenges facing law enforcement agencies in the twenty-first century.

INTRODUCTION

POLICING SPOTLIGHT

In October 2019, the bodies of 39 Vietnamese nationals were found in the trailer of an articulated refrigerated lorry in Essex. The trailer had been shipped from the port of Zeebrugge, Belgium, to the UK; the lorry cab and its driver originated from Northern Ireland. Investigations were led by Essex Police and involved law enforcement agencies from the UK and abroad (Sky News, 2019; BBC, 2021).

This chapter begins with a policing spotlight which highlights one of a number of contemporary threats to public safety: the challenges faced by policing and law enforcement agencies in the UK, and internationally. Government and policing bodies suggest with increasing frequency that the police alone cannot deal with crime and a more joined-up approach with a range of other agencies is required (Home Office, 2004; College of Policing, 2015). Policing has long been posited as 'everyone's business' (Remington, 1965), and for some time this has been evident when addressing threats such as terrorism and youth violence. The World Health Organization (WHO) recently urged member states to tackle youth violence by adopting an evidence-based public health approach (WHO Europe, 2021). As policing and threats increase in complexity, so does the need for a greater focus on partnerships and a skilled professional workforce. The Policing Vision 2025 highlighted a need for collaboration, and for police officers to be 'confident professionals able to operate with a high degree of autonomy and accountability' (APCC and NPCC, 2016). This is embedded in the Police Education Qualification Framework (PEQF), the National Policing Curriculum (NPC) and in the Competency and Values Framework (CVF) which sets out nationally recognised behaviours and values expected of a constable (College of Policing, 2017b, 2020e, 2021b). This chapter will explore the core elements of the NPC, before identifying the role and responsibilities of key law enforcement agencies, revealing how the role of the constable supports them in keeping communities safe. Finally, it will explore the 'now' threats facing policing, before critically exploring the future challenges faced by policing in the twenty-first century.

THE NATIONAL POLICING CURRICULUM

Chapter 1 introduced the notion of the College of Policing being the custodian of both the National Policing Curriculum (NPC) and the educational quality framework, and the entry routes into policing. The College has developed its curriculum and courses for delivery in collaboration with higher education institutions (HEIs) providing educational programmes. While some have been critical that a prescriptive approach to curriculum content limits the ability of HEIs to influence real change in policing (Williams et al, 2019), nevertheless it provides a useful benchmark to highlight the educational principles that underpin the PEQF. These include consistency, promoting a values-based ethical approach to policing and education, and continuous professional development. Crucially it aims to help policing meet the professional requirements of the twenty-first century, setting out learning and development themes across a range of policing professional situations and contexts (College of Policing, 2021b). Level 4 (PCDA) and level 5 (DHEP) follow similar themes with a broad focus on the role and legal responsibilities of the police, human rights, decision making in complex situations and the use of reflection to improve practice. Acquiring this knowledge and associated skills *'is essential to ensuring that police constables can discharge their duties and responsibilities effectively'* (College of Policing, 2021b, p 8).

The police CVF introduced by the College of Policing (2017b) presents the relevant competencies and values expected of police officers. It sets out the behaviours and beliefs expected of constables, framed alongside complex challenges facing policing, like those highlighted in the policing spotlight. It will be helpful to consider this broad range of knowledge, skills and behaviours through some of the core elements of the NPC: professional practice, response, and investigative and community policing.

Professional practice is underpinned by the way in which police officers act and in the decisions they make. The national decision model with the code of ethics at its centre is embedded into policing practice in England and Wales (College of Policing, 2012, 2014a). While the policing spotlight presents a long and complex case, it began with response officers attending the scene, gathering and assessing information, and making decisions. Literature and policing have long suggested that the initial response is the most critical part of an investigation (Hess and Hess, 2012; College of Policing, 2013a). The knowledge and skills required of those charged to get this right cannot be understated. There is a public expectation that officers dealing with any serious incident would do so effectively, and in a way that stands up to scrutiny; those attending such incidents should ask themselves the following questions.

- *Is what I am considering consistent with the code of ethics?*

- *What would the victim or community expect of me in this situation?*

- *What does the police service expect of me in this situation?*

- *Is my action or decision likely to reflect positively on my professionalism and policing generally?*

- *Could I explain my action or decision in public?*

(College of Policing, 2014a)

It is not enough to recognise a serious incident; police officers must understand increasing criticality when dealing with the incidents they attend. A critical incident is defined by the College of Policing as *'any incident where the effectiveness of the police response is likely to have a significant impact on the confidence of the victim, their family and/or the community'* (College of Policing, 2013b). Using a critical thinking matrix, officers are expected to recognise the three phases of critical incident management: being prepared for it, managing it and restoring public confidence (College of Policing, 2013b, 2021c). It is the preparation of first responders through learning that provides officers with the confidence to do this. It is important to note that some critical incidents may also be major incidents, but in all cases a major incident will be by default a critical incident.

The initial and most critical part of an investigation is often referred to as *'the golden hour'*. This initial action, whether the arrest of a suspect, the preservation of a crime scene or the seizure of evidence, has a significant impact on the effectiveness of the investigation. Put forward by Cooke et al (2013, p 40) and helpful for consideration during all stages of response and investigation is the mnemonic ABC.

- **A**ssume nothing.

- **B**elieve nothing.

- **C**hallenge and check everything.

In the policing spotlight, officers quickly identified a critical major incident and once it was established that nothing could be done for the occupants, took positive steps to arrest the driver and secure the scene. These decisions were critical as forensic examinations later identified the fingerprint of a witness who had survived a previous journey; this person was able to supply crucial evidence to the investigative team. The incident presented significant challenges to the investigators ranging from the identification of victims and their families, the international aspect of the crime, and the impact on members of vulnerable communities who had experienced similar exploitation.

The Crime and Disorder Act 1998 arguably enhanced policing and mandated that a broad range of partners should work together to address crime in communities. Seen by some as a criminalisation of social policy, it required the police and local authorities to think about harm prevention in all aspects of their business (Crawford, 1997). There has been criticism that the Policing Vision 2025 (APCC and NPCC, 2016) looked retrospectively at community policing, while recognising that it also alluded to a greater focus on understanding communities and improving links between the police and those they serve (The Police Foundation, 2017). Survivors of human trafficking are likely to be out of reach in terms of traditional community policing approaches, and more sophisticated engagement is required to identify and safeguard this group. In Essex, support came from the Vietnamese community in London who helped in relation to family liaison (BBC, 2021). Cuts to police funding and officer numbers have arguably impacted on the effectiveness of community policing. In 2017, the chair of the NPCC, Sarah Thornton, suggested that reductions in neighbourhood officers would cut off the intelligence required to prevent terror attacks and risked undermining public trust (Dodd, 2017). This presents a risk to effectively policing other threats highlighted in the Strategic Policing Requirement (SPR), including action to tackle those involved in human trafficking (Home Office, 2015). Now consider the policing spotlight example below and the critical thinking activity which follows.

POLICING SPOTLIGHT

In 2018, Usman Khan, a convicted terrorist, was automatically released from prison on temporary licence. In 2019, he travelled to an event in London to participate in an event organised by a university programme. Wearing a fake suicide vest, Khan stabbed five people at the event – two fatally – before being shot dead on Westminster Bridge by police. The coroner's inquest reported that failings by law enforcement agencies contributed to the deaths (HM Coroner, 2021).

CRITICAL THINKING ACTIVITY 7.1

Reflecting on the policing spotlight, as a police officer arriving at the scene, can you explain your primary task?

A sample answer is provided at the end of this book.

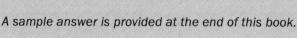

LAW ENFORCEMENT AGENCIES

The Policing Vision 2025 suggested how policing would meet the challenges of maintaining public safety through a *'professional workforce equipped with the skills and capabilities necessary for policing in 2025'* (APCC and NPCC, 2016, p 5). It recognised how the police, its partners and other law enforcement agencies would need to operate more collaboratively to meet and enhance their response to emerging threats. UK law enforcement is a collaboration between different police and non-police agencies, with specific powers and responsibilities. To better understand the complex network of UK law enforcement it is useful to do so through the shared national threat of serious organised crime (SOC) given that each has a role in tackling it. The National Audit Office (NAO) suggests there are over 100 law enforcement agencies and other bodies involved in addressing SOC in the UK (NAO, 2019). It is beyond the reach of this chapter to look at all agencies, so we focus on those that predominantly operate in England and Wales:

- National Crime Agency (NCA);

- regional organised crime units (ROCU);

- special police forces;

- Border Force (BF);

- immigration enforcement (IE);

- HM Revenue and Customs (HMRC);

- Serious Fraud Office (SFO);

- Government Communications Headquarters (GCHQ);

- Security Service (MI5);

- Secret Intelligence Service (SIS).

THE NATIONAL CRIME AGENCY (NCA)

The NCA was formed in 2013 under Part 1 of the Crime and Court Act 2013 and has two functions specified in law – crime reduction and criminal intelligence. The UK government's aim for the NCA was that it would *'make the UK a hostile environment for serious and organised criminality'*. It put forward a vison that the NCA would deal with serious and organised crime, working with other UK law enforcement agencies and confiscating the profits of crime (HM Government, 2011). In its own mission statement, the NCA aims to *'cut serious and organised crime, protecting the public by targeting and pursuing those criminals who pose the greatest risk to the UK'* (NCA, 2022). In the SOC strategy there is an expectation that the majority of activity directed at SOC will be carried out by territorial police forces, while the NCA's role is one of co-ordination, leadership, support and close collaboration with forces. The NCA has more than 5500 staff, many of whom are accredited with the operational powers of a constable, immigration and customs officer. To inform its partners and to meet its statutory requirements, the NCA publishes a national strategic assessment that highlights the threats posed by SOC (NCA, 2021a).

REGIONAL ORGANISED CRIME UNITS (ROCU)

Established in 2009, there are 10 ROCU in England and Wales covering between three and seven force areas. Their role is set out in their regional plans, but their collective focus is on the protection of communities from SOC. The importance of ROCU is highlighted both in the SPR (Home Office, 2015), and more recently in the SOC strategy, which describes them as *'the principal link between the NCA and police forces in England and Wales'* (HM Government, 2018a, p 22). ROCU provide a range of specialist capabilities to support forces, including surveillance, cyber investigations, intelligence and asset recovery. To meet the changing nature of SOC, ROCU have developed a further range of core digital capabilities, including undercover online teams, dark web and digital investigations, modern slavery and human trafficking, as highlighted in the first policing spotlight (HMICFRS, 2021d). ROCUs seek to tackle crime centred on a '4P' approach set out in the government's SOC Strategy (HM Government, 2018a):

- pursue offenders through prosecution and disruption;

- prepare for when SOC occurs and mitigate impact;

- protect individuals, organisations and systems;

- prevent people from engaging in SOC.

SPECIAL POLICE FORCES

The term *'special police force'* can be found referenced in UK legislation (Serious Organised Crime and Police Act 2005; Police, Public Order and Criminal Justice (Scotland) Act 2006; Police and Justice Act 2006). It relates to police organisations whose governance lies with other governmental departments and not with the Home Office. Three special forces that operate in the UK are:

1. the British Transport Police;

2. the Civil Nuclear Constabulary;

3. the Ministry of Defence Police (MDP).

THE BRITISH TRANSPORT POLICE (BTP)

The BTP is responsible for policing the rail network of England, Wales and Scotland; its aim is 'to keep the railways safe and protect people from crime, ensuring that levels of disruption and the fear of crime are as low as possible' (BTPA, 2018, p 11). BTP officers share the same powers of constables in territorial forces. Section 100 of the Anti-terrorism, Crime and Security Act 2001 provides authority for a BTP officer away from the railway infrastructure to assist a constable when requested to act where an offence is being committed and/or to prevent injury or to save a life. The organisation employs 3123 police officers, 233 police community support officers, 1452 police staff and 306 special constables (BTP, 2020). The Force is headed by a chief constable who is appointed and accountable to the British Transport Police Authority (BTPA). The BTPA is responsible for publishing its policing strategy and for funding, which is not obtained through tax but from the railway industry (Railways and Transport Safety Act 2003).

THE CIVIL NUCLEAR CONSTABULARY (CNC)

Formerly known as United Kingdom Atomic Energy Authority Constabulary, the CNC was established in 2005. Its responsibility is the security of nuclear facilities in England, Scotland and Wales; these responsibilities are set out in legislation (Energy Act 2004). A predominantly armed service, the CNC is led by a chief constable who is accountable to the Civil Nuclear Police Authority. It is responsible for ten nuclear sites, employing 1500 police officers and staff; 1060 officers are authorised firearms users. The aim of the CNC is explained through its ambition statement:

> *To be recognised nationally and internationally as the United Kingdom's leading organisation for the provision of protective policing for the civil nuclear industry and other critical national infrastructure.*

(CNPA, 2021, p 7)

CNC police officers may use the powers of a constable in certain circumstances outside their jurisdiction (Energy Act 2004); however, unlike the BTP and MDP this does not include the extra powers provided by the Anti-terrorism, Crime and Security Act 2001.

THE MINISTRY OF DEFENCE POLICE (MDP)

The merger of the Air Force Department Constabulary, the Army Department Constabulary and the Admiralty Constabulary saw the creation of the MDP in 1971. The Ministry of Defence Police Act 1987 redefined the role and jurisdiction of the organisation. The force comprises around 2900 mostly armed police officers and 260 non-uniform civilian staff. According to the organisation's Corporate Plan 2020–2025, the overarching purpose of the organisation is to protect the UK's defences and infrastructure (MDP, 2020, p 7).

Though not a Home Office force, the MDP work regularly in support of territorial forces across the UK. High-profile examples have included collaboration with the City of London Police as part of the armed response element of Project Servator. This deployment sought to deter, disrupt and detect terrorist activity while offering public reassurance following terrorist attacks like those described in the second policing spotlight (*Daily Express*, 2017).

EVIDENCE-BASED POLICING

Project Servator is a policing tactic using high-visibility, often armed, teams to disrupt serious criminal activity and provide a reassuring presence for the public. It has been successful in gathering intelligence helping Counter Terrorism Units across the UK to investigate and prevent acts of terror (Counter Terrorism Policing, 2021).

Finding prohibited articles like weapons or drugs following stop and searches conducted during Project Servator compared positively to national figures in 2018/19. Servator achieved a 37 per cent positive outcome rate compared to a national average of 17 per cent (Bains, 2019). Disruption tactics are becoming more important in managing 'risky people' as intelligence services identify more individuals that stretch the capability of law enforcement agencies with limited resources (Innes et al, 2011).

THE FUTURE

Initially mooted in the National Security Strategy and Strategic Defence and Security Review (HM Government, 2015) was the suggestion of a *national infrastructure police force*. This was posited to amalgamate the BTP, MDP and CNC. In Scotland, devolved powers and the Railway Policing (Scotland) Act 2017 presented the absorption of BTP Scotland into Police Scotland. The UK government has not advanced the idea of a national infrastructure police force, and Scotland's government have delayed a merger indefinitely; uncertainty remains in respect of reforming these special forces.

BORDER FORCE (BF)

Created in 2012, Border Force (BF) is a law enforcement command within the Home Office; headed by a director general, and overseen by the Minister of State for Immigration, it employs around 7700 staff (Home Office, 2017). The organisation is responsible for immigration controls at the multiple air, sea and rail ports that afford entry to goods and passengers to the UK. The priorities of BF focus on managing the legitimate flow of people and goods to and from the UK while preventing harm from them (HM Government, 2013). Designated officers from BF can under Section 2 of the UK Borders Act 2017 detain anyone for a criminal offence, or under the authority of an arrest warrant for the period of three hours while waiting for the arrival of a police officer. Officers are dual warranted, which means that they possess the legal powers of both a customs and immigration officer. The Independent Chief Inspector of Borders and Immigration (ICIBI) monitors and reports on the efficiency and effectiveness of BF (HM Government, 2014a). Migration to the UK continues to be a significant political issue and the ICBI have reported critically on the effectiveness of tactics such as *intensification exercises* that focus on clandestine entry routes and methods like those presented in the first policing spotlight. It reported that these exercises ran before and after the incident but there is little evidence of the long-term effectiveness of such strategies (ICIBI, 2019).

IMMIGRATION ENFORCEMENT (IE)

Immigration Enforcement (IE) is a law enforcement directorate within the Home Office. The vision of IE is *'to reduce the size of the illegal population and the harm it causes'*, and it has three core objectives relating to preventing illegal migration, the threats relating to it and the repatriation of illegal migrants (HM Government, 2014b). The difference between BF and IE is in terms of responsibilities and powers. IE is responsible for investigating immigration offences, detention, administrative removal and deportation; however, it prioritises the prevention of loss of life. The organisation is led by a director general and employs around 5000 staff (National Audit Office, 2019).

The public interest in immigration has resulted in significant scrutiny of the way in which IE operates. The Independent Chief Inspector of Borders and Immigration (ICIBI) is responsible for inspecting the work of IE and reporting to government. The ICIBI reported a mixed picture in terms of focus on modern-day slavery, suggesting *'siloed and disjointed'* operational directorates (ICIBI, 2021, p 35). Furthermore, the Committee of Public Accounts reported broader concerns about the Home Office being *'not sufficiently curious about the impact of its actions and the underlying reasons for the challenges it faces'* (House of Commons, 2020, p 3).

HM REVENUE AND CUSTOMS (HMRC)

Her Majesty's Revenue and Customs (HMRC) was created in 2005 following the merger of Her Majesty's Inland Revenue and Her Majesty's Customs and Excise. The Commissioners for Revenue and Customs Act 2005 provides the legislative framework for HMRC and the powers it has to fulfil its roles and responsibilities. The purpose of HMRC is *'to collect the money that pays for the UK's public services and give financial support to people'*. It employs 58,170 staff and is led by a First Permanent Secretary and Chief Executive, working closely with other law enforcement agencies such as BF in the collection of customs revenues at the border (HMRC, 2021a; ONS, 2021). HMRC is a significant partner in the UK's serious crime strategy, working with the NCA, and it has a number of staff seconded to ROCU. HMRC staff processed 10,000 requests for support in the 2020/21 financial year (HMRC, 2021a).

The HMRC's Outcome Delivery Plan sets out the organisation's five strategic objectives, which include protecting society from harm (HMRC, 2021b). HMRC are provided with investigative powers in England and Wales by the Police and Criminal Evidence Act 1984. Additionally, the Proceeds of Crime Act 2002 gives investigators powers to search suspects and premises following arrest, and recover criminal assets. Not all powers provided by this legislation are available to HMRC staff; for example, only police officers can take fingerprints or charge and bail suspects.

SERIOUS FRAUD OFFICE (SFO)

Dissatisfaction in the 1970s and 1980s about the investigation of serious fraud resulted in the commissioning of a fraud trials committee. The report resulting from this committee became commonly known as the Roskill Report and recommended the creation of a new body to investigate fraud (Roskill, 1986). The Criminal Justice Act 1987 enacted Roskill's recommendations, and in 1987 the Serious Fraud Office (SFO) was created. The SFO is headed by a director who leads a team of around 500 staff. The director is accountable to the Attorney General for England and Wales and the organisation is subject to inspection by Her Majesty's Crown Prosecution Service Inspectorate (HMCPSI) (SFO, 2021). The mission statement of the SFO focuses on the rule of law, victims, and the independent investigation and prosecution of top-tier crimes such as serious or complex fraud, bribery and corruption (SFO, 2019). SFO staff have a number of powers that require those under investigation to provide answers when questioned and to surrender documents.

THE UK INTELLIGENCE SERVICES

Three agencies, GCHQ, MI5 and SIS, are responsible for most of the UK's intelligence and security work. It has been reported that the work of the UK intelligence services and law enforcement agencies has prevented 27 terrorist plots in the UK since 2017 (BBC News, 2021). While we are broadly discussing law enforcement agencies, both MI5 and SIS are actually publicly accountable civilian intelligence organisations. Their staff have no powers of detention or arrest but work closely with the police and other agencies to stop significant threats to the UK at home and abroad. World events undoubtably impact on the threats faced by the UK and it is important to understand the basic role and responsibilities of these services.

GCHQ

Formed in 1919 and originally called the Government Code and Cypher School, it became well known for breaking the German Enigma codes during the Second World War. After the war it was renamed the Government Communications Headquarters (GCHQ). Today it is split into two cells, Joint Operations, in which the NCA is a partner, and the National Cyber Security Centre. It is led by a director and overseen by the Foreign and Commonwealth Office; employing 7107 staff, its primary role is the interception, analysis and sharing of information to keep the UK safe (House of Commons, 2021; GCHQ, 2022).

MI5

MI5 (Military Intelligence Section 5) was formed in 1909 and is a government department that reports to the Home Secretary. Led by a director general, it employs 5200 staff whose main role is to protect democracy in the UK and to protect against threats from terrorism and espionage. The director general is referred to as 'K' from the surname of the first person to hold the post, Sir Vernon Kell. MI5 works closely with the police to mitigate the risk presented to the UK in respect of terrorism and lead on the collection of intelligence to support operational activity. The Joint Terrorism Analysis Centre (JTAC) based within MI5 is responsible for setting the national terrorism threat level for the UK. MI5 have highlighted the threat that espionage, including cyber espionage, poses to the UK, pointing to Russia and China as areas of serious concern (House of Commons, 2021; MI5, 2022).

SIS

The Special Intelligence Service, often referred to as MI6 (Military Intelligence Section 6), focuses on gathering intelligence from outside the UK. It is led by a 'Chief', known as 'C' taken from the surname of the first person to hold the post, Captain Sir Mansfield

Smith-Cumming. The Chief of SIS reports directly to the Foreign Secretary and leads 4107 staff who collectively seek to meet the organisation's core aims of *'stopping terrorism, disrupting the activity of hostile states, and giving the UK a cyber advantage'* (House of Commons, 2021; SIS, 2022). The threat of terrorism in the UK and that presented by the actions of rogue nations present particular challenges for the intelligence services.

There has been criticism of the intelligence services and their role in such incidents as shown in the second policing spotlight. The role of constables working in communities, building legitimacy and trust, will enable the flow of intelligence to support the broader intelligence services and address contemporary and future challenges facing the UK.

CONTEMPORARY THREATS AND POLICING CHALLENGES

The UK Home Office is required under the Police Reform and Social Responsibility Act 2011to publish the SPR, in which the Home Secretary sets out the most significant national threats. The reviewed SPR was encapsulated in the 2025 Vision (Home Office, 2015; APCC and NPCC, 2016). Importantly, both publications recognise the need and challenges of capacity building, and point to the strength of connected partnerships, emphasising the importance of a skilled and knowledgeable workforce. The SPR was created in consultation with a range of law enforcement agencies, including the police, National Police Chiefs' Council, Association of Police and Crime Commissioners, the National Crime Agency and the Security Service. Through the SPR the UK government sets out the requirement of territorial forces to work effectively with a range of law enforcement agencies to keep the UK safe. The six areas of focus highlighted in the SPR are:

1. *terrorism*;

2. *civil emergencies;*

3. *organised crime;*

4. *public order threats;*

5. *large-scale cyber incidents;*

6. *child sexual abuse.*

(Home Office, 2016)

Importantly, the SPR promotes a joined-up approach to policing with other law enforcement agencies. In support, the curriculums for both the Police Constable Degree Apprenticeships (PCDA) and the Degree Holder Entry Programme (DHEP) are underpinned by the educational principles of the PEQF. These promote consistency in education, focus on continuous professional development, and prepare a workforce to address the immediate threats as outlined in the SPR and the future challenges of twenty-first-century policing (College of Policing, 2020b).

FUTURE POLICING CHALLENGES

This chapter has highlighted many of the strategic plans that law enforcement agencies create and publish to share their vision statements, mission and what they intend to do to deliver their service. Some of these are intertwined with more national strategic requirements such as the SPR. Arguably, law enforcement agencies tend to focus on more immediate organisational and community needs when what is required is a more long-term understanding of likely future challenges that lie *just over the horizon*. Research has provided a view of post-Covid-19 life suggesting that 2025 could see worsening economic equality, a growth in the power of technology companies using artificial intelligence, and the manipulation of public perception through the spread of misinformation (Anderson et al, 2021). The College of Policing (2020f) have looked further forward in publishing their *Future Operating Environment 2040* report. Informed by analysts, scientists, technologists and police practitioners, it provides resources to assist in the development of plans, strategies and capabilities to address trends that are likely to emerge and impact on public safety over the next 20 years. The report and predictions echo the post-Covid-19 research but present a broader set of trends and future challenges that relate specifically to policing. Ten trends have been highlighted as the most consequential for policing and decision makers are encouraged to consider them not as a firm prediction of what might happen, nor in isolation, but to think how these might occur, connect with and impact on policing (College of Policing, 2020f). The ten trends are:

1. social inequality;

2. unregulated mass information;

3. changes in 'trust', influenced by technology;

4. accelerating technology;

5. artificial intelligence;

6. workforce automation;

7. demographics;

8. changing economies;

9. private and commercial security growth;

10. global warming.

Recognising the limitations of trend-based analysis, the College offers four scenarios to stimulate thought and discussion. Analysis of the trends and scenarios has presented five key challenges that it suggests policing will face over the next 20 years:

1. balancing the benefits and risks of artificial intelligence in an emerging surveillance society;

2. policing digital disinformation;

3. building trust in a digital era;

4. shaping the future police workforce;

5. operating in conditions of increasing complexity.

Again, there can be no certainty of what the future might bring, but these five challenges are to some degree evident in different levels of maturity in contemporary policing. Returning to the policing spotlights, imagine how criminals might adapt and use more advanced techniques to facilitate human trafficking, or who and what will be the UK terror threat. Considering these challenges and the inevitable acceleration of technology also presents fundamental questions about policing and its traditional doctrines such as the *Peelian* principles and the code of ethics. It is questionable whether these are fit for purpose and if they will enhance or hinder police organisational and cultural change, and impact public legitimacy in a future operating environment. Interestingly, the College of Policing are in the process of reviewing the code of ethics and at the time of writing are at the consultation phase (College of Policing, 2021d). Equally, the broad nature of threats highlighted in the SPR, and the need for partnerships and collaboration to tackle them, demonstrates the range of complex knowledge, skills and behaviours required of serving police officers right now. The analysis presented by the College of Policing offers a glimpse of an enhanced skill set and the potential need for further reviews of doctrines that will ensure a competent police service, one that communities in the future can trust and have confidence in.

CRITICAL THINKING ACTIVITY 7.2

LEVEL 4

a) Having explored the role of other law enforcement agencies in addressing national and overseas threats to the UK, can you explain how your role of constable can support them?

LEVEL 5

b) What do you determine are the ethical implications of policing in the digital age?

Sample answers are provided at the end of this book.

REFLECTIVE PRACTICE 7.1

LEVEL 4/5

Look at the documents presented in *Preparing Policing for Future Challenges and Demands* on the College of Policing website (College of Policing, 2020d). Reflect on the learning from this chapter and the skills that a police officer serving in 2040 will be required to possess. You should focus on academic, practical and personal requirements of the role.

A sample answer is provided at the end of this book.

SUMMARY OF KEY CONCEPTS

This chapter has explored the following key concepts.

 There are competing '*now*' challenges and a growing understanding of '*future*' challenges facing policing.

- The National Policing Curriculum (NPC) supports the development of police education programmes.

- The landscape of UK law enforcement agencies is complex and has evolved over time, with different schemes of accountability and governance.

- The publication of the Strategic Policing Requirement is a collaborative process and updated periodically.

- Future challenges identified by the College of Policing are supported by broader international research.

CHECK YOUR KNOWLEDGE

1. Name the framework that sets out the behaviours, competencies and values expected of a constable.

2. Which UK law enforcement agency were tasked by government to 'make the UK a hostile environment for serious organised criminals'?

3. Name the three 'special forces' that serve the UK.

4. Which law enforcement agency was created following the Roskill report?

5. Led by 'C', which intelligence service is responsible for gathering intelligence outside the UK?

6. Can you name three of the five key challenges that the College of Policing claim that policing will face in the twenty-first century?

Sample answers are provided at the end of this book.

FURTHER READING

BOOKS

Hale-Ross, S (2019) *Digital Privacy, Terrorism and Law Enforcement: The UK's Response to Terrorist Communication.* 1st ed. London: Routledge.

Kilgallon, M and Wright, M (eds) (2022) *Behavioural Skills for Effective Policing.* St Albans: Critical Publishing.

JOURNALS

Brown, D (2020) Criminal Justice in an Age of Austerity: The London Bridge Killings. *Alternative Law Journal*, 45(4): 238–46.

CHAPTER 8
POLICING AND THE VULNERABLE

PETER WILLIAMS

LEARNING OBJECTIVES

AFTER READING THIS CHAPTER YOU WILL BE ABLE TO:

- critically evaluate the concept of harm;

- understand the definition of vulnerable;

- understand the historical context in relation to safeguarding children;

- evaluate critically police responses to serious sexual assault, domestic violence and mental health.

INTRODUCTION

It could be argued that this is the most operationally relevant chapter in the entire book, given the amount of police time and resources in contemporary policing that are now dedicated to dealing with vulnerable members within society. That was not typically the case and there are reasons for that. One reason is historical, in that these matters were traditionally dealt with by other agencies, specialists within their discipline and consequently lay outside the proficiency of the police service. Secondly, other agencies were explicitly resourced and capable of responding when called upon. This however has changed since 2010 with the implementation of austerity measures across the wider public services, reducing their capability of delivering a service comparable to that in the pre-2010 times. This is where the police service has been asked to fill the void, as the agency of last resort in many circumstances, creating challenges not just for individual officers and staff, but across the police service nationally.

Furthermore, legislative change, such as the Crime and Disorder Act 1998, as discussed in Chapter 3, has mandated that agencies must work closer in resolving specific community problems.

In addition to that, and potentially even more influential, has been the consistent stream of official inquiries, together with recommendations into multi-agency failings into high-profile, avoidable and tragic child abuse cases, in particular. Some of those will be referred to in this chapter. Furthermore, the then Home Secretary, Amber Rudd MP, at an address at the College of Policing on 1 December 2016, said the following:

> *I am very pleased to see that this year the subject of the conference is vulnerability – one of the most pressing issues facing policing today, and as Alex Marshall has said, one of my priorities as Home Secretary.*
>
> *Because, while forces have been very effective at decreasing the rates of so-called traditional volume crime, which is now at an all-time low, more needs to be done to protect the vulnerable victims of sexual abuse, modern slavery and domestic violence.*
>
> *For too long crimes against vulnerable people have simply not been taken seriously enough and their voices have not necessarily been heard. They've been treated as second class crimes and not always been given the attention that they deserve.*
>
> *And as I made clear in my first major speech on policing to the Association of Police and Crime Commissioners and the National Police Chiefs Council, protecting the vulnerable is a priority of mine as Home Secretary and as I'm sure you'll agree, it must be the key focus for all police officers and staff too.*
>
> *The role of the college in the fight to protect the vulnerable is key and the government is here to help the college to reach those goals.*

(Rudd, 2016)

This of course sets out the priorities for the government as endorsed by the Association of Police and Crime Commissioners and the National Police Chiefs' Council, and sets the agenda for policing in the future.

The diverse roles within modern-day policing that are now associated with 'vulnerability' cannot all be covered within this chapter. Instead, we dip in and out and in doing so gain an understanding of this complex and ever-changing topic. Therefore, the chapter will focus on child abuse, sexual offences against women, and people suffering from mental health.

We also need to understand within the police service what is meant by 'vulnerable', which is defined by the College of Policing as follows:

> *A person is vulnerable if, as a result of their situation or circumstances, they are unable to take care of or protect themselves or others from harm or exploitation.*

(College of Policing, 2021e)

In order to gain that understanding, we also need to appreciate the concept and wider meaning of a word we hear a lot of these days within policing, and that word is *harm*.

THE MEANING OF 'HARM'

The history of the word 'crime', *crimen* in Latin, indicates that it was cited within notions of harm. *Crimen* was historically applied to acts that attracted scandal, dishonor, harm, blame and insult, not just to those that contravened state legislation (Muncie et al, 2010). While we are socialised to the word 'crime' referring to to the contraventions of criminal law, the concept of 'harm' has a much wider meaning, with an historical legacy and as a result some criminologists have formulated a 'social harm approach'.

The 'social harm approach' has been devised to appreciate both the social problems and injurious practices that are within the remit of the criminal justice system and those that are not. Consequently, Hillyard and Tombs (2007), quoted in Muncie et al (2010), have formulated four interrelated theories intended to challenge the traditional boundaries of criminology. One or two are worthy of further exploration to provide a realistic context from which to consider the remainder of this chapter.

1. *Social harms are greater and more differentially distributed than criminal law allows.*

2. *The concept of harm incorporates notions of financial/economic, emotional and cultural harms as well as physical harms.*

Criminal law has a propensity to view crime narrowly and, according to Hillyard and Tombs (2007, p 18), as either interpersonal violence or transgression of property ownership. This simply means that some actions that are considered harmful in some way are subject to legislation and therefore criminal sanctions. Others that may be even more harmful are not. This assertion requires further explanation in relation to policing and needs to be considered given the contemporary involvement by police with the vulnerable or, in other words, people or victims that have been subject to harm.

Obviously, the *raison d'etre* of the police service is the enforcement of criminal law and as per the definition of a constable, the protection of life and property. However, as we have established, that responsibility historically was confined to actions that had been legislated against and in practice it was confined to the immediate danger. Nonetheless, harmful practices that were not subject to a criminal sanction, as identified by Hillyard and Tombs (2007), fell outside that remit and historically the police service did not see a role for itself in such circumstances. That function would be taken up by other agencies, such as social services or local health services, those whose core business was that of welfare or medicine, or indeed both. The vulnerable people that we are concerned with in this chapter fell within that category and to fully understand the contemporary arrangements, we need to appreciate the reasons why and how this changed and what the future holds in store. Now consider the following reflective practice which provides an insight into the way ahead for the police service.

REFLECTIVE PRACTICE 8.1

LEVEL 4

Access the Policing Vision 2025 available online, published by the National Police Chiefs' Council and the Association of Police and Crime Commissioners. Having accessed it, provide answers to the following questions.

a) Under Section 1, 'Policing mission and values 2025', what are core priorities for the police service?

b) Under Section 3, 'Why does policing need to change?', what are the new and evolving crime challenges?

c) What does the public expect from the police service and how will that be achieved?

d) Under Section 4.1, 'Local policing', what will be aligned by 2025, with who and for what purpose?

e) To achieve an enhanced understanding on 'vulnerability', what must police do locally?

f) In relation to data sharing and technological solutions, what two partners are specifically referred to?

g) What is a 'whole place' approach intended to achieve?

Sample answers are provided at the end of this book.

The document *Future Operating Environment*, published by the College of Policing (2020f) relates to what policing will look like in 2040. This is obviously further ahead than 2025, but it is certainly worth being aware of its contents.

CHILD ABUSE

This chapter now focuses on the topic of 'child abuse', as this provides a lens through which to better understand 'vulnerability' and the indispensable role of the police officer within that continual and crucially important area of responsibility. In this chapter we will continue to use the term 'child abuse' as a descriptive term for each category of abuse that will be referred to, but it is important to highlight that phrases such as 'child protection' and 'safeguarding' are almost interchangeable, but have come about at different times in the historical discovery of abuse committed against children.

It is an important subject to study within this chapter, simply because we are almost sequentially discovering different categories of abuse against children and as a society are caught by surprise by each individual one, as the historical development illustrates. However, the abuse of children is also an extremely emotive issue and needs to be responded to sensitively and professionally, especially in an operational capacity.

A suitable place to start and one that highlights the ambiguous status of children, not merely uniquely within the criminal justice system, but also within wider society, is with the establishment of the National Society for the Prevention of Cruelty to Children (NSPCC). This occurred in Liverpool in 1889 and the NSPCC was awarded its Royal Charter in 1895 (Saraga, 2001). Ironically, the idea originated at a meeting of the Society for the Prevention of Cruelty to Animals, later the Royal Society for the Prevention of Cruelty to Animals, or what we know as the RSPCA. It is worthy of note here that this provision and potential intervention was charity funded and not state funded. Therefore, the ambivalence of the state towards offences and harms committed against children was a common and recurring theme throughout the twentieth century and one that has continued into the twenty-first century.

The year 1908 witnessed some symbolic legislation being passed that focused on children with provisions that included neglect and violence, although these elements were rarely enforced (Saraga, 2001). The main issues concerned the employment of children, their participation in dangerous performances and being sold intoxicants. While the juvenile court operated under the auspices of the criminal justice system, it also had elements of welfare incorporated into it, or 'rescue' as the phrase was at that time; it ideally illustrates the ambiguity of status of children within society: welfare-v-enforcement, or offenders or victims?

The Children and Young Persons Act 1933 created for the first time a 'welfare principle', which in practice meant that courts in the process of decision making in respect of children must take into account the welfare of the child. The Act also instigated the offence of *'willfully assaulting a child'*; however, it did place on a statutory footing the common law defence of *'reasonable chastisement'* of a child but offered no definition as to what it was (Saraga, 2001) and retained the rights of parents and teachers in charge of children to administer punishment.

In respect of teachers, nursery staff and other officials in charge of children, this has now been revoked by the Children Act 2004, together with enhanced caveats in the case of parents (Gov.UK, 2004).

However, two major developments were incorporated: the creation of the juvenile courts and also that of specific detention facilities for young people aged 16–21, named after the first establishment that opened in Borstal, Kent (Blake et al, 2010). In 1982, Borstals were renamed 'youth custody centres' and six years later 'young offender institutions'.

This point is underlined by the more recent changes in terminology, referred to earlier in this chapter. For example, the official designation of 'child abuse' refers to a 'medical-social' model and approach to the issue, whereas the change to 'child protection' refers to a different approach or a 'social-legal' model. In the case of the former, the objective was to diagnose the disease and offer therapeutic assistance, whereas the latter was to secure evidence and a subsequent conviction (Saraga, 2001).

The wartime period had highlighted the plight of some children with evidence of neglect and deprivation. Post-war policies were implemented that encouraged family life and a stable one being the panacea in resolving the most prominent issue concerning children, child neglect. Criminal offences committed against children, especially within the family, were not considered and certainly children were not perceived as victims. Therefore, under this working regime, there was little or no involvement by the police and the matter was almost exclusively dealt with by welfare service staff.

PHYSICAL ABUSE: 'THE REDISCOVERY'

It was not until the 1960s that an American paediatrician, Dr Henry Kempe, published work on findings in the United States into what he called 'battered babies', a series of unexplained physical injuries inflicted on the youngest of children. This promulgation of his work is often referred to as the 'rediscovery of child abuse' (Saraga, 2001).

Eventually this work was picked up by the NSPCC in the United Kingdom and throughout the 1970s in particular there was a series of child abuse scandals, starting with the death of Maria Colwell in Brighton in 1973, which resulted in an official inquiry. Throughout this decade there were a number of official inquiries into the tragic deaths of children as a result of physical abuse, which is referred to as non-accidental injury. From these inquiries common themes emerge in respect to agencies' responses and we will look at what they are shortly. It should be noted, however, that even though at the moment we are looking retrospectively over a period of some 50 years, in the most recent cases the same themes are consistently identified as agency failures, which include the police service.

It should be noted, however, that even at this stage, in the 1970s, the response was very much a 'medical-social' model one and the cause being a breakdown of family life (Saraga, 2001). There was little involvement by the police, which prompts the following question: within wider society, was child abuse perceived as a crime or not?

CHILD SEXUAL ABUSE

The arrival of child sexual abuse (CSA) as a final recognition of abuse against children came in May 1987, in Cleveland in north-east England when 121 children were taken into care on the professional advice of two consultant paediatricians, Dr Marietta Higgs and Dr Geoffrey Wyatt, based at Middlesbrough General Hospital. Their medical findings were based upon a medical diagnosis that was controversial within the profession and one that the senior Cleveland police surgeon at that time, Dr Alistair Irvine, disagreed with. Consequently, there was a major rift between the medical services, social services and the police.

At the centre of this were the children who were allegedly subject to sexual abuse and their families. Eventually, the families via their Member of Parliament Stuart Bell brought the matter to the attention of the government, which ordered an independent review of the medical evidence and announced an official inquiry under Lady Justice Butler-Sloss.

Most of the children were returned home and the issue here is not specifically the credibility of the means of diagnosis, but how the agencies reacted and in doing so totally disregarded the interests of the children.

Following the recommendations of Butler-Sloss, the government introduced legislation with the Children Act 1989 and an accompanying practice document, called *Working Together* (HM Government, 2018b). This legislation and *Working Together* left no doubt that in future child protection inquiries are to be conducted within a multi-agency framework, and that this includes the police service. In all cases, the overriding consideration should be the '*welfare of the child*' (Children Act 1989).

REFLECTIVE PRACTICE 8.2

LEVEL 4

Access the *Working Together to Safeguard Children* (2018) document online, and consider the following questions:

Refer to the section headed 'A child centred approach to safeguarding' and answer the following questions.

a) What does a 'child-centred approach' mean?

b) Children may be vulnerable to neglect, abuse or exploitation, but what are these specific threats to their safety?

c) What should guide the behaviour of practitioners?

Answer the following question relating to the section headed 'Assessment of risk outside the home'.

d) Outside of the family setting, what are the categories of harm that children may be vulnerable to outside of their families?

Refer to the section headed 'Police' and answer the following questions.

e) Exactly *what* may be indirect and non-physical?

f) Children who are dealt with as offenders are entitled to what?

g) Under section 46 of the Children Act 1989 the police have power to remove a child to suitable accommodation providing what threshold is met?

Sample answers are provided at the end of this book.

The Children Act 1989 and *Working Together* were key milestones in the discovery of CSA and provided the framework for the multi-agency approach to child protection. This mandated that the local authority are the lead agency for protection and the police the lead agency for investigation, albeit there is an expectation that agencies should work and communicate together throughout the process, 'in the interests of the child'.

As indicated earlier, other legislative changes were instigated which were aimed at the investigation process, in addition to enhanced punishments for offences such as child neglect. These changes underpinned overall development in the recognition and knowledge of the diverse categories of abuse against children and provided a framework for professionals to work within in order to respond appropriately. Post-Cleveland, many believed that the worst was behind us. That assessment lasted until 2000 and ended with the tragic case of Victoria Climbié. This is a story that must be told, not only to remember the memory of Victoria, but because the case had major ramifications for the protection of vulnerable children and also the contemporary child protection system.

VICTORIA CLIMBIÉ

POLICING SPOTLIGHT

Victoria was an eight-year-old girl that had come to Britain from the Ivory Coast. She was subject to horrific abuse and eventually died at the hands of her carers, who were her great aunt and her partner. While Haringey Social Services were responsible at the time, two child protection teams from the Metropolitan Police were involved. Lord Laming, who chaired an inquiry into the case, noted the inadequacy and inexperience of the police investigators into child abuse:

> *I was very concerned to hear from a large number of officers who gave evidence before me, that child protection teams (CPT) within the Metropolitan Police Service were considered to be somehow 'different' from other police units. Several officers told me that CPTs were the 'poor cousins' or 'Cinderellas' of the force (2003: 331).*

(Heidensohn, 2008, p 657)

Between Maria Colwell and Victoria Climbié there were approximately 30 official inquiries into individual child abuse cases. This raises the question of whether the police service was fully committed and properly resourced to investigate incidents of harm inflicted on vulnerable children.

$\longrightarrow$

Due to the tragic nature of the case and the recognition that this was a watershed event, together with the apparent abject failure of the agencies involved, the government ordered an official and wide-ranging inquiry that lasted for almost two years, and this was chaired by Lord Laming (2003).

When Lord Laming reported, he made 108 recommendations. Many were incorporated into the Children Act 2004, which also introduced local safeguarding children boards (LSCB), which were placed on a statutory footing for the first time and the lexicon changed again from 'child protection' to 'safeguarding'. This was a watershed moment in the development of abuse against children and you will have the opportunity to learn more about what Lord Laming recommended specifically for the police service in reflective practice 8.3 (Gov.UK, 2004).

REFLECTIVE PRACTICE 8.3

LEVEL 6

Access the report by Lord Laming online and read Part Four of the report that deals with the police. Identify answers to the following.

a) In paragraph 13.24 what is the recommendation from Lord Laming?

b) In paragraph 14.15 what is the recommendation from Lord Laming?

c) In paragraph 14.57 what is the recommendation from Lord Laming?

d) In paragraph 15.16 what is the recommendation from Lord Laming?

e) In paragraph 15.46 what are the two recommendations from Lord Laming?

f) Having read Part Four of the report and considered some of the key issues in this chapter concerning society's response historically to the abuse of children, what factors can you identity that may have added to the ambivalent response by the Metropolitan Police?

Sample answers are provided at the end of this book.

LSCBs have now increased their role to incorporate vulnerable adults who are at risk of harm and also the responsibility for administering the 'Prevent' referrals under the United Kingdom Counter Terrorism Strategy 'Contest 3'. They have had this role since being placed on a statutory basis in the Counter Terrorism and Security Act 2015, as referred to in Chapter 3 in relation to multi-agency working arrangements.

However, even since the inception of the LSCB we have still witnessed tragic deaths of children that could have been avoided and below are links to some of the high-profile cases; in the case of the final two, the official inquiries are still ongoing:

- Baby Peter Connolly (2007) (BASW, 2009, www.basw.co.uk/resources/serious-case-review-baby-peter);

- Daniel Pelka (2012) (BASW, 2014, www.basw.co.uk/resources/daniel-pelka-review-retrospective-deeper-analysis-progress-report-implementation);

- Arthur Labinjo-Hughes and Star Hobson (2021) (Gov.UK, 2022, www.basw.co.uk/media/news/2022/may/national-review-murders-arthur-labinjo-hughes-and-star-hobson).

It was noted earlier in this chapter that we are still discovering categories of abuse against children, which is one of the reasons that it is the ideal lens through which to consider the issue of 'vulnerability'. However, what we have not referred to are the categories of abuse that are perpetrated via the internet, therefore remotely and almost certainly covertly, which renders accurate figures and rates difficult to validate. Notwithstanding that, between 2019 and 2021 a total of 35,000 child abuse offences were recorded, which is a 16 per cent increase (Dathan, 2021).

The government have responded to this and introduced the Online Safety Bill (2021) which has yet to receive Royal Assent (Gov.UK, 2022b). Just by looking at the historical development of the abuse of children illustrates how the police role in connection to dealing with vulnerable members of society has been shaped and continues to evolve in reacting to ever-changing and challenging circumstances.

The next issue that we will look at is equally, if not more of, a challenge in the contemporary climate and that is the sexual abuse of women. This links in with the government publishing a policy paper in November 2021 entitled *Tackling Violence against Women and Girls Strategy* (Gov.UK, 2021c).

SEXUAL OFFENCES AGAINST WOMEN

Sexual offences against women are an ongoing issue concerning the vulnerability of women. The conviction of Wayne Couzens in 2021, a serving Metropolitan Police officer, who was imprisoned for the murder of Sarah Everard, initially abducted by Couzens for sexual gratification, outraged the whole country. The case further emphasised the vulnerable status of females and underlined the almost insurmountable task that the police service now face in rebuilding confidence and trust with female victims of crime. Accordingly, the government has published the strategy, referred to above, but the responsibility for rebuilding trust falls upon each and every one of us in the police family.

Furthermore, issues related to the sexual harms experienced by women within the criminal justice system have been subject to both public and academic debate for a considerable period of time. The current situation does not indicate that there will be an improvement in the near to medium term, notwithstanding the confidence and legitimacy issues caused by the murder of Sarah Everard.

Firstly, the issue highlighted by Hillyard and Tombs (2007) in relation to how the criminal law defines harm 'narrowly' is echoed in relation to sexual offences committed against women. For example, it was not until the early 1990s that rape within marriage was criminalised, and as recently as 2003 that the Sexual Offences Act 2003 introduced a number of offences directly aimed at the vulnerability of women and children as victims in relation to sexual assaults.

Also, as identified by Betsy Stanko in 1985, following research in the United States and Britain, the police and the courts are described as the 'second assailant' because in practice it has been extremely difficult to secure charges or convictions against offenders (Segal, 2003). What Stanko is referring to in practice is the medical examination of the victim, the investigation by the police and the eventual prosecution process, and their cumulative approach.

Nils Christie identified this issue back in 1977, in his paper 'Conflicts as property' which focused on the status of a victim within a criminal trial where both parties, prosecution and the defence, are represented by lawyers. Remember, as we identified in Chapter 3, the system in England and Wales is an adversarial process, which is simply the prosecution-v-the defence. Therefore, for Christie, the victim who started the process off in the first place is sidelined by the legal process which is dominated by lawyers on both sides and the victim isolated and marginalised (Christie, 1977).

The factors identified years ago by both Christie and Stanko are clearly key issues now and the Ministry of Justice is introducing specialist courts that would handle cases of rape, as a pilot scheme initially (Gov.UK, 2021d).

At the time of writing in 2022, it appears there is on average a 706-day wait for cases to get to court and many cases resulted in acquittals, which has resulted in a collapse of public confidence in the police and prosecutors to deliver successful prosecutions. These and other findings were published in a joint report (HMICFRS, 2022) by the police and courts watchdog (Hamilton, 2022).

HISTORICAL CONTEXT

An historical analysis will be useful here and add a constructive perspective in which to consider these issues.

Obviously, there has been a consistent reluctance by female victims of sexual assault to engage with the police and the criminal justice process, for reasons that are identified in this chapter. Therefore, alternative support networks emerged, normally from the voluntary or what is now referred to as the third sector.

The first Rape Crisis Centre opened its doors in 1976 in London and by 1988 they numbered over 40 centres (Walklate, 2013). In 1984, the London Rape Crisis Centre described its *raison d'etre* in the following terms.

> *Our primary aim is to provide a place where women and girls who have been raped or sexually assaulted can talk with other women at any time of the day or night.*
>
> *Unlike most agencies that women come into contact with we always believe any woman that calls us. We also offer emotional support and/or legal or medical information according to what each woman wants. We are also committed to educating and informing the public about the reality of rape, to refute many myths and misconceptions which distort and deny women's experiences.*
>
> (Walklate, 2013, p 141)

In 1982, a documentary BBC series about Thames Valley Police was broadcast and one of the series was called *A Complaint of Rape*, which referred to an allegation of rape and the filming of the initial stages of the investigation. The female victim was interviewed by three male detectives who were trying to dissuade the victim from making a formal allegation and thereby not purse the allegation. In the days that followed there was almost universal condemnation of the questioning by the police. By recording the interview (BBC, 1982), the police had provided the evidence that vocal critics of their investigative methods, such as the feminist movement, had sought for years and proved that the vulnerable victim had been treated as anything but vulnerable.

Following the documentary, it was apparent that things would need to change in the police response reports of serious sexual assault. Police forces throughout England and Wales implemented policies that addressed some of the major concerns:

- the creation of designated examination suites, sited away from police premises;

- the introduction of special lists of doctors, predominately female, who were only contracted for sexual offences examinations;

- the selection of investigators who received specific training into interview techniques in relation to vulnerable victims of sexual offences.

In many forces, specially designated squads of detectives became operational and the police service re-opened for business; however, as the joint report confirms, despite the passage of time, serious problems still remain as Phase Two of the undermentioned report published by HMICFRS (2022) indicates.

CRITICAL THINKING ACTIVITY 8.1

LEVEL 6

Access Phase One of the report: *A Joint Thematic Inspection of the Police and Crown Prosecution Service's Response to Rape – Phase One: From Report to Police or CPS Decision to Take No Further Action* (HMICFRS, 2021).

Identify answers to the following questions.

a) According to the inspectors, in relation to first contact what is critical and why?

b) Who can play an important role?

c) What is hampering the progress of the case?

d) In relation to victims later withdrawing their willingness to prosecute, what could change this?

e) Why were some cases closed quickly?

Sample answers are provided at the end of this book.

A logical conclusion to this report is that very little has changed in the intervening years since Rape Crisis was founded in 1976 despite some key initiatives in most police forces, such as the creation of specialist squads. However, it is accepted that many vulnerable victims are not being professionally responded to by the criminal justice system. This, together with the challenges around credibility, legitimacy and confidence in respect of providing a sensitive victim-centred service, are the major issues in working towards regaining the trust of the public per se in the aftermath of the Wayne Couzens conviction.

DOMESTIC VIOLENCE

The issue of domestic violence has been a critical one for the police service for some years, and again an important area to appreciate how the recognition of 'vulnerability' has both emerged and developed sequentially. It is estimated that one in four women and one in ten men have been subject to domestic abuse during their life, with 100,000 victims of severe domestic abuse in the United Kingdom annually (Williams et al, 2020).

In 1975, the Association of Chief Police Officers (ACPO), now replaced by the National Police Chiefs' Council (NPCC), gave this evidence to the House of Commons Select Committee on Violence in Marriage:

> *Whilst such problems take up considerable police time during say, 12 months, in the majority of cases the role of the police is a negative one. We are, after all, dealing with persons 'bound in marriage' and it is important, for a host of reasons, to maintain the unity of the spouses. Precipitate action by the police could aggravate the position to such an extent as to create a worse situation than the one they were summoned to deal with. The lesser of the two evils principle is often a good guideline in these situations.*

(Saraga, 2001, p 208)

Since this evidence there has been a complete change in that attitude, but it has been a gradual one and again this is a perfect example of how the criminal law viewed harm 'narrowly' (Hillyard and Tombs, 2007).

The collective failure of the criminal justice system, particularly the reluctance of the police to take assertive action in relation to 'domestics', became one of the main targets of the feminist campaigns of the 1970s (Saraga, 2001).

For example, the offence of common assault, section 39 of the Offences Against the Person Act, arguably the most frequently encountered when the police attended a domestic incident, until the 1988 Criminal Justice Act merely attracted a maximum sentence of six months' imprisonment. At the time, this meant in practice that the police were unable to arrest for this offence unless 'found committing' and therefore the police routinely took little or no action at all. Often, irrespective of the degree of injury inflicted on the victim, the victim was advised to call at the police station in the following days in order to provide a written statement. Therefore, police officers called to the scene by the victim witnessed the harm suffered, yet practice at that time dictated that they took no action, basically to avoid taking agency action later: for example if the victim withdrew the complaint after the police having arrested the offender at the time and at the scene.

As a consequence, victims were left in a situation where they were at risk of further harm. The routine response of the police was unsatisfactory and negligent and, together with the criminal justice system, did not provide a professional service or protection to vulnerable victims who had clearly suffered harm.

However, there is now considerable oversight of police action at domestic abuse incidents with safeguarding of the victim a priority (Williams et al, 2020).

There has been significant research into domestic abuse that has resulted in changes in legislation, policy and practice. However, there is too much to detail in this single chapter, but it is suffice to summarise that the police service and the wider criminal justice system have recognised the many complex issues that surround domestic violence, from the attitudes and working practices as articulated by ACPO in 1975. But, as with the case of child abuse, we are still witnessing different categories of harm inflicted on victims. Notwithstanding that, some initiatives are worthy of further development to illustrate some of the changes, one of which is the work undertaken by the police, CPS and the courts themselves to instigate a fast-track domestic violence court. Research has highlighted this as a key issue. Specifically, this can impact on decisions by victims to withdraw their complaint or not (Williams et al, 2020).

THE NEEDS OF VICTIMS

There have been other key developments aimed at addressing the needs of victims *per se* and a critical development has been the publication of the updated Victims' Code (Ministry of Justice, 2021).

The Code provides 12 basic rights for victims and details arrangements that must be taken in the case of vulnerable victims. Basically, victims need to be dealt with professionally and ethically by the police and this Code needs to be read, understood and applied in practice.

Furthermore, the Domestic Abuse Act 2021, which coincided with the updated Victims Code, has introduced some provisions aimed at protecting the vulnerable such as the domestic abuse protection orders, which can be issued by a senior police officer. Again, there are many other provisions aimed at reducing harm in the Act.

In November 2021, the College of Policing (2021e) introduced guidelines in relation to vulnerability-related risk in order to assist officers and adopted the THRIVE definition of vulnerability (threat, harm, risk, investigation, vulnerability and engagement).

REFLECTIVE PRACTICE 8.4

LEVEL 4

Access the College of Policing website and the THRIVE guidance. Having done so, identify answers to the following questions.

a) On page 1 when does harm occur?

b) What does the four-step approach involve?

c) On page 2 what is the purpose of the guidelines?

d) What do the 3 'C's refer to?

e) What are the College's 'Principles of Risk'?

Sample answers are provided at the end of this book.

POLICING AND MENTAL HEALTH

In recent years the professional liability of dealing with mental health has developed enormously, one of the reasons being that due to austerity cuts in the public services, some key agencies have had to rationalise their services and other agencies, notably the police, have had to fill the gap. As indicated at the start of the chapter, in many circumstances the police have now become the agency of first resort as opposed to the last resort and this has necessitated police officers dealing with people in vulnerable situations, in circumstances where they have little or no professional knowledge, and this is presenting problems for resources, both individually and organisationally.

This section will look at issues presented in the community and what has been done to address them and also for persons brought into police custody and potentially the wider criminal justice system.

COMMUNITY ISSUES

In respect to incidents concerning mental disorder in the community, there is evidence to suggest that the police are dealing with mental health in a manner that does not address the root cause of the issue and in doing so it is almost certain that the individual will again come to police attention. This is creating further difficulties for the management of demand on the police (Solar and Smith, 2022). The authors looked at the burden of mental health related calls on North Yorkshire Police and identified specific issues which will be replicated across all forces in the country. Police interviews indicated that the cuts to the public services were preventing a practical solution to the scope and form of service provision and this was creating higher demand on an already struggling police force.

In North Yorkshire, police personnel commented that A&E departments are reluctant to assess people in crisis that do not meet criteria for admission or if assessed and admitted, they are quickly discharged. Accordingly, the police were left dealing with people cut off from the health service (Solar and Smith, 2022). This of course raises issues concerning the correct and professional response regarding threat harm and risk in respect of these vulnerable people and how that can be properly met.

However, most forces have adopted a partnership approach with a street triage car, which involves the police attending incidents in company with a nurse or paramedic, who can advise officers attending and hopefully access the correct welfare and medical services. The purpose of the street triage is to lower the amount of people detained under Section 136 of the Mental Health Act (MHA) 1983 (Solar and Smith, 2022). For example, from January to September 2014, out of 255 people detained in North Yorkshire under the MHA, 57 per cent were taken to 'places of safety', 13 per cent to A&E and 30 per cent into police custody.

CUSTODY ISSUES

Research by the National Police Chiefs' Council in 2017 involving 21 police forces making use of section 136 discovered that in 264 cases the police felt they were obliged to keep someone safe by holding them in custody longer than legally empowered to do so, due to difficulties in finding a hospital bed. This is further evidence of the increasing number of incidents concerning mental health (Solar and Smith, 2022).

Of course, dealing with persons who are already vulnerable by retaining them in custody is not ideal, but is symptomatic of the enhanced burden on the police in respect of mental health.

The issue of mental health and police custody has been an issue for some time now and there are examples of good practice where provision has been put in place to alleviate the situation. While there is no automatic link between mental health and persons at risk of self-harm and suicide, it is clear that the increasing number of vulnerable detainees who do present this risk necessitates some considerable resources within the custody suite, such as being placed on constant observations, in order to keep them safe. Therefore, some police custody suites in England and Wales have on-site access to a criminal justice mental health liaison and diversion service (CJMHL&D), which can assist in screening detainees for mental health issues, provide professional assessments and arrange further referral to community services (Noga et al, 2016). This provision is in addition to the nurse practitioners that offer other medical services to detainees and are now based in custody suites, on a 24-hour basis. This itself is an improvement on the previous arrangements where a forensic medical examiner (FME), previously known as a police surgeon, had to be called and summoned to attend in each and every medical case.

The involvement of the police service with vulnerable people who are suffering from mental health issues has been a growing one for some time, as this chapter has shown. While individual officers are operating outside of their professional knowledge, it is clear that there have been some measures put in place to improve the situation, but involvement with vulnerable people who fall into this category is likely to continue for the foreseeable future.

As identified at the start of this chapter, operationally this could be the most relevant one in the whole book and we have not covered many key issues, such as hate crime, human trafficking, modern slavery and online harms. However, by reflecting on how specialist knowledge is acquired in specific areas such as child abuse and domestic violence, that knowledge can be applied to the diverse situations that are presented by vulnerable people at risk of harm.

SUMMARY OF KEY CONCEPTS

This chapter has discussed the following key concepts.

⚙ The scale of vulnerability is ever increasing and will require broader skills and knowledge by the police to meet the demand professionally and appropriately.

⚙ The concept of harm incorporates notions of financial/economic, emotional and cultural harms as well as physical harms; however, it is defined narrowly by the criminal justice system.

⚙ We are still discovering categories of abuse committed against children and one of the first categories to be discovered, physical abuse, was not 'discovered' until the 1960s.

⟶

- One of the major issues in relation to multi-agency working within safeguarding is the lack of communication between agencies. It is therefore vital that *Working Together* is strictly complied with.

- Local safeguarding children boards have now taken statutory responsibility for referrals under the counter-terrorism 'Prevent' strategy.

- Historically, it has been difficult to secure convictions in the criminal courts for sexual offences committed against women.

- The police service and wider criminal justice system do not have an enviable record when responding to reports of sexual offences committed against women.

- There have been measures and facilities put in place that have been designed to meet the needs of the victim during the investigation process, but more is needed.

- The whole police family has a responsibility in regaining the trust of the public in the aftermath of the murder of Sarah Everard.

- There is now far greater oversight of the police when dealing with domestic violence incidents.

- Research has indicated that fast-track domestic violence courts are important to victims not withdrawing their statements.

- The College of Policing has adopted the 'THRIVE' definition of vulnerability when assessing vulnerability and risk.

- All police forces are witnessing an increased demand from the community concerning incidents linked to mental health issues.

- Most forces operate a 'street triage' car to alleviate the demand.

- Most forces operate a system where medical professionals are available on a 24-hour basis to meet the demand from detained persons with mental health needs.

CHECK YOUR KNOWLEDGE

1. Who published the Policing Vision 2025?

2. What are more differentially distributed than criminal law allows?

3. Lord Laming made 108 recommendations. Many were incorporated into what subsequent legislation?

4. In 1985, the academic Betsy Stanko published her research and described the role of the police and the courts in the investigation of sexual offences against women as what?

5. Who said this and when?

'Precipitate action by the police could aggravate the position to such an extent as to create a worse situation than the one they were summoned to deal with.'

Sample answers are provided at the end of this book.

FURTHER READING

BOOKS

Bird, R (2015) *Domestic Violence: Law and Practice*. 6th ed. Bristol: Family Law.
This text explores family, violence, law and legislation, and domestic relations.

Brown, J and Walklate, S (2012) *Handbook on Sexual Violence*. London: Routledge.
This book theoretical perspectives, acts of sexual violence and responding to sexual violence.

McAlinden, A M (2012) *'Grooming' and the Sexual Abuse of Children: Institutional, Internet, and Familial Dimensions*. Oxford: Oxford University Press.
This text explores the nature and extent of sexual grooming, legislative frameworks and offender risk management, and institutional grooming.

Quayle, E and Ribisl, K (2012) *Understanding and Preventing Online Sexual Exploitation of Children*. London: Routledge.
This book covers online sexual predators, pornography online and preventing child sexual abuse on the internet.

Wilkins, D, Shemmings, D, Pascoe, C and Corby, B (2019) *Child Abuse: An Evidence Base for Confident Practice.* 5th ed. London: McGraw Hill.
This title covers the history of child abuse, history of child abuse and neglect from 1870 onwards, protecting children from harm, defining child abuse, the causes of abuse against child, the evidence base for child protection practices and global challenges.

JOURNALS

Chambers, J (2021) Meaningful Engagement to Save Lives – Working Relationship of a Service User Organisation with Police and Mental Health Services. *Journal of Psychiatric and Mental Health Nursing*, 28(1): 83–9.
This journal article explores police and mental health partnership working in practice.

CHAPTER 9
CRIME IN THE TWENTY-FIRST CENTURY

SEAN PALEY

LEARNING OBJECTIVES

AFTER READING THIS CHAPTER YOU WILL BE ABLE TO:

- understand how crime has evolved and the key events driving those changes;

- understand the enablers to current crime and the challenges in that working environment;

- identify the methods used in tackling the different crime types;

- understand how to maintain confidence in policing within the changing face of crime.

INTRODUCTION

Crime and policing in the twenty-first century require legitimate practice, and police officers are increasingly required to demonstrate lawful interference with an individual's qualified right to privacy. This chapter explores changing crime and the use of digital data by the police, which has more recently received additional scrutiny because of campaign groups expressing concern about the level of police intrusion (Privacy International, 2018). For example, in February 2019 the Investigatory Powers Tribunal ruled in their first case against Hampshire Constabulary that the use of body-worn video in a victim's private home was unlawful and amounted to surveillance because the officers had not told the victim that the camera was operating (IPT, 2019).

The chapter briefly highlights the new enablers to modern crime, looking at past inadequacies of legislation and the impact of big data on police performance regimes. It explores resourcing and risk to vulnerable victims, followed by the expansion in accountability and compliance with human rights, including applying the four-stage proportionality test set out by the Supreme Court in the case of *Bank Mellat v Her Majesty's Treasury* (2013). The chapter concludes by examining counter-terror policing, and the issues that currently surround public confidence in policing.

HISTORICAL PERSPECTIVES OF CRIME

Key events in the changing face of crime are reflected in government strategy (Policing Vision, 2016) and included in the various responses by governments of the day in creating legislation to tackle new and changing criminal behaviour, and keeping pace with the enabling factors that society and technology bring. The challenge is to tackle the emerging and technical crime while maintaining individual rights and freedoms, something that has seen much recent scrutiny from privacy groups. Balancing continued criminalisation of behaviour with rights of society will become an ever-increasing challenge.

Changes in material possessions have seen new crime evolving, one example being vehicle-related crime. Car ownership has risen from around 19 million in 1971 to an estimated 37 million in 2020 (Leibling, 2020). These changes have resulted in huge increases in vehicle crime; take the 1980s as an example, where it was relatively simple to break into a car and remove the stereo radio. This led to government action to design out vehicle crime, placing new pressures on car makers to improve security. These changes led to evolving criminal techniques, most notably in recent times the ability to steal a car using a remote device or laptop. This example reflects the enormous impact advances in technology have had on the nature of crime.

Cases which expose the inadequacies of legislation at the time are the best way to understand the changing face of crime, and none more so than the failure of the Forgery and Counterfeiting Act 1981 in prosecuting two computer enthusiasts of hacking the BT Prestel System in 1984, *R v Gold & Schifreen* (1988).

This was a landmark case, and while the motive was more mischief than financial gain, the facts of the case demonstrated the shape of things to come not just in the methods criminals would use in the following decades, but the technical challenges in bringing those cases to justice.

The Prestel case was high profile, not just in the facts which involved hacking Prince Philip's account, but in exposing the lack of legislation to regulate such activity, and this directly led to the creation of the Computer Misuse Act 1990. The explosion of the computer virus from tens of thousands in the early 1990s to 5 million a year by 2007 (Chadd, 2020) has led to the most notable change in criminal activity in history, with the ability to commit crime without any form of physical act, executing the crime from any place, anywhere in the world.

NATIONAL STATISTICS

The Home Office are the guardian of national police statistics, covering a diverse range of subjects from modern slavery referrals, arrests for football hooliganism, to police use of force. The annual data requirement (ADR) contains all requests for data made to all police forces in England and Wales under the Home Secretary's statutory powers and is used to report crime and policing related statistics. Key developments in measuring police performance through statistics started in the early 1990s under the Audit Commission, with recommendations often implemented (Mawby and Wright, 2005). This foundation provided a platform for sustained performance management in policing, leading to the Police Performance Assessment Framework and subsequently through to modern-day accountability through its successor, the Assessment of Policing Community Safety. As previously covered in Chapter 3, the desire to hold the police to account is often seen to improve performance, particularly in ethical processes in police recording systems.

The practice of using statistics to direct police activity is complex now that prioritisation and risk have such influence. However, it remains a significant part of financial and resourcing decisions at a strategic level. Another important aspect of statistics is the ability to bring about long-term change and reducing harm. A good example is the significant reduction in people killed and seriously injured (KSIs) on UK roads around the turn of the twenty-first century because of demanding long-term multi-agency targets, set by the Department of Transport in 1987 and 1999 respectively, where reductions in fatalities fell from over 5000 in 1987 to under 2000 by 2010. The fall was the result of a range of performance measures based on statistics and represented the largest reduction in KSIs since the war (Hibberd, 2021).

PRIORITISATION OF RESOURCES

The single most challenging issue for the police in meeting public need and legitimacy is identifying demand, and then applying models to deploy resources in both efficient and effective ways. Identifying risk and harm has become a complex business for policing. Crowhurst (2017) suggests that the rapidly changing nature of crime to a digital platform and more murky environments requires a new approach to modelling the police response. Higgins (2019, p 2) suggests:

> *The recent announcement of 20,000 new police recruits offers an opportunity to narrow the gap but police leaders face difficult decisions about how to use new resources.*

FOCUS ON HARM

Since the adoption of the National Intelligence Model in 2000, there has been a change in focus from the original approach of resourcing across most areas of policing to a risk-based approach to tackling crimes of most harm. This has partly come about through more sophisticated systems to capture intelligence, together with risk management models, such as the Management of Risk in Law Enforcement (MoRiLE) matrix (Home Office, 2018b). There has also been an increase in demand, requiring more scientific approaches to iden-tifying harm. This demands an approach that will reduce harm through community engage-ment as opposed to traditional enforcement methods.

EVIDENCE-BASED POLICING

The guidance *Recognising and Responding to Vulnerability and Risk*, based on 110 studies of interviews with victims of domestic abuse, provides the concept that vulnerabilities are features of individuals, and that harm – or the risk of harm – occurs when relevant vulnerabilities interact with the individual's situation (College of Policing, 2021f).

As a frontline officer you are encouraged to explore the following clues to vulnerability and harm (College of Policing, 2021f, p 18).

* fear, bullying or coercion;

* disempowerment;

* dependence;

* lack of recognition of abuse;

* cultural and societal influences;

* perception of authority;

* past experience;

* feeling blamed or not believed;

* impact of trauma.

COUNTY LINES

Where a group not necessarily affiliated as a gang establishes a network between an urban hub and county location, into which drugs (primarily heroin and crack cocaine) are supplied, it is now commonly referred to as '*County Lines*' (NCA, 2017). These remote dealers regularly exploit vulnerable people, not just children, to maximise financial gain (Densley et al, 2018).

Findings suggest that distinctive supply practices including 'cuckooing' have emerged and that out-of-town dealers regularly exploit vulnerable populations to maximise economic gain in these new 'host' drug markets (Coomber and Moyle, 2017).

You will come across vulnerable people who have been coerced into allowing their home to become the out-of-town dealer's marketplace, known as cuckooing (Spicer, 2021), where victims are often isolated and suffering from harm. Critical skills are required in situations as illustrated below, with often the victim being subjected to serious violence. In addition to using several properties within a local setting, organised drug gangs will use accommodation in rural places, including serviced apartments, holiday homes, budget hotels and caravan parks. Research has shown that in many cases, county line gangs will target children to travel to towns far away from home and deliver on their behalf (NCA, 2016). It is therefore vital to consider this in any report of a child missing from home or care setting.

CRITICAL THINKING ACTIVITY 9.1

LEVEL 4

Imagine that you are deployed to attend a flat situated in a social housing complex; the report is of a burglary in progress. On arrival there is no reply at the house, but eventually you see a young male in the rear of the flat, and he lets you in. The male, aged 19, has apparent learning difficulties and explains he knows nothing about a burglary at his flat.

Consider the scenario above. What issues of vulnerability will you be thinking are present here, specifically county lines, and what steps would you take before leaving the premises to safeguard him? Also, what might be behind the anonymous call, and how could you explore what is happening at the flat?

A sample answer is provided at the end of this book.

ACQUISITIVE CRIMES

This is a category of crime usually resulting in material gain for the offender and can include a wide range of offences, including theft, robbery and vehicle crimes (Theft Act 1968), and in recent times this has been placed under a thematic threat desk structure within policing models. An interesting aspect of acquisitive crime is that it encourages analysis of the causes leading to the commission of these crime types (Becker, 1974). Economic frameworks for crime have shown the presence of rational choice theory if rewards of a criminal behaviour outweigh the negative consequences (Cornish and Clarke, 1986). This is particularly relevant to acquisitive crime because of the financial benefit usually gained. This perceived financial spotlight has placed intense pressure on policing to tackle and be seen to be managing acquisitive crime effectively and led to the creation of a national operation called '*Opal*' (to find out more, search 'Operation Opal Police' on the internet). One of its primary aims is to link investigations where common methods or suspects are identified.

The policing response to acquisitive crime is through recognition and prioritisation of the threat, which results in the utilisation of a range of assets and capabilities, from local policing through to force level and onto those assets regionally held within regional organised crime units (ROCUs). Despite the historical context of dedicated units set at regional levels (ROCUs), working more locally to tackle the perceived greater challenges of organised criminals, we now see a more holistic model to tackling it through a 'whole-system approach'. The core model that offered efficiency in resources through the delivery of the specialist capabilities programme in 2014 has been subject to scrutiny regarding the level of independence and fairness in the allocation of resource to forces inside the regions, and by February 2022 chief officers responsible for serious and organised crime in each region had to ensure that a chief officer is appointed with responsibility for that ROCU, working autonomously of force responsibilities. Force intelligence units (FIU) play a key role and are responsible for identifying offences and proactively sharing intelligence across local policing areas and with other forces, and are also responsible for intelligence sharing in daily management meeting (DMM) structures as part of the National Intelligence Model process. The identification of emerging crimes such as cash machine (ATM) attacks and commercial burglaries result in target-specific briefings and trigger plans; these then inform the acquisitive crime content of monthly tactical assessments at local and force level. Establishing and disseminating comprehensive understanding of those involved can then allow for offenders to be identified as 'organised crime groups' to support targeting and co-ordinate activity across boundaries. External intelligence sharing through well-established partnerships with industry is a proven method of tackling criminal activity. This work supports closer local partnership activity through recently established multi-agency partnership arrangements known as Serious Organised Crime Joint Action Groups, in each policing area and within the existing community safety partnership structure. The partnership approach supports mutual understanding and ownership to tackle serious organised crime.

DIGITAL CHALLENGE

One of the greatest challenges to modern-day policing is maintaining pace with the digital world. In January 2020, and not for the first time in modern policing, an ambitious digital strategy was launched (NPCC, 2020).

According to the Policing Minister (Malthouse, 2020), the strategy is '*an incredible vision*' that would drive the police service in meeting current and future challenges. Significant progress will need to be made from previous initiatives to improve the service, as HMIC, when examining levels of support in responding to digital crime (HMIC, 2014, p 13), found that the victim's perception of an investigating officer's competence was not directly related to the depth of the officer's knowledge of digital crime, but more about the officer's ability to provide thoughtful advice and practical guidance about what the victim could do to protect him or herself from any further criminality. The ability of the police to meet this often relies upon significant financial investment in training those officers for the challenges ahead.

The gathering of data to inform policing and investigate crime continues to grow with the rapid advances in technology offering new ways and efficient processes to support policing practice. These include CCTV, automatic number plate recognition (ANPR), communications, financial transactions and use of the internet. One challenge in this digital world is the need for new legislation to ensure accountability and compliance with rights to privacy for the individual. This has led to concerns around police methods (Privacy International, 2018) and required the Information Commissioner's Office (ICO) to intervene not only in breaches of legislation, but in providing guidance to the police in meeting these important individual rights. The Human Rights Act 1998, and specifically Article 8, the right to privacy, is central to any decision to gather and use digital data in a criminal investigation.

To lawfully interfere with the right to privacy, there must be a legitimate aim, and the action must be necessary and proportionate. The use of digital data by the police has more recently received additional scrutiny because of campaign groups expressing concern about the police use and extraction of data from mobile phones. The College of Policing have issued a code of practice to comply with the recent ICO recommendations (College of Policing, 2021f). The code of practice has nine principles which require significant consideration before a mobile phone extraction can take place, with a new emphasis that seizure of a phone and extraction from it are two separate stages that require new considerations.

The main change is the widening application of the Data Protection Act 2018, which has always applied to police processing of personal data, extending to the processing of data that occurs during and following an evidential mobile phone extraction. This attempts to meet concerns around a plug and play approach that may impact individual rights of privacy, specifically processing sensitive personal information. The Court of Appeal considered the issues in the case of *R v Bater-James and Mohammed* (2020). Police practice must now reflect both this judgement and the recommendations of the ICO. Practitioners will need to firstly consider the lawful basis for the seizure of the mobile phone, using powers under Section 32 of the Police and Criminal Evidence Act 1984, where the device is connected to the investigation and there are reasonable grounds to believe it is evidence of an offence. There will also be cases where mobile phones are written specifically in the items sought on a search warrant, therefore providing a power to seize.

Further consideration in exercising the powers of mobile phone seizure and extraction from victims and witnesses is required, as illustrated in reflective practice 9.1 below. Police officers must now consider if less intrusive measures are available to achieve the aim of the investigation. Any interference with the right to privacy must satisfy the four-stage pro-portionality test set out by the Supreme Court in the case of *Bank Mellat v Her Majesty's Treasury* (2013) . The officer is duty bound to ask if the objective is sufficiently important to limit fundamental rights, whether a less intrusive measure could be used, and whether the measure taken was rationally connected to the objective sought, resulting in a fair balance between the individual and community interests.

The Code of Practice to the Criminal Procedure and Investigation Act 1996 provides the duty for officers to pursue all reasonable lines of inquiry, whether they point towards or away from the suspect, and to gather and retain relevant material. Although this lawful basis remains, officers will still need to consider if a less intrusive method is an option in meeting this duty.

The extraction of mobile phone data code of practice (College of Policing, 2021g) rightly concerns the main data source for the police, mobile phones, placing emphasis on obtaining consent and ensuring this is informed consent, requiring officers to go through detailed provisions with victims and witnesses, including why the device is connected to the investigation and what it will achieve. Individual police forces will be issuing data notices to support the code requirements. Officers will have to pay particular attention to the sensitive data that may be present within the phone, and the new code extends this consideration to suggest that victims and witnesses cannot consent to third party material within their personal device, and therefore officers should consider applying the powers of processing sensitive data. The code goes on to state that police practitioners are unable to assess the nature of the material without viewing it. Therefore they should assume it is sensitive and comply with Section 42, Part 3 of the Data Protection Act 2018 and ensure the additional measures under Section 35(8) of the Data Protection Act 2018 for processing sensitive personal data are met, such as revealing racial or ethnic origin, political opinions, religious or philosophical beliefs, trade union membership, genetic or biometric data, data concerning health or information concerning an individual's sex life or sexual orientation. This requires officers to consider the processing as strictly necessary for the law enforcement purpose, and that a law enforcement purpose applies, such as investigating and detecting crime, and further, that at least one of the conditions in Schedule 8 of the Act applies, for example, it being necessary for judicial or statutory purposes, or for safeguarding children and individuals at risk.

REFLECTIVE PRACTICE 9.1

LEVEL 4

A report of domestic abuse and harassment from a previous partner is received and you attend the complainant's house. The complainant explains that her mobile phone has communication with the suspect over some time, including threats, but she is reluctant to hand the phone over. Reflect how seizing the phone with informed consent impacts on the victim and how you will reassure the victim.

A sample answer is provided at the end of this book.

CYBER CRIME

Cyber crime is an umbrella term used to describe two linked, but distinct, ranges of criminal activity. The government's National Cyber Security Strategy defines these as follows.

- *Cyber-dependent crimes – crimes that can be committed only using information and communications technology (ICT) devices, where the devices are both the tool for committing the crime and the target of the crime, for example, developing and propagating malware for financial gain; hacking to steal, damage, distort or destroy data and/or network or activity.*

- *Cyber-enabled crimes – traditional crimes which can be increased in scale or reach using computers, computer networks or other forms of ICT such as cyber-enabled fraud and data theft.*

(Gov.UK, 2022c)

The explosion in online crime and its fiscal impact has led to a strategic approach through a multitude of joint programmes, in response to the fact that fraud is now one of the most common crime types in England and Wales. The scale of the problem can be seen with some £479 million lost in 2020 to scams where people were tricked into making money transfers to fraudsters, according to the data from UK Finance. Over the past fiscal year, the Crown Prosecution Service (CPS) has prosecuted 10,000 economic crime cases (CPS, 2021).

Cyber crime is a rapidly changing category of crime, with 86 per cent of reported fraud now thought to be cyber-enabled (CPS, 2021b), exploiting advances in technology to execute crimes. Phishing emails are often used to deploy ransomware, where a user is tricked into clicking on a malicious file or link that hosts malware (NCSC, 2021). Opportunistic criminals have also tried to exploit the government's financial lending scheme by posing as businesses to fraudulently receive money (Makortoff and Jolly, 2022).

During the Covid-19 pandemic, the banks' basic 'know-your-customer' requirements were dispensed with for self-certification. The National Crime Agency investigated two organised criminals from Lithuania, who were jailed for 33 years for laundering £70m on behalf of criminal gangs from around the world – including £10m in bounce-back loans (BBC, 2021).

The National Fraud Intelligence Bureau (NFIB), within the City of London Police, now receives all of Action Fraud's reports. Millions of reports of fraud are used by the NFIB to identify serial offenders, organised crime groups and find emerging crime types (NFIB, 2010). The reports are assessed by NFIB experts. Data matching allows reports from various parts of the country to be linked through analysis, identifying the criminals behind the frauds. Reports are sent to local police forces for investigation.

The increased volume of cyber-enabled crime has led to significant changes in structure and the introduction of the National Cyber Security Centre (NCSC). Since the NCSC was created in 2016 as part of the government's National Cyber Security Strategy, we have seen increasing numbers of cyber crimes, such as ransomware attacks, with one fifth (17 per cent) of UK adults having been the victim of fraud in the 12 months up to November 2021 (Cybersecurity Intelligence, 2021).

Ransomware is a form of malware that encrypts a victim's files, denying access until you pay a fee (Action Fraud, 2018). Victims are given instructions for how to pay a fee to access the decryption key. The costs can range from a few hundred pounds to thousands, payable to cyber criminals in Bitcoin. This is a digital currency founded in 2008, and is not centralised in a bank, enabling pseudonymous use by anyone, which is why it is favoured by cyber criminals (McWhinney, 2021).

The impact upon victims is often unseen due to the perceived monetary loss being viewed as less harmful than the more physical harm resulting from other crime. However, it is known that the impact of digital crimes upon victims is far greater than we may believe. Increases in child exploitation through online harm and cyber-enabled offending has led to changes in legislation, such as section 33 of the Criminal Justice and Courts Act 2015, which created an offence of disclosing private sexual photographs or films without the consent of an individual who appears in them and with intent to cause that individual distress. The offence is known colloquially as *revenge pornography*, which is a broad term that usually refers to the actions of an ex-partner, who uploads a sexually intimate photograph or a video where a person is engaged in a sexual activity onto the internet, or shares by text or email, with the intent of causing the victim humiliation or embarrassment as revenge for the breakup of their relationship.

Sextortion is another harmful form of online blackmail where a perpetrator threatens to reveal intimate images of the victim online unless they give in to their demands. These demands are typically for money or further intimate images. Perpetrators commonly target their victims through dating apps, social media or webcams. Webcam blackmail usually involves people being lured into taking off some or all their clothes in front of their webcam, only to be told that you have been recorded and that the video will be posted online and/or shown to the victim's contacts unless a fee is paid – usually a substantial sum of money.

POLICING SPOTLIGHT

Recently we have seen how legitimate encryption services have enabled criminals to operate in this underworld, but at the same time creating opportunities for law enforcement to use new methods. In 2020, the NCA, working with the French *gendarmerie* under operation *Emma*, created shockwaves throughout the criminal underworld after hundreds of organised crime groups' use of a bespoke encrypted global communication service, *encrochat*, was infiltrated using lawfully authorised hacking methods. The case demonstrated the ability for law enforcement to cross new boundaries using covert techniques to arrest substantial numbers of significant criminals in one operation across several countries.

The case raises questions about the extent to which new technologies and tactics can be used lawfully when related to covert policing, and of illegality and disproportionality in its use.

CRITICAL THINKING ACTIVITY 9.2

LEVEL 5

The Investigatory Powers Tribunal was established to ensure that the United Kingdom meets its obligations under Article 13 of the European Convention on Human Rights (ECHR). Visit the following website and familiarise yourself with its general powers, functions and judgements regulating covert policing activity: www.ipt-uk.com/content.asp?id=10

- What conclusions can you draw from the recent judgements made and how can policing adapt to ensure fundamental rights are protected?

A sample answer is provided at the end of this book.

TERRORIST THREAT

Following the attacks in London and Manchester between March and June 2017, several detailed internal reviews were conducted by MI5 and the police with the final report making more than a hundred recommendations for change (Intelligence and Security Committee of Parliament, 2018). A key recommendation for improvement was to increase and widen information sharing across agencies and to allow local police and other agencies to be alerted to threats of which they are currently unaware. Included in the review was the attack by Khuram Butt on London Bridge, June 2017, which established that Butt was known to the authorities in relation to investigations into the proscribed extremist group Al Muhajiroun. In fact, Butt was actively investigated by MI5 between mid-2015 and 2017. The investigation into Butt remained open at the time of the attack; however, MI5 had not detected any signs of attack planning. This and other cases highlighted the challenges to counter-terror policing and the need for wider communication and improved threat assessment.

The constantly changing terrorist threat with increasing unpredictability places enormous demands on resources. Added to this, in recent years, there has been a considerable change in terrorists' tactics. Islamic extremism has seen a trajectory from co-ordinated attacks to isolated acts by lone actors, who can be associates or members of a terrorist network acting autonomously or may be unconnected to any network, but have been influenced by terrorist or extremist propaganda (HM Government, 2018c). The classification of Extinction Rebellion as a key threat by UK counter-terror police also demonstrates the range of ideologies that are now identified as extreme. There are many reasons behind terrorism, and threat levels can change following events linked to a broad range of ideologies. The Joint Terrorism Analysis Centre (JTAC) and MI5 are responsible for setting the international and domestic threat levels, respectively, considering available intelligence, terrorist intentions and capability as well as potential timescales for attacks. A list of all terrorist organisations or groups proscribed under legislation (Terrorism Act 2000) and the criteria for proscription is maintained by the government and can be found through an internet search (proscribed terrorist groups or organisations).

'CONTEST' is the government's comprehensive strategy to reduce the risk faced from international terrorism, launched in 2003, with revised publications in 2011 and 2018. The strategy directs activity through intelligence officers, the emergency services, local authorities, businesses, voluntary and community organisations, governments and other partners in joint working at an international, national and local level. The Home Secretary has responsibility for 'CONTEST' and is supported by the Office for Security and Counter-Terrorism in the Home Office.

The framework of the 'CONTEST' strategy is based on four 'P' work strands.

- *Prevent: to stop people becoming terrorists or supporting terrorism.*

- *Pursue: to stop terrorist attacks.*

- *Protect: to strengthen our protection against a terrorist attack.*

- *Prepare: to mitigate the impact of a terrorist attack.*

(HM Government, 2018c)

A Prevent statutory duty was introduced through the Counter Terrorism and Security Act 2015. The duty requires local authorities, schools, colleges, higher education institutions, health bodies, prisons and probation, and the police to consider the need to safeguard people from being drawn into terrorism.

Sensitivity in the 'CONTEST' strategy exists, where frontline workers who have a concern about an individual they think might be vulnerable to radicalisation can refer them for appropriate support or intervention. It is suggested that the 'CONTEST' strategy creates Islamophobia in its uneven surveillance of Muslim communities (Qurashi, 2018, citing Fiske, 1998). This concern supports the need for continued and effective dialogue to ensure an inclusive approach in delivering the 'CONTEST' strategy.

PUBLIC CONFIDENCE IN POLICING

The ability to determine levels of public confidence in our police service is viewed as a complex issue, although the recent murder of Sarah Everard by a serving police officer, and the taking of photographs of deceased victims, Bibba Henry and Nicole Smallman, has had significant negative impact on this prominent issue. One aspect is the method used to establish levels of confidence and interpreting such data, such as public surveys. Morrell et al (2019) assert that we need to know what it means when we ask the public whether they have confidence in policing. The need for clarity on general feelings of confidence and that of personal trust in receiving fair treatment has led to the term trust and confidence in policing. Bradford and Jackson (2010) suggest that trust might include the interpersonal relationship between the public and individual police officers, whereas confidence might be more of a set of negative attitudes towards the police as an institution, and when this confidence reaches crisis levels, it has led to resignations, including two Metropolitan Police Commissioners, Ian Blair and Cressida Dick, in 2008 and 2022, respectively. As modern policing continues to develop, the need for higher standards of service has never been higher on the policing agenda.

SUMMARY OF KEY CONCEPTS

This chapter has discussed the following key concepts.

- The challenges emerging from technical crime and maintaining individual rights and freedoms.

- Methods in holding the police to account to improve performance, particularly in police recording systems.

- The recruitment of 20,000 new police recruits offering an opportunity to narrow the gap in service standards.

- Vulnerable people can be exploited into allowing their home to become the out-of-town drug dealer's marketplace.

- Use of the whole-system approach to succeed in tackling serious and organised crime.

- The Force Intelligence Unit's role is identifying offences and proactively sharing intelligence across other forces.

- Scrutiny of the use of digital data by the police by privacy campaign groups.

- Cyber criminals' use of Bitcoin as an alternative for criminal funds.

- Illegal commodities' migration from the street to online platforms in the dark web.

- The challenges to counter-terror policing and the need for wider communication and improved threat assessment.

- Scrutiny on legitimacy of policing methods.

CHECK YOUR KNOWLEDGE

1. What are the four 'P's' of the 'CONTEST' strategy?

2. How has the issue of consent in seeking digital evidence been tightened?

3. What risk factors may indicate county lines exploitation when dealing with victims?

4. What is the annual data requirement and how can this support crime reduction campaigns?

FURTHER READING

Harding, S (2020) *County Lines: Exploitation and Drug Dealing Among Urban Street Gangs*. Bristol: Bristol University Press.
A detailed look at county lines using research and theory on why young people are drawn into county lines. This offers a particularly good holistic view of the models involved and the concept of commodities in street crime.

Joyce, P and Laverick, W (2021) *Policing, Development and Contemporary Practice*. London: Sage.
An up-to-date book including chapters on women in policing and the use of social media, and changes to cross-border working because of Brexit.

Roycroft, M (2021) *Modern Police Leadership: Operational Effectiveness at Every Level*. London: Palgrave Macmillan.
This book is academic and practitioner based with core themes of community relations, fast-time intelligence, human rights and mental health, and dealing with demand, diversity and partnerships.

SAMPLE ANSWERS

CHAPTER 1

CHECK YOUR KNOWLEDGE

1. A systematically developed and organised body of knowledge, authority to use professional judgement to advise a client, sanction by the community to use formal and informal powers, ethical codes of practice which ensure the provision of a service to whoever requests it, a culture of professional practice (Greenwood, 1957)

2. A Vollmer (1933)

3. Establish and maintain the educational requirements for policing ensuring quality and the recognition of professional expertise.

   Build knowledge of what really works in policing so that in time evidence-based practice can replace custom.

   Set the standards for policing and the service through, for example, the implementation of Authorised Professional Practice and a Code of Ethics to ensure standards of professional behaviour (College of Policing, 2020a)

4. Police Constable Degree Apprenticeship (PCDA) and Professional Policing Degree (PPD)

5. College of Policing

CHAPTER 2

REFLECTIVE PRACTICE 2.1

a) To maintain order mainly in rural areas and prevent faction fighting

b) Organised along colonial policing lines as an armed quasi-military force as opposed to conventional police forces on the British mainland

CRITICAL THINKING ACTIVITY 2.1

If 'yes' – conservative histories as per Reiner (2010) and Brogden et al (1988)

If 'no' – revisionist histories as per Brogden et al (1988), Elmsley (2001) and Storch (1975)

CRITICAL THINKING ACTIVITY 2.2

Argument for: standardisation across policing, one Senior Leadership Team, ability to pool and share resources

Argument against: the same objections as Peel faced when initially proposing a national force, lack of local accountability and consent of the public

CHECK YOUR KNOWLEDGE

1. Maintain order and British sovereignty in Ireland

2. 'a system of police would make every servant a spy upon his master and all classes of society spies on each other'

3. Avoiding a centralised force; 'Peelian' principles

4. This view sees the requirement for a professional preventative police service as the logical response to the problems posed by urban and industrial revolution

5. To police the working classes specifically in order to facilitate capitalism

6. Unarmed, local, non-military and non-political, police by consent

7. Earlier in the chapter we referred to the unique features of the police on the British mainland and to that short list we can add that we police by consent, it is focused locally, and accordingly the police are accountable locally. Notwithstanding the policing by consent issue which is linked to several of the Peelian principles.

8. Free from political interference

9. 1974

10. Basic Command Unit

CHAPTER 3

CRITICAL THINKING ACTIVITY 3.1

a) The adversarial system that turns a search for the truth into a contest between opposing lawyers according to a set of rules that the jury neither understands or accepts.

b) The innocent defendant including unnecessary detention prior to trial

c) Italy has sought to introduce a more adversarial approach and there have been criticisms of the juge d'instruction in France

d) The English and Welsh systems due to the rights and protections of defendants contained in PACE, 1984. Far less pre-trial investigation with the adversarial system and pre-trial detention does not exist. The roles of the police, prosecutor and judge are separate.

CRITICAL THINKING ACTIVITY 3.2

a) Contained in pages 5–6 of the policy

b) Page 24 under 'Rolling Up the County Lines Model'

c) Pages 32–33 under 'How This Strategy Will Change Things for the Better'

d) Pages 50–51 of the policy

e) Page 61 of the policy

REFLECTIVE PRACTICE 3.2

a) 14 Areas in England and Wales headed by a Chief Crown Prosecutor work closely with the police and other criminal justice agencies

b) Depends where you live – or work

c) Code for Crown Prosecutors

d) The evidential stage: The public interest stage

e) 'Realistic prospect of conviction' 'Must decide if a prosecution is needed in the public interest'

CHECK YOUR KNOWLEDGE

1. The prosecution brings the case to court and presents their case.

2. Maxwell Confait.

3. Royal Commission into Criminal Procedure, 1981 (Phillips Commission).

4. Lord Justice Auld.

5. Lord Chief Justice.

CHAPTER 4

REFLECTIVE PRACTICE 4.2

It was established within the chapter that the Police and Crime Panel have limited powers to hold a PCC to account. They can veto certain decisions such as the council tax precept and the appointment of a chief constable. They can also make recommendations, but the PCC does not necessarily have to comply with them. Longer term they may seek re-election when the people will have the opportunity to hold a PCC to account by electing another candidate.

The Police Authority was made up of local councillors representing different political parties and a number of independent members who made decisions as a collective. Some may argue that PCCs have too much power being able to make decisions as a single entity rather than a collective.

CRITICAL THINKING ACTIVITY 4.1

Nothing can be taken for granted, but considerable changes have been made by responding positively to lessons learned from previous miscarriages of justice. Legislation, supporting codes of practice, policy, new accredited processes, and developing technology have all made significant contributions. A vulnerable person is now afforded protections through CCTV monitoring, digital investigative interviewing, and the support of a legal representative, and appropriate adult. During interview the focus is now a search for the truth rather than obtaining a confession. Disclosure laws introduced in 1996 ensure that all material that is collected during an investigation is now disclosed in full to both the prosecution and defence teams, providing an open and transparent approach.

CRITICAL THINKING ACTIVITY 4.2

a) The problem is identified as the police using their stop and search powers disproportionately on different ethnic groups, causing suspicion amongst affected communities believing that they are being unfairly targeted.

b) At the time of writing, it is too early to say. There are 8 recommendations that include training, monitoring, and scrutiny. Future events, scrutiny reports, policing statistics, and performance measurement may possibly indicate some problem resolution. If you are a student police officer checkout how your police force is responding to these recommendations and find out what progress is being made.

c) The author of the report Wendy Williams, states:

'The police service must be able to show the public evidence that their use of the powers is fair, lawful and appropriate, or risk losing the trust of the communities they serve.'

Legitimacy will be enhanced by rising confidence in policing by communities affected by disproportional use of police powers.

CHECK YOUR KNOWLEDGE

1. Home Secretary, Police Authority, Chief Constable.

2. These are set out in the Police Reform and Social Responsibility Act (PRSR 2011). Look up the answer.

3. Sections 28(6)(a) and 28(6)(b) of the PRSR 2011 requires a police and crime panel to review and scrutinise decisions made, or other action taken by the PCC, and to make reports or recommendations to the PCC. They cannot hold the PCC to account. (See reflective practice exercise 4.2).

4. The plan sets out a series of objectives that relate to a strategy for policing the area and how crime and disorder reduction will be tackled. It will also contain information about the policing area, the financial resources that are available, how performance will be measured, and grants available to reduce crime and disorder.

5. Police effectiveness, efficiency, and legitimacy.

CHAPTER 5

REFLECTIVE PRACTICE 5.1

A whole range of behaviour could breach the standards of professional behaviour and lead to an investigation against a police officer. For example:

An officer lying in a statement about what they saw a suspect do would be a breach of the standard of *'honesty and integrity'*.

An officer telling a relative what information the police national computer contained about their neighbour would be a breach of the standard of *'confidentiality'*.

REFLECTIVE PRACTICE 5.2

There are many policing examples where HMICFRS have been commissioned by the Home Secretary following high-profile events, and two examples are set out below.

a) A review of the recording and investigation of allegations of child abuse by the late Jimmy Saville.

b) A review commissioned in October 2020 to inspect how effectively the police manage protests. This followed several protests including Black Lives Matter protests in Bristol where the statue of Edward Colston was toppled by protesters.

CRITICAL THINKING ACTIVITY 5.1

a) Police officers and staff should not accept gifts or gratuities from members of the public which could been viewed as compromising their impartiality. They are expected to decide for themselves whether this is the case. Factors such as the value of the gift and whether it is connected to a business may be relevant. The officer or staff member can also consider whether refusing the gift may cause offence.

Police forces have policies covering gifts and gratuities and for all offers of gifts, gratuities, favours and hospitality it should be recorded whether they are accepted or refused.

b) The driver of the vehicle should be treated the same as you would treat a member of the public and in accordance with the law. Your colleague is in breach of a number of the standards of professional behaviour with his proposed actions, including honesty and integrity, duties and responsibilities, orders and instructions and discreditable conduct. If you agree to take the driver home, in addition to those breaches you also breach the standard which requires you to challenge and report improper conduct.

CRITICAL THINKING ACTIVITY 5.2

a) The alleged actions would amount to serious corruption and is, therefore, a mandatory referral.

b) The alleged action would amount to an abuse of authority to pervert the course of justice. This would be a mandatory referral as the offence of perverting the course of justice carries a maximum sentence of life imprisonment.

CRITICAL THINKING ACTIVITY 5.3

Police officers and staff have access to a lot of information which should only be accessed and shared for a policing purpose. They are also expected to maintain the highest standards of behaviour at all times. Any reduction in those standards can impact not just on the individual officer or staff member but on the whole service. Police officers both on and off duty should consider at all times whether their actions could discredit the police service or undermine public confidence in it.

CHECK YOUR KNOWLEDGE

1. Police Reform Act 2002.

2. The Code of Ethics applies to police officers and police staff including those working on permanent or temporary contracts and a casual or voluntary basis.

3. Organisational factors, situational factors, and individual characteristics.

4. Seven years or more.

5. Final written warning, reduction in rank and dismissal without notice.

CHAPTER 6

CRITICAL THINKING ACTIVITY 6.2

Firstly, whatever your actions, at the heart of your decision making will be the code of ethics. You will be acting with fairness, integrity, respect and selflessness, and will be accountable for any decisions you make.

You are likely to have little information or intelligence about the person you are dealing with and will quickly have to take steps to find out what has happened, and who the person is. Where is this information or intelligence going to come from? There may be people nearby who can provide the information you need, and if the identity of the person is known a call to the police control room may provide you with more information about the person you are dealing with.

Consider the risks in this scenario to you as a police officer, the collapsed person and members of the public. Are you dealing with a medical issue, is the person drunk or under the influence of drugs, is the person dangerous (for example, the police control room may provide information that the person is known for carrying weapons), is the person a danger to others? The person may even be a victim of crime and still at risk from the perpetrator. Any risks identified need to be quickly considered and mitigated, and it may be appropriate to call for assistance and seek advice; however, in some situations, decisions will need to be made quickly.

Having obtained as much information as you can in the time available, and considered the risks, you will need to identify the powers available to you and consider any force policy that may be appropriate to the situation you are dealing with. If it is a criminal offence you are dealing with, legislation will provide powers of arrest, search and seizure. If it is a safeguarding issue, you will have a duty of care set out in both legislation and local policy. If your action requires the use of force, this too will be set out within legislation and common law.

Next a decision will have to be made in relation to how you are going to deal with the incident and there may be a range of options available to you. If it is a medical issue, it would be appropriate to seek medical assistance or to arrange removal directly to hospital. You may decide to arrest the person for a criminal offence, although you could use your discretion and decide not to make an arrest. You may report the person for a criminal offence rather than making an arrest, or you may consider that a caution would be appropriate in the circumstances. If safeguarding is required, you may decide to refer direct to another agency to provide appropriate support. For example, this could be social services, other organisations concerned with drink or drugs addiction, or victim services. There are often many options for you to consider.

Finally, having taken the decision, following implementation it is always good practice to later reflect on the incident and the decisions you have made. Was the incident effectively dealt with, were good decisions made, what went well, what didn't go so well, what did you learn from the experience, and what, if anything, would you do differently next time?

CHECK YOUR KNOWLEDGE

1. Use the mnemonic CIAPOR – Code of Ethics, Information gathering, Assessment of risk, Powers available, Options, Action and review.

2. The code of ethics originate from the 'Principles of Public Life' published in 1995, by the Parliamentary Committee on Standards in Public Life.

3. Common law.

4. A vulnerable victim at risk of harm, an offence committed as a series within a community, a prolific or priority offender, and any person who is being managed under multi agency public protection arrangements (MAPPA)

5. Racism awareness and valuing cultural diversity.

6. The two main acts cited were the Criminal Law Act 1967 (section 1), and Human Rights Act 1998 (articles 2, 3, and 5).

CHAPTER 7

CRITICAL THINKING ACTIVITY 7.1

Your primary role would be the protection of life.

CRITICAL THINKING ACTIVITY 7.2

a) Constables need to act at all times in accordance with the code of ethics and to understand and gain the trust and confidence of the communities they serve. This 'legitimacy' will ensure that the vulnerable can be identified or have the confidence to seek help, and that the intelligence picture to prevent or mitigate the harm caused in the examples presented in the policing spotlights is enhanced.

b) The College of Policing highlights the risk of artificial intelligence, machine learning and predictive analysis, and how this presents ethical concerns around human rights, private data and questions of bias. It also recognises the challenge of building trust in a digital age and the need for transparent debate and scrutiny. The NPCC, the Independent Digital Ethics Panel for Policing (IDEPP), was formed in 2015 and is a group of experts from law enforcement, academia, community and other legal/policy professionals whose aim is to test the emerging ethical issues of policing the digital age.

REFLECTIVE PRACTICE 7.1

A police officer serving in 2040 will need to operate within a complex legal, technological and social environment and will require a high degree of professional competency and integrity. All officers will require training to prepare them for predictable societal change and must be committed to continuous professional development. Police officers will understand their role and relationship with their communities, the powers they possess and the impact on that relationship when those powers are used. They will be required to understand the national threats to public safety in the UK, and how international events might impact on those. Subsequently, emotional intelligence and cultural awareness will be core skills to serve effectively in the office of constable. More broadly, police organisations need to attract recruits who are committed to lifelong learning, especially those from unrepresented groups. This will secure its legitimacy as a public service that reflects the community it serves.

CHECK YOUR KNOWLEDGE

1. Competency Values Framework (CVF).

2. National Crime Agency (NCA).

3. British Transport Police, Civil Nuclear Constabulary, Ministry of Defence Police.

4. Serious Fraud Office (SFO).

5. Secret Intelligence Service (SIS).

6. Risk of artificial intelligence, policing misinformation, building trust in a digital age, workforce balance/skills, operating in an increasingly complex arena.

CHAPTER 8

REFLECTIVE PRACTICE 8.1

a) Paragraph 1.1 in the bold print

b) P 6 especially paragraphs 3.2–3.9

c) To protect them from harm and transforming the approach to policing

d) With other local public services to improve outcomes for citizens and protect the vulnerable

e) Adapting evidence of what works in targeting vulnerability in areas of high demand and need

f) College of Policing and Police ICT Company

g) Better response to assessments of threat, harm, risk and vulnerability

REFLECTIVE PRACTICE 8.2

a) Means keeping the child in focus when making decisions about their lives and working in partnership with them and their families

b) Sexual, physical and emotional abuse; domestic abuse; controlling or coercive behaviour; exploitation by criminal gangs and organised crime groups; trafficking; online abuse and the influences of radicalisation

c) Paragraph 13 p9/10

d) Paragraphs 40/41 p25

e) Harm may be indirect such as some domestic abuse and controlling and coercive behaviour

f) The same safeguards as any other child

g) Reasonable cause to believe that they would otherwise suffer significant harm

REFLECTIVE PRACTICE 8.3

a) Crimes against children are every bit as serious as crimes against adults. Chief constables must ensure that crimes involving a child victim are dealt with promptly and efficiently, and to the same standard as equivalent crimes against adults

b) Chief constables must ensure that the investigation of crime against children is as important as the investigation of any other form of serious crime. Any suggestion that child protection is of a lower status than other forms of policing must be eradicated.

c) The *Working Together* arrangements must be amended to ensure the police carry out completely and exclusively, any criminal investigation elements in a case of suspected injury or harm to a child, including the evidential interview with a child victim. This will remove confusion about which agency takes the 'lead' or is responsible for certain actions.

d) The Home Office, through Centrex (now the College of Policing) and the Association of Chief Police Officers (now the National Police Chiefs Council) must devise and implement a national training curriculum for child protection officers as recommended in 1999 by Her Majesty's Inspectorate of Constabulary in its thematic inspection report, *Child Protection*

e) Included in the list of ministerial priorities for the police and chief constables must give child protection investigations a high priority in their policing plans to ensure they are well-resourced, well-managed and well-motivated.

f) Conflicting evidence of senior officers as to who was ultimately accountable for the Child Protection Teams.

REFLECTIVE PRACTICE 8.4

a) When relevant vulnerabilities interact with the individual's situation

b) Identify an individual's vulnerability or vulnerabilities

c) Understand how these interact with the situation to create harm or the risk of harm

d) Assess the level of risk or harm

e) Take appropriate and proportionate action, involving partners where they have the relevant skills and resources

f) Spot the clues associated with vulnerability-related risk

g) Communication, Clues and Curiosity

h) Ten principles of risk (page 4)

CRITICAL THINKING ACTIVITY 8.1

a) The first contact in building trust and building the case

b) Independent sexual advisers

c) The absence of a victim-centred approach, founded on targeted specialist support for victims is hampering the progress of the case.

d) Getting the first response right is crucial

e) When a case involved complex features such as a victim with poor mental health or alcohol or drug dependency.

CHECK YOUR KNOWLEDGE

1. National Police Chiefs' Council and the Association of Police and Crime Commissioners.

2. Social harms.

3. Children Act 2004.

4. Second assailant.

5. Association of Chief Police Officers in 1975.

CHAPTER 9

CRITICAL THINKING ACTIVITY 9.1

The primary aim is to safeguard the young male and identify his needs. In this scenario the second aim is to establish any exploitation using him and his home to deal controlled drugs, known as cuckooing. Some of the actions would be to:

- carry out intelligence checks;

- contact housing and establish the named occupiers on their system for this address;

- ask the occupant for details of immediate family or services he is in receipt of;

- look out for unexplained injuries or signs of assault;

- follow national and local safeguarding guidance and share the incident with the local authority.

CRITICAL THINKING ACTIVITY 9.2

a) Policing needs to ensure structures are in place to limit collateral intrusion into the private lives of people outside of specific operations where covert policing takes place.

b) Covert policing authorising officers need to reflect the seriousness of the offence and the extent to which it constitutes a pressing social need, thereby deeming the activity '*necessary in a democratic society*'.

c) Improved training, leadership and supervision are a core foundation to ensuring fundamental rights are protected and balanced against the need to prevent and detect crime.

REFLECTIVE PRACTICE 9.1

a) Confirm ownership and ask the victim for their informed agreement when acquiring the device; consider whether the individual needs independent support and/or time to consider their decision. Explain the reasons for needing to obtain material and what will happen to it.

b) Seek to understand the concerns of the victim to allay them as far as possible and, where necessary, mitigate any safeguarding risks raised.

c) Explain you will only extract the minimum amount of data.

CHECK YOUR KNOWLEDGE

1. Prevent, Pursue, Protect, Prepare.

2. Digital extraction is now subject to a Code of Practice issued as APP by the College of Policing, May 2021.

3. a) Increased visitors to your area surrounding a house or flat

b) Frequent change of residents

c) Drug paraphanalia in the street

d) Unexplained new things or wealth

e) Young residents going missing

f) Exclusion from school, truancy.

4. The annual data requirement (ADR) contains all requests for data made to all police forces in England and Wales under the Home Secretary's statutory powers and is used to support crime and policing related statistics.

REFERENCES

Action Fraud (2018) Ransomeware. [online] Available at: www.actionfraud.police.uk/campaign/ransomware (accessed 20 June 2022).

Advance HE (2020) Unconscious Bias. [online] Available at: www.advance-he.ac.uk/guidance/equality-diversity-and-inclusion/employment-and-careers/unconscious-bias (accessed 12 June 2022).

Alderson, J (1992) 'The Police'. In Stockdale, E and Casale, S (eds) *Criminal Justice Under Stress* (pp 10–33). London: Blackstone.

All Party Parliamentary Group for Domestic and Sexual Violence (2015) The Changing Landscape of Domestic and Sexual Violence Services. [online] Available at: www.womensaid.org.uk/wp-content/uploads/2015/11/APPG_Report_20151.pdf (accessed 12 June 2022).

Anderson, J, Rainie, L and Vogels, E A (2021) Experts Say the 'New Normal' in 2025 Will Be Far More Tech-Driven, Presenting More Big Challenges. Pew Research Center: Internet, Science & Tech. [online] Available at: www.pewresearch.org/internet/2021/02/18/experts-say-the-new-normal-in-2025-will-be-far-more-tech-driven-presenting-more-big-challenges (accessed 12 June 2022).

Anti-terrorism, Crime and Security Act 2001 [online] Available at: www.legislation.gov.uk/ukpga/2001/24/contents (accessed 12 June 2022).

Association of Chief Police Officers (ACPO) (2012) *The National Decision Model*. [online] Available at: www.squaredapplesuk.co.uk/app/download/23383435/201201PBANDM.pdf (accessed 12 June 2022).

Association of Police and Crime Commissioners and National Police Chiefs' Council (APCC and NPCC) (2016) *Policing Vision 2025*. London: Association of Police and Crime Commissioners/National Police Chiefs' Council.

Auld, R (2001) *Review of the Criminal Courts in England and Wales* (Chapter 10). [online] Available at: www.criminal-courts-review.org.uk/chpt10.pdf (accessed 12 June 2022).

Bains, P (2019) *Project Servator Evaluation Study 2018/19 Report*. [online] Available at: https://le.ac.uk/-/media/uol/docs/news/project-servator-report.pdf (accessed 12 June 2022).

Bank Mellat v Her Majesty's Treasury (No 2) [2013] UKSC 39.

Banton, M (1964) *The Policeman in the Community*. London: Tavistock.

BBC (1982) The Police Rape Interview That Shocked Britain. [online] Available at: www.bbc.co.uk/programmes/p09lqp6t (accessed 12 June 2022).

BBC (2021) *Hunting the Essex Lorry Killers*. [online] Available at: www.bbc.co.uk/programmes/m0010ldl (accessed 12 June 2022).

BBC News (2013) Avon and Somerset Police Boss Colin Port Loses Court Action. [online] Available at: www.bbc.co.uk/news/uk-england-20944403 (accessed 12 June 2022).

BBC News (2018) Bury PC Who Dived in River Earwell to Save Man 'Can't Swim'. [online] Available at: www.bbc.co.uk/news/uk-england-manchester-43110296 (accessed 12 June 2022).

BBC News (2021) MI5: 31 Late-stage Terror Plots Foiled in Four Years in UK. [online] Available at: www.bbc.co.uk/news/uk-58512901 (accessed 12 June 2022).

Beattie, J M (1986) *Crime and the Courts in England 1660–1800*. Oxford: Oxford University Press.

Becker, G (1974) Crime and Punishment: An Economic Approach. In Becker, G and Landes, W (eds) *Essays in the Economics of Crime and Punishment*. [online] Available at: www.nber.org/system/files/chapters/c3625/c3625.pdf (accessed 12 June 2022).

Bitner, E (1970) *The Functions of the Police in Modern Society*. Chevy Chase, MD: Center for Studies of Crime and Delinquency, National Institute of Mental Health.

Blair, I (2009) *Policing Controversy*. London: Profile Books.

Blake, C, Sheldon, B and Williams, P (2010) *Policing and Criminal Justice*. Exeter: Learning Matters.

Boulton, L, Phythian, R, Kirby, S and Dawson, I (2020) Taking an Evidence-Based Approach to Evidence-Based Policing Research. *Policing: A Journal of Policy and Practice*, 15(2): 1290–305.

Bradford, B and Jackson, J (2010) *Trust and Confidence in the Police: A Conceptual Review*. [online] Available at: www.researchgate.net/publication/228242091_Trust_and_Confidence_in_the_Police_A_Conceptual_Review (accessed 12 June 2022).

British Association of Social Workers (BASW) (2009) Serious Case Review Baby Peter. [online] Available at: www.basw.co.uk/resources/serious-case-review-baby-peter (accessed 12 June 2022).

British Association of Social Workers (BASW) (2014) Daniel Pelka Review Retrospective: Deeper Analysis Progress Report on Implementation of Recommendations. [online] Available at: www.basw.co.uk/resources/daniel-pelka-review-retrospective-deeper-analysis-progress-report-implementation (accessed 12 June 2022).

British Transport Police (2020) *Annual Report 2020/21*. [online] Available at: www.btp. police.uk/SysSiteAssets/foi-media/british-transport-police/reports/annual-reports-2020-21/btp_annual_report_2020_21.pdf (accessed 12 June 2022).

British Transport Police Authority (2018) *Strategic Plan 2018–2025*. [online] Available at: https://btpa.police.uk/wp-content/uploads/2018/07/BTPA-Strategic-Plan-201821-1.pdf (accessed 12 June 2022).

Brogden, M (2005) The Emergence of the Police – the Colonial Dimension. In Newburn, T (ed) *Policing: Key Readings* (pp 69–80). Cullompton: Willan Publishing.

Brogden, M J, Jefferson, T and Walklate, S (1988) *Introducing Policework*. London: Unwin Hyman.

Brown, J (2014) *The Future of Policing*. London: Routledge.

Brown, J, Belur, J, Tompson, L, McDowall, A, Hunter, G and May, T (2018) Extending the Remit of Evidence-based Policing. *International Journal of Police Science & Management*, 20(1): 38–51.

Burnside, J (nd) The Stefan Kiszco Case. [online] Available at: www.julianburnside.com.au/law/the-stefan-kiszko-case (accessed 12 June 2022).

Cambridge Dictionary (2020) Definition of 'Governance'. [online] Available at: https://dictionary.cambridge.org/dictionary/english/governance (accessed 12 June 2022).

Cambridge Dictionary (2022) Definition of 'Bias'. [online] Available at: https://dictionary.cambridge.org/dictionary/english/bias (accessed 19 June 2022).

Cameron, D (2010) Invitation to join the Government of Britain – The Conservative Manifesto 2010. [online] Available at: https://issuu.com/conservatives/docs/cpmanifesto2010_hires (accessed 12 June 2022).

Campion, J (2020) *Safer West Mercia Plan 2016–2021* (updated July 2020). Worcester: Office of Police and Crime Commissioner.

Carlan, P and Lewis, J (2009) Dissecting Police Professionalism: A Comparison of Predictors within Five Professionalism Subsets. *Police Quarterly*, 12(4): 370–87.

Carter, H (2011) Rapist Police Officer Jailed for Life. *The Guardian*, 11 January. [online] Available at: www.theguardian.com/uk/2011/jan/11/rapist-police-officer-life-sentence (accessed 12 June 2022).

Chadd, K (2020) The History of Cybercrime and Cybersecurity, 1940–2020. *Cybercrime Magazine*. [online] Available at: https://cybersecurityventures.com/the-history-of-cybercrime-and-cybersecurity-1940-2020 (accessed 29 March 2022).

Children Act 1989 [online] Available at www.legislation.gov.uk/ukpga/1989/41/contents (accessed 4 May 2022).

Children Act 2004 [online] Available at: www.legislation.gov.uk/ukpga/2004/31/contents (accessed 12 June 2022).

Christie, N (1977) Conflicts as Property. *British Journal of Criminology*, 17(1): 1–15.

Civil Nuclear Police Authority (2021) *Civil Nuclear Authority Strategic Plan 2021/24*. [online] Available at: https://assets.publishing.service.gov.uk/government/uploads/system/uploads/attachment_data/file/1021292/CNPA_three_year_strategic_plan_2021-24.pdf (accessed 12 June 2022).

Cockcroft, T, Bryant, R and Keval, H (2016) The Impact of Dispersal Powers on Congregating Youth. *Safer Communities*, 15(4): 213–22.

College of Policing (2012) National Decision Model. [online] Available at: www.app.college.police.uk/app-content/national-decision-model/the-national-decision-model (accessed 12 June 2022).

College of Policing (2013a) Investigation Process. [online] Available at: www.app.college.police.uk/app-content/investigations/investigation-process/ (accessed 12 June 2022).

College of Policing. (2013b) Introduction and Types of Critical Incidents. [online] Available at: www.app.college.police.uk/app-content/critical-incident-management/types-of-critical-incident (accessed 12 June 2022).

College of Policing (2014a) National Decision Model. [online] Available at: www.app.college.police.uk/app-content/national-decision-model/the-national-decision-model (accessed 12 June 2022).

College of Policing (2014b) *Code of Ethics*. [online] Available at: https://assets.college.police.uk/s3fs-public/2021-02/code_of_ethics.pdf (accessed 12 June 2022).

College of Policing (2015) Partnership Working and Multi-agency Responses. [online] Available at:www.app.college.police.uk/app-content/major-investigation-and-public-protection/domestic-abuse/partnership-working-and-multi-agency-responses (accessed 12 June 2022).

College of Policing (2017a) Evidence-based Policing. [online] Available at: www.college.police.uk/research/evidence-based-policing-EBP (accessed 12 June 2022).

College of Policing (2017b) *Competency and Values Framework: Guidance.* [online] Available at: https://assets.college.police.uk/s3fs-public/2020-11/competency_and_values_framework_guidance.pdf (accessed 12 June 2022).

College of Policing (2018a) Risk. [online] Available at: www.app.college.police.uk/app-content/risk-2/risk (accessed 12 June 2022).

College of Policing (2018b) Tactical Planning. [online] Available at: www.app.college.police.uk/app-content/operations/operational-planning/tactical-planning (accessed 12 June 2022).

College of Policing (2020a) About Us. [online] Available at: www.college.police.uk/About/Pages/default.aspx (accessed 12 June 2022).

College of Policing (2020b) PCSO Entry Routes. [online] Available at: www.college.police.uk/What-we-do/Learning/Policing-Education-Qualifications-Framework/PCSO-entry-routes/Pages/PCSO-entry-routes.aspx (accessed 12 June 2022).

College of Policing (2020c) Special Constables Learning Programme. [online] Available at: www.college.police.uk/guidance/involving-citizens-policing/training-special-constables (accessed 10 July 2022).

College of Policing (2020d) Preparing Policing for Future Challenges and Demands. [online] Available at: www.college.police.uk/article/preparing-policing-future-challenges-and-demands (accessed 12 June 2022).

College of Policing (2020e) Policing Education Qualifications Framework (PEQF). [online] Available at: www.college.police.uk/guidance/policing-education-qualifications-framework-peqf (accessed 12 June 2022).

College of Policing (2020f) *Policing in England and Wales: Future Operating Environment 2040.* [online] Available at: https://paas-s3-broker-prod-lon-6453d964-1d1a-432a-9260-5e0ba7d2fc51.s3.eu-west-2.amazonaws.com/s3fs-public/2020-08/Future-Operating-Environment-2040_0.pdf (accessed 14 April 2022).

College of Policing (2021a) Body-worn Cameras. [online] Available at: https://whatworks. college.police.uk/toolkit/Pages/Intervention.aspx?InterventionID=66 (accessed 12 June 2022).

College of Policing (2021b) *Police Constable Degree Apprenticeship National Policing Curriculum* (pp 6–7), v 4.

College of Policing (2021c) Phase 2 – Managing Critical Incidents. [online] Available at: www.app.college.police.uk/app-content/critical-incident-management/phase-2-managing-critical-incidents (accessed 12 June 2022).

College of Policing (2021d) Help Shape the Code of Ethics Review. [online] Available at: www. college.police.uk/article/help-shape-review-code-of-ethics (accessed 12 June 2022).

College of Policing (2021e) *Recognising and Responding to Vulnerability and Risk*. [online] Available at: https://assets.college.police.uk/s3fs-public/2021-11/Recognising-responding-vulnerability-related-risks-guidelines.pdf (accessed 12 June 2022).

College of Policing (2021f) Introduction to Vulnerability-related Risk. [online] Available at: www. college.police.uk/guidance/vulnerability-related-risks/introduction-vulnerability-related-risk (accessed 12 June 2022).

College of Policing (2021g) *Authorised Professional Practice: Extraction of Material from Digital Devices*. [online] Available at: https://library.college.police.uk/docs/college-of-policing/APP-the-extraction-of-material-from-digital-devices-2021.pdf (accessed 12 June 2022).

College of Policing. Covid-19 Restrictions. [online] Available at: www.college.police.uk/ guidance/covid-19/understanding-law (accessed 12 June 2022).

Commissioners for Revenue and Customs Act 2005 [online] Available at: www.legislation. gov.uk/ukpga/2005/11/contents (accessed 12 June 2022).

Computer Misuse Act 1990 [online] Available at: www.legislation.gov.uk/ukpga/1990/18/ crossheading/computer-misuse-offences (accessed 12 June 2022).

Constitutional Reform Act 2005 [online] Available at: www.legislation.gov.uk/ukpga/2005/ 4/contents (accessed 12 June 2022).

Cook, T, Hibbit, S and Hill, M (2013) *Blackstone's Crime Investigator's Handbook*. Oxford: Oxford University Press.

Coomber, R and Moyle, L (2017) The Changing Shape of Street-Level Heroin and Crack Supply in England: Commuting, Holidaying and Cuckooing Drug Dealers Across 'County Lines'. *The British Journal of Criminology*, 58(6): 1323–42.

Cordner, G (2016) The Unfortunate Demise of Police Education. *Journal of Criminal Justice Education*, 27(4): 485–96.

Coronavirus Act 2020 [online] Available at: www.legislation.gov.uk/ukpga/2020/7/contents/enacted (accessed 12 June 2022).

Cornish, D and Clarke, R V (1986) *The Reasoning Criminal: Rational Choice Perspectives on Offending*. Hague: Springer-Verlag.

Cottrell, S (2017) *Critical Thinking Skills*. 3rd ed. London: Palgrave.

Counter Terrorism Policing (2021) Project Servator. [online] Available at: www.counter terrorism.police.uk/servator (accessed 12 June 2022).

Counter-Terrorism and Security Act 2015 [online] Available at: www.legislation.gov.uk/ukpga/2015/6/contents/enacted (accessed 12 June 2022).

Couper, D (1994) Notable Speeches: Seven Seeds for Policing. *Law Enforcement Bulletin*, 63(3): 12–14.

Courts Act 2013 [online] Available at: www.legislation.gov.uk/ukpga/2003/39/contents (accessed 22 June 2022).

Cowley, R and Todd, P (2006) The History of Her Majesty's Inspectorate of Constabulary: The First 150 Years. [online] Available at: www.justiceinspectorates.gov.uk/hmicfrs/media/the-history-of-hmic-the-first-150-years.pdf (accessed 19 June 2022).

Crawford, A (1997) *The Local Governance of Crime: Appeals to Community and Partnerships*. Oxford: Oxford University Press.

Crime and Disorder Act 1998 [online] Available at: www.legislation.gov.uk/ukpga/1998/37/section/6 (accessed 12 June 2022).

Criminal Justice Act 1987 [online] Available at: www.legislation.gov.uk/ukpga/1987/38/contents (accessed 12 June 2022).

Criminal Justice Act 2003 [online] Available at: www.legislation.gov.uk/ukpga/2003/44/contents (accessed 12 June 2022).

Criminal Justice and Courts Act 2015 [online] Available at: www.legislation.gov.uk/ukpga/2015/2/contents (accessed 12 June 2022).

Criminal Law Act 1967 [online] Available at: www.legislation.gov.uk/ukpga/1967/58/section/3 (accessed 5 12 June 2022).

Criminal Procedure and Investigations Act 1996 [online] Available at: www.legislation.gov.uk/ukpga/1996/25/contents (accessed 12 June 2022).

Crowhurst, L (2017) Improving policing for the benefit of the public. [online] Available at: www.police-foundation.org.uk/2017/wp-content/uploads/2017/08/pf_cgi_digital_justice.pdf (accessed 22 December 2021).

Crown Prosecution Service (CPS) (2021) CPS Launches Ambitious Plan to Combat Economic Crime. [online] Available at: www.cps.gov.uk/cps/news/cps-launches-ambitious-plan-combat-economic-crime (accessed 12 June 2022).

Cyber Security Intelligence (2021) One Fifth of British Adults Suffer Online Fraud. [online] Available at: www.cybersecurityintelligence.com/blog/one-fifth-of-british-adults-suffer-online-fraud-5973.html (accessed 12 June 2022).

Daily Express (2017) Police 'Terror' Operation Stops Vehicles Just Yards from London Bridge Attack. [online] Available at: www.express.co.uk/news/uk/827773/Terror-checks-vehicles-London-Bridge-attack-Project-Servator-City-London-Police-terrorism (accessed 12 June 2022).

Data Protection Act 2018 [online] Available at: www.legislation.gov.uk/ukpga/2018/12/contents/enacted (accessed 2 January 2022).

Dathan, M (2021) Online Crimes Double as Promised Laws Are Delayed. *The Times*, 19 December. [online] Available at: www.thetimes.co.uk/article/online-crimes-double-as-promised-laws-are-delayed-56ds6djs3 (accessed 12 June 2022).

Densley, J, McLean, R, Deuchar, R and Harding, S (2018) An Altered State? Emergent Changes to Illicit Drug Markets and Distribution Networks in Scotland. *International Journal of Drug Policy*, 58: 113–20.

Dixon, B (2018) Who Needs Critical Friends? Independent Advisory Groups in the Age of the Police and Crime Commissioner. *Policing Journal*, 14(3): 686–97.

Dodd, V (2017) Don't Cut Police Anti-Terror Budget as Threat Grows, Warns Top Officer. *The Guardian*, 22 September. Available at: www.theguardian.com/uk-news/2017/sep/22/dont-cut-general-police-budget-amid-terror-threat-says-top-officer (accessed 12 June 2022).

Dodd, V and Siddique, H (2021) Sarah Everard Murder: Wayne Couzens Given Whole Life Sentence. *The Guardian*, 30 September. Available at: www.theguardian.com/uk-news/2021/sep/30/sarah-everard-murder-wayne-couzens-whole-life-sentence (accessed 12 July 2022).

Domestic Abuse Act 2021 [online] Available at: www.legislation.gov.uk/ukpga/2021/17/contents/enacted (accessed 12 June 2022).

Donoghue, J (2014) Reforming the Role of Magistrates: Implications for Summary Justice in England and Wales. *The Modern Law Review*, 77(6): 928–63.

Doss, D, Glover Jr, W, Goza, R and Wigginton Jr, M (2015) *The Foundations of Communication in Criminal Justice Systems.* Boca Raton, FL: CRC Press.

Drake, D, Muncie, J and Westmarland, L (2010) *Criminal Justice: Local and Global.* Cullompton: Willan.

East Midlands Police Academic Collaboration (EMPAC) (2018) The Science of Management of Risk in Law Enforcement. [online] Available at: www.empac.org.uk/science-management-risk-law-enforcement (accessed 22 June 2022).

Easteal, G (2021) North Yorkshire Police Boss Resigns Amid Criticism Over Sarah Everard Comments. [online] Available at: www.itv.com/news/tyne-tees/2021-10-14/panel-passes-vote-of-no-confidence-in-north-yorkshire-police-boss-philip-allott (accessed 12 June 2022).

Emsley, C (2001) The Origins and Development of the Police. In McLaughlin, E and Muncie, J (eds) *Controlling Crime*. 1st ed (pp 11–52). London: Sage.

Emsley, C (2003) The Birth and Development of the Police. In Newburn, T (ed) *Handbook of Policing* (pp 66–83). Cullompton: Willan.

Emsley, C (2007) Historical Perspectives on Crime. In Maguire, M, Morgan, R and Reiner, R (eds) *The Oxford Handbook of Criminology* (pp 122–38). Oxford: Oxford University Press.

Emsley, C (2014) Peel's Principles, Police Principles. In Brown, J M (ed) *The Future of Policing* (pp 11–22). Abingdon, Oxon: Routledge.

Energy Act 2004 [online] Available at: www.legislation.gov.uk/ukpga/2004/20/contents (accessed 12 June 2022).

Fitzgerald, M, McLennan, G and Pawson, J (1981) *Crime and Society: Readings in History and Theory*. Routledge: London.

Fleming, J and Rhodes, R (2018) Can Experience Be Evidence? Craft Knowledge and Evidence-Based Policing. *Policy and Politics*, 46(1): 3–26.

Forgery and Counterfeiting Act 1981 [online] Available at: www.legislation.gov.uk/ukpga/1981/45/contents (accessed 12 June 2022).

Fuller, A (2014) *West Midlands PCC: Strategic Policing and Crime Board – Victims and Restorative Justice Funding Update.* [online] Available at: www.westmidlands-pcc.gov.uk/wp-content/uploads/2019/05/SPCB-140204-Victims-and-Restorative-Justice-Funding-Update.pdf (accessed 12 June 2022).

Fyfe, N (2014) A Different and Divergent Trajectory? Reforming the Structure, Governance and Narrative of Policing in Scotland. In Brown, J (ed) *The Future of Policing* (pp 493–506). London: Routledge.

GCHQ (2022) GCHQ Overview. [online] Available at: www.gchq.gov.uk/section/mission/overview (accessed 12 June 2022).

Gov.UK (2004) *Review of Section 58 of the Children Act 2004.* [online] Available at: https://assets.publishing.service.gov.uk/government/uploads/system/uploads/attachment_data/file/344503/Review_of_Section_58_of_the_Children_Act_2004.pdf (accessed 12 June 2022).

Gov.UK (2021a) Beating Crime Plan. [online] Available at: www.gov.uk/government/publications/beating-crime-plan/beating-crime-plan (accessed 18 April 2022).

Gov.UK (2021b) Criminal Court Statistics Quarterly: April to June 2021. [online] Available at: www.gov.uk/government/statistics/criminal-court-statistics-quarterly-april-to-june-2021/criminal-court-statistics-quarterly-april-to-june-2021 (accessed 12 June 2022).

Gov.UK (2021c) Tackling Violence Against Women and Girls Strategy. [online] Available at: www.gov.uk/government/publications/tackling-violence-against-women-and-girls-strategy/tackling-violence-against-women-and-girls-strategy (accessed 18 April 2022).

Gov.UK (2021d) New Courtroom Protections for Victims of Rape Piloted in London and North East. [online] Available at: www.gov.uk/government/news/new-courtroom-protections-for-victims-of-rape-piloted-in-london-and-north-east (accessed 18 April 2022).

Gov.UK (2022a) National Review into the Murders of Arthur Labinjo-Hughes and Star Hobson: Terms of Reference. [online] Available at: www.gov.uk/government/publications/child-safeguarding-practice-review-panel-national-review-following-the-murder-of-arthur-labinjo-hughes (accessed 12 June 2022).

Gov.UK (2022b) Online Safety Law to Be Strengthened to Stamp Out Illegal Content. [online] Available at: www.gov.uk/government/news/online-safety-law-to-be-strengthened-to-stamp-out-illegal-content (accessed 12 June 2022).

Gov.UK (2022c) National Cyber Security Strategy 2022. [online] Available at: www.gov.uk/government/publications/national-cyber-strategy-2022/national-cyber-security-strategy-2022 (accessed 12 June 2022).

Green, D (2013) Home Department – Police Funding, UK Parliament Written Question; 18 December 2013; Column 112WS. [online] Available at: www.bcu.ac.uk/library/services-and-support/referencing/harvard/other-sources (accessed 12 June 2022).

Green, T and Gates, A (2014) Understanding the Process of Professionalisation in the Police Organisation. *Police Journal: Theory, Practice and Principles*, 78: 75–91.

Greenwood, E (1957) Attributes of a Profession. *Social Work*, 2(3): 45–55.

The Guardian (2007) Boy Drowned as Police Support Officers 'stood by'. *The Guardian*, 21 September. [online] Available at: www.theguardian.com/uk/2007/sep/21/1 (accessed 12 June 2022).

Hamilton, F (2022) Specialist Rape Courts Demanded by Watchdogs to Protect Victims. *The Times*, 25 February. [online] Available at: www.thetimes.co.uk/article/specialist-rape-courts-demanded-by-watchdogs-to-protect-victims-6x5zhnvhp#:~:text=Specialist%20courts%20should%20be%20introduced,by%20the%20criminal%20justice%20system (accessed 12 June 2022).

Hansard (1984) Police Stations (Lay Visitors). Volume 65, debated on Tuesday 31 July 1984. [online] Available at: https://hansard.parliament.uk/Commons/1984-07-31/debates/90a94ded-eb96-44e6-bf18-1e9f0dc0d847/PoliceStations (accessed 12 June 2022).

Hardwick, N (2006) The Independent Police Complaints Commission. [online] Available at: www.crimeandjustice.org.uk/sites/crimeandjustice.org.uk/files/09627250608553115.pdf (accessed 22 June 2022).

Harfield, C (2021) *The Ethics of Policing: New Perspectives on Law Enforcement*. New York: New York University Press.

Harris, C J (2009) Police Use of Improper Force: A Systematic Review of the Evidence. *Victims and Offenders*, 4(1): 25–41.

Hayes, J (2015) UK Parliament, Hansard Volume 601: Chief Constable Dismissal Procedures. [online] Available at: https://hansard.parliament.uk/Commons/2015-10-29/debates/151 02963000001/ChiefConstableDismissalProcedures (accessed 12 June 2022).

Heidensohn, F (2008) Gender and Policing. In Newburn, T (ed) *Handbook of Policing*. 2nd ed (pp 642–65). London: Willan Publishing.

Her Majesty's Inspectorate of Constabulary (HMIC) (2006) *The History of Her Majesty's Inspectorate of Constabulary*. [online] Available at: www.justiceinspectorates.gov.uk/hmicfrs/media/the-history-of-hmic-the-first-150-years.pdf (accessed 12 June 2022).

Her Majesty's Inspectorate of Constabulary (HMIC) (2014) *Real Lives, Real Crimes*. [online] Available at: www.justiceinspectorates.gov.uk/hmicfrs/wp-content/uploads/real-lives-real-crimes-a-study-of-digital-crime-and-policing.pdf (accessed 12 June 2022).

Her Majesty's Inspectorate of Constabulary (HMIC) (2016) *PEEL: Police Legitimacy 2016*. [online] Available at: www.justiceinspectorates.gov.uk/hmicfrs/wp-content/uploads/peel-police-legitimacy-2016.pdf (accessed 12 June 2022).

Her Majesty's Inspectorate of Constabulary and Fire & Rescue Services (HMICFRS) 2016. 2014 PEEL assessment. [online] Available at: www.justiceinspectorates.gov.uk/hmicfrs/peel-assessments/how-we-inspect/2014-peel-assessment (accessed 12 June 2022).

Her Majesty's Inspectorate of Constabulary and Fire & Rescue Services (HMICFRS) (2017) *PEEL: Police Effectiveness 2017. A National Overview*. [online] Available at: www.justiceinspectorates.gov.uk/hmicfrs/wp-content/uploads/peel-police-effectiveness-2017-2.pdf (accessed 12 June 2022).

Her Majesty's Inspectorate of Constabulary and Fire & Rescue Services (HMICFRS) (2018) What We Do. [online] Available at: www.justiceinspectorates.gov.uk/hmicfrs/about-us/what-we-do (accessed 12 June 2022).

Her Majesty's Inspectorate of Constabulary and Fire & Rescue Services (HMICFRS) (2019) *PEEL Spotlight Report: Shining a Light on Betrayal*. [online] Available at: www.justiceinspectorates.gov.uk/hmicfrs/publications/shining-a-light-on-betrayal-abuse-of-position-for-a-sexual-purpose (accessed 12 June 2022).

Her Majesty's Inspectorate of Constabulary and Fire & Rescue Services (HMICFRS) (2020a) *State of Policing: The Annual Assessment of Policing in England and Wales 2019*. [online] Available at: www.justiceinspectorates.gov.uk/hmicfrs/wp-content/uploads/state-of-policing-2019.pdf (accessed 12 June 2022).

Her Majesty's Inspectorate of Constabulary and Fire & Rescue Services (HMICFRS) (2020b) Regional Organised Crime Units. [online] Available at: www.justiceinspectorates.gov.uk/hmicfrs/our-work/article/regional-organised-crime-units-2/ (accessed 12 June 2022).

Her Majesty's Inspectorate of Constabulary and Fire & Rescue Services (HMICFRS) (2021a) *Disproportionate Use of Police Powers: A Spotlight on Stop and Search and the Use of Force.* [online] Available at: www.justiceinspectorates.gov.uk/hmicfrs/wp-content/uploads/disproportionate-use-of-police-powers-spotlight-on-stop-search-and-use-of-force.pdf (accessed 12 June 2022).

Her Majesty's Inspectorate of Constabulary and Fire & Rescue Services (HMICFRS) (2021b) The Sarah Everard Vigil. [online] Available at: www.justiceinspectorates.gov.uk/hmicfrs/publication-html/inspection-metropolitan-police-services-policing-of-vigil-commemorating-sarah-everard-clapham-common (accessed 12 June 2022).

Her Majesty's Inspectorate of Constabulary and Fire & Rescue Services (HMICFRS) (2021c) *Policing the Pandemic: The Police Response to the Coronavirus Pandemic During 2020.* [online] Available at: www.justiceinspectorates.gov.uk/hmicfrs/wp-content/uploads/policing-in-the-pandemic-police-response-to-coronavirus-pandemic-during-2020.pdf (accessed 12 June 2022).

Her Majesty's Inspectorate of Constabulary and Fire & Rescue Services (HMICFRS) (2021d) *An Inspection of the Effectiveness of the Regional Organised Crime Units.* [online] Available at: www.justiceinspectorates.gov.uk/hmicfrs/publication-html/regional-organised-crime-units-effectiveness (accessed 12 June 2022).

Her Majesty's Inspectorate of Constabulary and Fire & Rescue Services (HMICFRS) (2021e) A *Joint Thematic Inspection of the Police and Crown Prosecution Service's Response to Rape – Phase One: From Report to Police or CPS Decision to Take No Further Action.* [online] Available at: www.justiceinspectorates.gov.uk/hmicfrs/publication-html/a-joint-thematic-inspection-of-the-police-and-crown-prosecution-services-response-to-rape-phase-one (accessed 12 June 2022).

Her Majesty's Inspectorate of Constabulary and Fire & Rescue Services (HMICFRS) (2022) *A Joint Thematic Inspection of the Police and Crown Prosecution Service's Response to Rape – Phase Two: Post-Charge.* [online] Available at: www.justiceinspectorates.gov.uk/hmicfrs/publications/a-joint-thematic-inspection-of-the-police-and-crown-prosecution-services-response-to-rape-phase-two-post-charge (accessed 12 June 2022).

Hess, K and Hess Orthmann, C (2012) *Criminal Investigation.* 10th ed. Clifton Park, NY: Cengage Learning.

Hibberd, M (2021) Police Targets: Knowing the Difference between Apparent Performance and Actual Performance. [online] Available at: www.police-foundation.org.uk/2021/08/police-targets-knowing-the-difference-between-apparent-performance-and-actual-performance (accessed 12 June 2022).

Higgins, A (2019) Understanding the Public's Priorities for Policing. [online] Available at: www.police-foundation.org.uk/2017/wp-content/uploads/2010/10/understanding-public-priorities-final.pdf [accessed 12 June 2022).

Highet, G (2021) Juvenal: Roman Poet. [online] Available at: www.britannica.com/biography/Juvenal (accessed 12 June 2022).

HM Coroner (2021) *Inquests Arising from the Deaths in the Fishmongers' Hall Terror Attack.* [online] Available at: https://fishmongershallinquests.independent.gov.uk/wp-content/uploads/2021/11/Fishmongers_-Hall-Inquests-PFD-Report-Final.pdf (accessed 12 June 2022).

HM Government (2011) *The National Crime Agency: A Plan for the Creation of a National Crime-Fighting Capability.* [online] Available at: https://assets.publishing.service.gov.uk/government/uploads/system/uploads/attachment_data/file/97826/nca-creation-plan.pdf (accessed 12 June 2022).

HM Government (2013) About Us: Border Force. [online] Available at: www.gov.uk/government/organisations/border-force/about (accessed 12 June 2022).

HM Government (2014a) About Us: ICIBI. [online] Available at: www.gov.uk/government/organisations/independent-chief-inspector-of-borders-and-immigration/about (accessed 12 June 2022).

HM Government (2014b) About Us: Immigration Enforcement. [online] Available at: www.gov.uk/government/organisations/immigration-enforcement/about (accessed 12 June 2022).

HM Government (2015) *National Security Strategy and Strategic Defence and Security Review 2015.* [online] Available at: https://assets.publishing.service.gov.uk/government/uploads/system/uploads/attachment_data/file/478933/52309_Cm_9161_NSS_SD_Review_web_only.pdf (accessed 12 June 2022).

HM Government (2018a) *Serious and Organised Crime Strategy.* [online] Available at: https://assets.publishing.service.gov.uk/government/uploads/system/uploads/attachment_data/file/752850/SOC-2018-web.pdf (accessed 12 June 2022).

HM Government (2018b) *CONTEST: The United Kingdom's Strategy for Countering Terrorism*. [online] Available at: https://assets.publishing.service.gov.uk/government/uploads/system/uploads/attachment_data/file/716907/140618_CCS207_CCS0218929798-1_CONTEST_3.0_WEB.pdf (accessed 12 June 2022).

HM Government (2018c) *Working Together to Safeguard Children*. [online] Available at: https://assets.publishing.service.gov.uk/government/uploads/system/uploads/attachment_data/file/942454/Working_together_to_safeguard_children_inter_agency_guidance.pdf (accessed 12 June 2022).

HM Government (2019) *PCC Victim Services Grant Allocation 2019/20*. [online] Available at: https://assets.publishing.service.gov.uk/government/uploads/system/uploads/attachment_data/file/806809/pcc-victim-services-grant-allocation-2019-20.pdf (accessed 12 June 2022).

HM Revenue & Customs (HMRC) (2021a) *Annual Report and Accounts 2020 to 2021*. [online] Available at: https://assets.publishing.service.gov.uk/government/uploads/system/uploads/attachment_data/file/1035550/HMRC_Annual_Report_and_Accounts_2020_to_2021__Print_.pdf (accessed 12 June 2022).

HM Revenue & Customs (HMRC) (2021b) *HMRC Outcome Delivery Plan: 2021 to 2022*. Available at: www.gov.uk/government/publications/hm-revenue-and-customs-hmrc-outcome-delivery-plan/hm-revenue-and-customs-outcome-delivery-plan-2021-to-2022–2 (accessed 12 June 2022).

HMIC (2011) The Rules of Engagement: A Review of the August 2011 Disorders. [online] Available at: www.justiceinspectorates.gov.uk/hmicfrs/media/a-review-of-the-august-2011-disorders-20111220.pdf (accessed 22 June 2022).

Hodgson, J (2005) *French Criminal Justice: A Comparative Account of the Investigation and Prosecution of Crime in France*. Oxford: Hart Publishing.

Holdaway, S (2017) The Re-professionalization of the Police in England and Wales. *Criminology and Criminal Justice*, 17(5): 588–604.

Home Office (2004) *Building Communities, Beating Crime: A Better Police Service for the 21st Century*. [online] Available at: https://assets.publishing.service.gov.uk/government/uploads/system/uploads/attachment_data/file/251058/6360.pdf (accessed 12 June 2022).

Home Office (2015) *The Strategic Policing Requirement.* [online] Available at: https://assets.publishing.service.gov.uk/government/uploads/system/uploads/attachment_data/file/417116/The_Strategic_Policing_Requirement.pdf (accessed 12 June 2022).

Home Office (2017) *Annual Report and Accounts 2017–18.* [online] Available at: https://assets.publishing.service.gov.uk/government/uploads/system/uploads/attachment_data/file/727179/6_4360_HO_Annual_report_WEB.PDF (accessed 12 June 2022).

Home Office (2018a) *Revised Financial Management Code of Practice.* Norwich: HMSO.

Home Office (2018b) *Management of Risk in Law Enforcement (MoRiLE) Based Scoring: Standards.* [online] Available at: https://assets.publishing.service.gov.uk/government/uploads/system/uploads/attachment_data/file/679814/Tactical-MoRiLE-Scoring-Standards-v1.0EXT.pdf (accessed 12 June 2022).

Home Office (2020a) *Conduct, Efficiency and Effectiveness: Statutory Guidance on Professional Standards, Performance and Integrity in Policing.* [online] Available at: https://assets.publishing.service.gov.uk/government/uploads/system/uploads/attachment_data/file/863820/Home_Office_Statutory_Guidance_0502.pdf (accessed 22 June 2022).

Home Office (2020b) Police to Receive More Than £15 Billion to Fight Crime and Recruit More Officers. [online] Available at: www.gov.uk/government/news/police-to-receive-more-than-15-billion-to-fight-crime-and-recruit-more-officers (accessed 12 June 2022).

Home Office (2020c) Priti Patel to Give Public Greater Say Over Policing Through PCC Review. [online] Available at: www.gov.uk/government/news/priti-patel-to-give-public-greater-say-over-policing-through-pcc-review (accessed 12 June 2022).

Home Office (2021a) National Statistics. Police Workforce, England and Wales: 31 March 2021. [online] Available at: www.gov.uk/government/statistics/police-workforce-england-and-wales-31-march-2021/police-workforce-england-and-wales-31-march-2021 (accessed 12 June 2022).

Home Office (2021b) *Policy Paper: Beating Crime Plan.* [online] Available at: www.gov.uk/government/publications/beating-crime-plan (accessed 12 June 2022).

Home Office (2021c) Police Use of Force Statistics, England and Wales: April 2019 to March 2020. [online] Available at: www.gov.uk/government/statistics/police-use-of-force-statistics-england-and-wales-april-2019-to-march-2020/police-use-of-force-statistics-england-and-wales-april-2019-to-march-2020 (accessed 12 June 2022).

Hough, M and Roberts, J V (2004) *Confidence in Justice: An International Review.* London: Home Office.

House of Commons (1977*) Report of an Inquiry by the Hon. Sir Henry Fisher into the Circumstances Leading to the Trial of Three Persons on Charges Arising Out of the Death of Maxwell Confait and the Fire at 27 Doggett Road, London SE6.* [online] Available at: https://assets.publishing.service.gov.uk/government/uploads/system/uploads/attachment_data/file/228759/0090.pdf (accessed 12 June 2022).

House of Commons (2014) *Public Administration Select Committee Thirteenth Report of Session 2013–14: Caught Red-Handed: Why We Can't Count on Police Recorded Crime Statistics.* [online] Available at: https://publications.parliament.uk/pa/cm201314/cmselect/cmpubadm/760/760.pdf (accessed 12 June 2022).

House of Commons (2020) *Public Accounts Committee Seventeenth Report of Session 2019–21: Immigration Enforcement.* [online] Available at: https://committees.parliament.uk/publications/2633/documents/26242/default (accessed 12 June 2022).

House of Commons (2021) *Intelligence and Security Committee of Parliament: Annual Report 2019–2021.* [online] Available at: https://isc.independent.gov.uk/wp-content/uploads/2021/12/ISC-Annual-Report-2019%E2%80%932021.pdf (accessed 12 June 2022).

Hughes, J (2012) Theory of Professional Standards and Ethical Policing. In MacVean, A (ed) *Handbook of Policing, Ethics, and Professional Standards* (pp 7–16). London: Routledge.

Human Rights Act 1998 [online] Available at: www.legislation.gov.uk/ukpga/1998/42/contents (accessed 12 June 2022).

Independent Chief Inspector of Borders and Immigration (ICIBI) (2019) *An Inspection of the Home Office's Response to In-country Clandestine Arrivals ('Lorry Drops') and to Irregular Migrants Arriving via 'Small Boats'.* [online] Available at: https://assets.publishing.service.gov.uk/government/uploads/system/uploads/attachment_data/file/933953/An_inspection_of_the_Home_Office_s_response_to_in-country_clandestine_arrivals___lorry_drops___and_to_irregular_migrants_arriving_via__small_boats_.pdf (accessed 12 June 2022).

Independent Chief Inspector of Borders and Immigration (ICIBI) (2021) *Independent Chief Inspector of Borders and Immigration: Annual Report for the Period 1 April 2020 to 31 March 2021.* [online] Available at: https://assets.publishing.service.gov.uk/government/uploads/system/uploads/attachment_data/file/1017864/ICIBI_Annual_Report_for_the_period_1_April_2020_to_31_March_2021_Large_Print.pdf (accessed 12 June 2022).

Independent Office for Police Conduct (IOPC) (2018) Becoming the IOPC. [online] Available at: https://policeconduct.gov.uk/becoming-iopc (accessed 12 June 2022).

Independent Office for Police Conduct (IOPC) (2020) *Statutory Guidance on the Police Complaints System*. London: IOPC.

Independent Office for Police Conduct (IOPC) (2021) Former Gwent Police Officer Sentenced for Misconduct in Public Office. [online] Available at: www.policeconduct.gov.uk/news/former-gwent-police-officer-sentenced-misconduct-public-office-cyn-swyddog-heddlu-gwent-wedi-ei (accessed 12 June 2022).

Independent Police Complaints Commission (IPCC) (2012) The Abuse of Powers to Perpetrate Sexual Violence. [online] Available at: www.policeconduct.gov.uk/sites/default/files/Documents/research-learning/abuse_of_police_powers_to_perpetrate_sexual_violence.pdf (accessed 12 June 2022).

Independent Police Complaints Commission (IPCC) (2016a) Police Use of Force: Evidence from Complaints, Investigations and Public Perception. [online] Available at: www.policeconduct.gov.uk/sites/default/files/Documents/research-learning/IPCC_Use_Of_Force_Report.pdf (accessed 12 June 2022).

Independent Police Complaints Commission (IPCC) (2016b) *Focus: Practical Guidance on Handling Complaints, Conduct Matters, and Death or serious Injury Matters within the Police Reform Act 2002*. London: IPCC.

Innes, M, Roberts, C and Innes, H (2011) *Assessing the Effects of Prevent Policing*. [online] Available at: www.npcc.police.uk/documents/TAM/2011/PREVENT%20Innes%200311%20Final%20send%202.pdf (accessed 11 July 2022).

Intelligence and Security Committee of Parliament (2018) *The 2017 Attacks: What Needs to Change?* [online] Available at: https://assets.publishing.service.gov.uk/government/uploads/system/uploads/attachment_data/file/776162/HC1694_The2017Attacks_WhatNeedsToChange.pdf (accessed 12 June 2022).

Investigatory Powers Tribunal (IPT) (2016) Who We Are: General Overview and Background. [online] Available at: www.ipt-uk.com/content.asp?id=10 (accessed 12 June 2022).

Investigatory Powers Tribunal (IPT) (2019) *Judgments: AB v Hampshire Constabulary*. [online] Available at: www.ipt-uk.com/judgments.asp?id=50 (accessed 12 June 2022).

Jones, T (2008) The Accountability of Policing. In Newburn T (ed) *Handbook of Policing*. 2nd ed (pp 693–724). Cullompton: Willan Publishing.

Joyce, P (2011) *Policing: Development and Contemporary Practice*. London: Sage.

Joyce, P (2017) *Criminal Justice: An Introduction*. 3rd ed. London: Routledge.

Kendall, J (2020) Custody Visiting: The Watchdog That Didn't Bark. *Journal of Criminology & Criminal Justice*, 22(1): 115–31.

Klockars, C B, Haberfeld, M and Kutjnak Ivkovich, S (2004) *The Contours of Police Integrity*. Thousand Oaks, CA: Sage.

KPMG (2000) *Feasibility of an Independent System for Investigating Complaints Against the Police*. Police Research Series Paper 124. London: Home Office.

Laming, L (2003) *The Victoria Climbié Inquiry*. [online] Available at: https://assets.publishing. service.gov.uk/government/uploads/system/uploads/attachment_data/file/273183/ 5730.pdf (accessed 12 June 2022).

Leibling, D (2020 [2008]) *Car Ownership in Great Britain*. RAC Foundation. [online] Available at: www.racfoundation.org/wp-content/uploads/2017/11/car-ownership-in-great-britain-leibling-171008-report.pdf (accessed 12 June 2022).

Leppard, A (2011) *Independent Advisory Groups: Advice and Guidance on the Role, Function and Governance of IAGs*. [online] Available at: https://library.college.police.uk/docs/ appref/independent-advisory-groups-iag-guidance-revised-september-2011.pdf (accessed 19 June 2022).

Lewis, C (1999) *Complaints Against the Police: The Politics of Reform*. New South Wales: Hawkins Press.

Liberty (2020) Pandemic of Police Powers: Liberty Reveals Scale of Misuse of Police Powers Under Lockdown. [online] Available at: www.libertyhumanrights.org.uk/issue/pandemic-of-police-powers-liberty-reveals-scale-of-misuse-of-police-powers-under-lockdown (accessed 12 June 2022).

Local Government Act 1999 [online] Available at: www.legislation.gov.uk/ukpga/1999/27/ section/3 (accessed 12 June 2022).

Local Government Association (LGA) (2018) *LGA Review of the Future of Community Safety Services*. [online] Available at: www.local.gov.uk/sites/default/files/documents/10.22%20- %20LGA%20review%20of%20the%20future%20of%20community%20safety%20services. pdf (accessed 12 June 2022).

Local Government Association (LGA) (2020) Review into the Role of Police and Crime Commissioners (Part 1): LGA Response 2020. [online] Available at: www.local.gov.uk/review-role-police-and-crime-commissioners-part-one-lga-response-september-2020 (accessed 12 June 2022).

Lodge, A (2020) Criminology and Criminal Justice. In Pepper, I K and McGrath, R (eds) *Introduction to Professional Policing: Examining the Evidence Base* (pp 7–26). Abingdon: Routledge.

Longmore, W (2013) *The Police and Crime Plan for West Mercia 1st April 2013 to 31st March 2017 (Varied February 2014)*. [online] Available at: www.westmercia-pcc.gov.uk/app/uploads/2016/09/PCPlanvariedFeb2014-FINAL.pdf?x13793&x40206 (accessed 12 June 2022).

Loveday, B (2013) Police and Crime Commissioners: The Changing Landscape of Police Governance in England and Wales: Their Potential Impact on Local Accountability, Police Service Delivery and Community Safety. *International Journal of Police Science and Management*, 15(1): 22–9.

Macpherson W (1999) *The Stephen Lawrence Inquiry: Report of an Inquiry by Sir William Macpherson of Cluny*. [online] Available at: https://assets.publishing.service.gov.uk/government/uploads/system/uploads/attachment_data/file/277111/4262.pdf (accessed 12 June 2022).

MacVean, A (2012) *Handbook of Policing, Ethics and Professional Standards*. London: Routledge.

Maguire, M and McVie, S (2017) Crime Data and Criminal Statistics: A Critical Reflection. In Liebling, A, Shadd, M and McAra, L (eds) *Oxford Handbook of Criminology*. 6th ed (pp 163–89). Oxford: Oxford University Press.

Makortoff, K and Jolly, J (2022) How the UK Government Lost £4.9bn to Covid Loan Fraud. *The Guardian*, 29 January. [online] Available at: www.theguardian.com/politics/2022/jan/29/how-the-uk-government-lost-49bn-to-covid-loan (accessed 12 June 2022).

Malthouse, K (2020) Policing's First Ever National Policing Digital Strategy Launched. [online] Available at: www.transformation.police.uk/news/policings-first-ever-national-policing-digital-strategy-launched (accessed 12 June 2022).

Mawby, R and Wright, A (2003) The Police Organisation. In Newburn, T (ed) *Handbook of Policing*. Cullompton: Willan Publishing, pp 224–52.

Mawby, R and Wright, A (2005) *Police Accountability in the UK*. Commonwealth Human Rights Initiative. [online] Available at: www.humanrightsinitiative.org/programs/aj/police/res_mat/police_accountability_in_uk.pdf (accessed 12 June 2022).

Mayhall, P D (1985) *Police–Community Relations and the Administration of Justice*. 3rd ed. New York: John Wiley & Sons.

Mayor of London (2020) Ministry of Justice Funding for Services to Victims of Crime. [online] Available at: www.london.gov.uk/what-we-do/mayors-office-policing-and-crime-mopac/governance-and-decision-making/mopac-decisions-0/ministry-justice-funding-services-victims-crime (accessed 12 June 2022).

McCartney, S and Parent, R (2015) *Ethics in Law Enforcement*. Victoria, BC: BCcampus. [online] Available at: https://opentextbc.ca/ethicsinlawenforcement (accessed 12 June 2022).

McConville, M and Marsh, L (2020) England Criminal Justice System Was On Its Knees a Long Time Before Covid. *The Guardian*, 6 September. [online] Available at: www.theguardian.com/commentisfree/2020/sep/06/england-criminal-justice-system-coronavirus-covid-19-cuts-2010 (accessed 12 June 2022).

McDowall, A, Quinton, P, Brown, D, Carr, I, Glorney, E, Russel, S, Bharj, N, Nash, R and Coyle, A (2015) *Promoting Ethical Behaviour and Preventing Wrongdoing in Organisations: A Rapid Evidence Assessment*. [online] Available at: https://research.aston.ac.uk/en/publications/promoting-ethical-behaviour-and-preventing-wrongdoing-in-organisa (accessed 12 June 2022).

McLaughlin, E (2007) *The New Policing*. London: Sage.

McLaughlin, E and Muncie, J (eds) *Controlling Crime*. 1st ed. London: Sage.

McLaughlin, E, Muncie, J and Hughes, G (eds) (2003) *Criminological Perspectives*. 2nd ed. London: Sage.

McWhinney, J (2021) Why Governments Are Afraid of Bitcoin. *Investopedia*. [online] Available at: www.investopedia.com/articles/forex/042015/why-governments-are-afraid-bitcoin.asp (accessed 12 June 2022).

Mental Health Act 1983 [online] Available at: www.legislation.gov.uk/ukpga/1983/20/contents (accessed 12 June 2022).

Metropolitan Police (2005) *Policing and Performance Plan 2005/06*. London: Metropolitan Police Authority.

Metropolitan Police (2018) Freedom of Information Request: Storage and Cost of Body Worn Camera Licences. [online] Available at: www.whatdotheyknow.com/request/body_worn_cameras_details (accessed 19 June 2022).

Metropolitan Police Act 1829 [online] Available at: www.legislation.gov.uk/ukpga/Geo4/10/44/contents (accessed 19 June 2022).

MI5 (2022) Home page. [online] Available at: www.mi5.gov.uk (accessed 12 June 2022).

Ministry of Defence Police (2020) *Ministry of Defence Police: Corporate Plan 2020–2025.* [online] Available at: https://assets.publishing.service.gov.uk/government/uploads/system/uploads/attachment_data/file/943476/MDP_Corporate_Plan_2020_-_2025_-_FINAL_WEB_COPY.pdf (accessed 12 June 2022).

Ministry of Defence Police Act 1987 [online] Available at: www.legislation.gov.uk/ukpga/1987/4/contents (accessed 12 June 2022).

Ministry of Justice (2021) Code of Practice for Victims of Crime in England and Wales (Victim's Code). [online] Available at: www.gov.uk/government/publications/the-code-of-practice-for-victims-of-crime/code-of-practice-for-victims-of-crime-in-england-and-wales-victims-code (accessed 12 June 2022).

Morrell, K, Bradford, B and Javid, B (2019) What Does It Mean When We Ask the Public if They Are 'Confident' in Policing? The Trust, Fairness, Presence Model of 'Public Confidence'. *International Journal of Police Science & Management*, 22(2): 111–22.

Muncie, J and McLaughlin, E (eds) (2001) *The Problem of Crime.* London: Sage.

Muncie, J, Talbot, D and Walters, R (2010) *Crime: Local and Global.* Cullompton: Willan Publishing.

National Audit Office (2019) *Immigration Enforcement.* [online] Available at: www.nao.org.uk/wp-content/uploads/2020/06/Immigration-enforcement-Summary.pdf (accessed 12 June 2022).

National Audit Office (2021) *Reducing the Backlog in Criminal Courts.* [online] Available at: www.nao.org.uk/report/reducing-the-backlog-in-criminal-courts (accessed 12 June 2022).

National Crime Agency (NCA) (2016) *County Lines Gang Violence, Exploitation & Drug Supply 2016.* 0346-CAD National Briefing Report. [online] Available at: www.nationalcrimeagency.gov.uk/who-we-are/publications/15-county-lines-gang-violence-exploitation-and-drug-supply-2016/file (accessed 12 June 2022).

National Crime Agency (NCA) (2017) *County Lines Violence, Exploitation and Drug Supply*. [online] Available at: www.nationalcrimeagency.gov.uk/who-we-are/publications/234-county-lines-violen-ce-exploitation-drug-supply-2017/file (accessed 12 June 2022).

National Crime Agency (NCA) (2021a) *National Strategic Assessment of Serious and Organised Crime*. [online] Available at: https://nationalcrimeagency.gov.uk/who-we-are/publications/533-national-strategic-assessment-of-serious-and-organised-crime-2021/file (accessed 12 June 2022).

National Crime Agency (NCA) (2021b) Annual Plan 2021–2022. [online] Available at: www.nationalcrimeagency.gov.uk/who-we-are/publications/558-national-crime-agency-annual-plan-2021-2 (accessed 12 June 2022).

National Crime Agency (NCA) (2022) Who We Are. [online] Available at: www.nationalcrimeagency.gov.uk/who-we-are (accessed 12 June 2022).

National Cyber Security Centre (NCSC) (2021) Alert: Targeted Ransomware Attacks on the UK Education Sector by Cyber Criminals. [online] Available at: www.ncsc.gov.uk/news/alert-targeted-ransomware-attacks-on-uk-education-sector (accessed 12 June 2022).

National Police Chiefs' Council (NPCC) (2017) National Strategy to Address the Issue of Police Officers and Staff Who Abuse Their Position for a Sexual Purpose. [online] Available at: www.npcc.police.uk/documents/Abuse%20of%20position%20for%20sexual%20purpose%20National%20Strategy.pdf (accessed 12 June 2022).

National Police Chiefs' Council (NPCC) (2020) National Policing Digital Strategy. [online] Available at: https://pds.police.uk/wp-content/uploads/2020/01/National-Policing-Digital-Strategy-2020-2030.pdf (accessed 12 June 2022).

Newburn, T (ed) (2005) *Policing: Key Readings*. Cullompton: Willan Publishing.

Neyroud, P (2011) *Review of Police Leadership and Training*. [online] Available at: www.gov.uk/government/publications/police-leadership-and-training-report-review (accessed 12 June 2022).

Neyroud, P (2012) *Review of Police Leadership and Training: Volume 1*. [online] Available at: https://assets.publishing.service.gov.uk/government/uploads/system/uploads/attachment_data/file/118227/report.pdf (accessed 12 Jume 2022).

Noga, H, Foreman, A, Walsh, E, Shaw, J and Senior, J (2016) Multi-Agency Action Learning: Challenging Institutional Barriers in Policing and Mental Health Services. *Action Research*, 14(2): 132–50.

Nolan, M (1995) *Standards in Public Life: First Report of the Committee on Standards in Public Life. Volume 1: Report.* London, HMSO. [online] Available at: https://assets.publishing. service.gov.uk/government/uploads/system/uploads/attachment_data/file/336919/ 1stInquiryReport.pdf (accessed 12 June 2022).

North Yorkshire Police, Fire and Crime Panel (2021) *Complaints Raised with the Panel (October 2021).* [online] Available at: https://edemocracy.northyorks.gov.uk/documents/ s8179/Item%206_Complaints%20raised%20with%20the%20Panel%20October%202 021%20report%20and%20appendices.pdf (accessed 12 June 2022).

Nuefville, M (2021) Tri-county Specialist Operations Command Introduces Independent Community Scrutiny on Use of Force. *Policing Insight,* 19 October. [online] Available at:https://policinginsight.com/features/tri-county-specialist-operations-command-introduces-independent-community-scrutiny-on-use-of-force (accessed 12 June 2022).

Offences Against the Person Act 1861 [online] Available at: www.legislation.gov.uk/ukpga/ Vict/24-25/100/section/39 (accessed 22 June 2022).

Office for National Statistics (ONS) (2021) Public Sector Employment. [online] Available at: www.ons.gov.uk/employmentandlabourmarket/peopleinwork/publicsectorpersonnel/ datasets/publicsectoremploymentreferencetable (accessed 12 June 2022).

Owers, A (2012) Independent Oversight of Police Complaints: The IPCC Eight Years On. John Harris Memorial Lecture, 3 July 2012. [online] Available at: www.police-foundation.org.uk/ 2017/wp-content/uploads/2010/10/jhml2012.pdf (accessed 12 June 2022).

Oxford Learner's Dictionary (2020) Definition of 'Governance'. [online] Available at: www. oxfordlearnersdictionaries.com/definition/english/governance?q=governance (accessed 12 June 2022).

Parliament.UK (2021) The Enforcement of Covid-19 Offences. [online] Available at: https:// publications.parliament.uk/pa/cm5802/cmselect/cmjust/71/7106.htm (accessed 12 June 2022).

Paterson, C (2011) Adding Value? A Review of the International Literature on the Role of Higher Education in Police Training and Education. *Police Practice and Research,* 12(4): 286–97.

Pearce, S (2014) *Code of Ethics: A Code of Practice for the Principles and Standards of Professional Behaviour for the Policing Profession of England and Wales.* Coventry: College of Policing Limited.

Pepper, I and McGrath, R (2019) Embedding Employability Within Higher Education for the Profession of Policing. *Higher Education, Skills and Work-based Learning*, 9(3): 319–28.

Pepper, I, Brown, I and Stubbs, P (2021) A Degree of Recognition Across Policing: Embedding a Degree Apprenticeship Encompassing Work-Based Research. *Journal of Work Applied Management*, 14(1).

Police Act 1964 [online] Available at: www.legislation.gov.uk/ukpga/1964/48/contents (accessed 12 June 2022).

Police Act 1996 [online] Available at: www.legislation.gov.uk/ukpga/1996/16/section/ 6AZA (accessed 12 June 2022).

The Police and Crime Panels (Precept and Chief Constables Appointments) Regulations (PCP regs) 2012. [online] Available at: www.legislation.gov.uk/uksi/2012/2271/regulat ion/5/made (accessed 12 June 2022).

Police and Criminal Evidence Act 1984 [online] Available at: www.legislation.gov.uk/ukpga/ 1984/60/contents (accessed 24 January 2021).

Police and Justice Act 2006 [online] Available at: www.legislation.gov.uk/ukpga/2006/48/ contents (accessed 12 June 2022).

Police and Magistrates' Courts Act 1994 [online] Available at: www.legislation.gov.uk/ ukpga/1994/29/contents (accessed 12 June 2022).

The Police Authority Regulations 2008 [Online] Available at: www.legislation.gov.uk/uksi/ 2008/630/contents/made (accessed 12 June 2022).

The Police (Complaints and Misconduct) Regulations 2020 [online] Available at: www. legislation.gov.uk/uksi/2020/2/made (accessed 12 June 2022).

The Police (Conduct) Regulations 2020 [online] Available at: www.legislation.gov.uk/uksi/ 2020/4/made (accessed 12 June 2022).

Police Federation (2018) *The Office of Constable: The Bedrock of Modern-Day British Policing*. [online] Available at: www.polfed.org/media/14239/the-office-of-constable-with-links-2018.pdf (accessed 12 June 2022).

The Police Foundation (2017) *Neighbourhood Policing: A Police Force Typology*. [online] Available at: www.police-foundation.org.uk/2017/wp-content/uploads/2017/06/neighbourhood_polici ng_a_police__force_typology.pdf (accessed 12 June 2022).

The Police (Performance) Regulations 2020 [online] Available at: www.legislation.gov.uk/uksi/2020/3/made (accessed 12 June 2022).

Police, Public Order and Criminal Justice (Scotland) Act 2006 [online] Available at: www.legislation.gov.uk/asp/2006/10/contents (accessed 12 June 2022).

Police Reform Act 2002 [online] Available at: www.legislation.gov.uk/ukpga/2002/30/section/12 (accessed 12 June 2022).

Police Reform and Social Responsibility Act 2011 [online] Available at: www.legislation.gov.uk/ukpga/2011/13/section/3/enacted (accessed 12 June 2022).

Police Success Blog (2021) What Are the Peelian Principles? [online] Available at: www.policesuccess.co.uk/blog/what-are-the-peelian-principles (accessed 12 June 2022).

Policing and Crime Act 2017 [online] Available at: www.legislation.gov.uk/ukpga/2017/3 (accessed 12 June 2022).

Prenzler, T (2009) *Police Corruption: Preventing Misconduct and Maintaining Integrity.* Boca Raton, FL: Routledge.

Privacy International (2018) Press Release: Privacy International Calls for Investigation into Whether the Police are Hacking Phones. [online] Available at: https://privacyinternational.org/press-release/2210/press-release-privacy-international-calls-investigation-whether-police-are (accessed 12 June 2022).

Proceeds of Crime Act 2002 [online] Available at: www.legislation.gov.uk/ukpga/2002/29/contents (accessed 12 June 2022).

Prosecution of Offenders Act 1985 [online] Available at: www.legislation.gov.uk/ukpga/1985/23 (accessed 12 June 2022).

Punch, M (2007) Cops with Honours: University Education and Police Culture. *Sociology of Crime, Law and Deviance,* 8: 105–28.

Punch, M (2009) *Police Corruption: Deviance, Accountability and Reform in Policing.* Cullompton: Willan Publishing.

Quality Assurance Agency for Higher Education (QAA) (2014) *UK Quality Code for Higher Education. Part A: Setting and Maintaining Academic Standards.* Gloucester: Quality Assurance Agency.

Qurashi, F (2018) The Prevent Strategy and the UK 'War on Terror': Embedding Infrastructures of Surveillance in Muslim Communities. *Palgrave Communications*, 4: 17.

R v Bater-James and Mohammed [2020] EWCA 790.

R v Gold & Schifreen [1988] 1 AC 1063 (HL).

Radzinowicz, L (1981) Towards a National Standard of Police. In Fitzgerald, M, McLennan, G and Pawson, J (eds) *Crime and Society. Readings in History and Theory* (pp 60–85). London: Routledge.

Railway Policing (Scotland) Act 2017 [online] Available at: www.legislation.gov.uk/asp/2017/4/contents/enacted (accessed 12 June 2022).

Railways and Transport Safety Act 2003 [online] Available at: www.legislation.gov.uk/ukpga/2003/20/contents (accessed 12 June 2022).

Regulation of Investigatory Powers Act 2000 [online] Available at: www.legislation.gov.uk/ukpga/2000/23/contents (accessed 12 June 2022).

Reiner, R (2010) *The Politics of the Police*. 4th ed. Oxford: Oxford University Press.

Remington, F J (1965) The Role of Police in a Democratic Society. *The Journal of Criminal Law, Criminology, and Police Science*, 56(3): 13.

Resick, C J, Hargis, M B, Shao, P and Dust, S B (2013) Ethical Leadershipm Moral Equity Judgments and Discretionary Workplace Behaviour. *Human Relations*, 66(7): 951–72.

Rogers, C (2020) *Policing Structures*. London: Routledge.

Roskill, E (1986) *Great Britain Fraud Trials Committee Report*. London. HMSO.

Rowe, M (2018) *Introduction to Policing*. 3rd ed. London: Sage.

Rudd, A (2016) Speech: Home Secretary's College of Policing Speech on Vulnerability. [online] Available at: www.gov.uk/government/speeches/home-secretarys-college-of-policing-speech-on-vulnerability (accessed 12 June 2022).

Runciman, W G (1993) *The Royal Commission on Criminal Justice: Report*. [online] Available at: https://assets.publishing.service.gov.uk/government/uploads/system/uploads/attachment_data/file/271971/2263.pdf (accessed 12 June 2022).

Sanders, A and Young, R (1994) *Criminal Justice*. London and Edinburgh: Butterworths.

Sanders, A and Young, R (2008) Police Powers. In Newburn, T (ed) *Handbook of Policing*. 2nd ed (pp 281–312). Cullompton: Willan Publishing.

Saraga, E (2001) Dangerous Places: The Family as A Site of Crime. In Muncie, J and McLaughlin, E (eds) *The Problem of Crime* (pp 191–238). London: Sage.

Scarman, L G (1981) *The Brixton Disorders, 10–12 April 1981: Report of an Inquiry by Lord Scarman*. London: HMSO.

Secret Intelligence Service (SIS) (2022) *SIS Home*. [online] Available at: www.sis.gov.uk (accessed 12 June 2022).

Segal, L (2003) Explaining Male Violence. In McLaughlin, E, Muncie, J and Hughes, G (ed) *Criminological Perspectives: Essential Readings* (pp 211–26). 2nd ed. London: Sage.

Serious Fraud Office (SFO) (2019) *Strategic Plan 2019–22*. [online] Available at: www.sfo.gov.uk/download/strategic-plan-2019-22 (accessed 12 June 2022).

Serious Fraud Office (SFO) (2021) *Annual Report and Accounts 2020–2021*. [online] Available at: www.sfo.gov.uk/download/annual-report-and-accounts-2020-2021 (accessed 12 June 2022).

Serious Organised Crime and Police Act 2005 [online] Available at: www.legislation.gov.uk/ukpga/2005/15/contents (accessed 12 June 2022).

Sexual Offences Act 2003 [online] Available at: www.legislation.gov.uk/ukpga/2003/42/contents (accessed 12 June 2022).

Sharpe, J (2001) Crime, Order and Historical Change. In Muncie, J and McLaughlin, E (eds) *The Problem of Crime* (pp 107–50). London: Sage.

Sherman, L (1978) *The Quality of Police Education*. Washington, DC: The Police Foundation.

Sherman, L (1998) *Evidence-Based Policing*. Ideas in American Policing Lecture. Washington, DC: The Police Foundation.

Sky News (2019) Essex Lorry Deaths: A Timeline of Events Leading Up to Discovery of 39 Bodies. [online] Available at: https://news.sky.com/story/essex-lorry-deaths-a-timeline-of-events-leading-up-to-discovery-of-39-bodies-11843663 (accessed 12 June 2022).

Smith, G (2005) A most Enduring Problem: Police Complaints Reform in England and Wales. *Journal of Social Policy*, 35(1): 121–41.

Solar, C and Smith, M (2022) Austerity and Governance: Coordinating policing and mental health policy in the UK. *Policy Studies*, 43(2): 352–69.

Spicer, J (2021) The Policing of Cuckooing in 'County Lines' Drug Dealing: An Ethnographic Study of an Amplification Spiral. *British Journal of Criminology*, 61(5): 1390–406.

Stewart, S (2013) Ethical Policing Practice in Community Policing. In Waddington, P A J, Kleinig, J and Wright, M (eds) *Professional Police Practice: Scenarios and Dilemmas.* (pp 98–108) Oxford: Oxford University Press.

Strom, K (2017) *Research on the Impact of Technology on Policing Strategy in the 21st Century, Final Report.* [online] Available at: www.ojp.gov/pdffiles1/nij/grants/251140.pdf (accessed 12 June 2022).

Sweeting, F, Arabaci-Hills, P and Cole, T (2021) Outcomes of Police Sexual Misconduct in the UK. *Policing: A Journal of Policy and Practice*, 15(2): 1339–51.

Taylor-Griffiths, C, Pollard, N and Stamatakis, T (2014) Assessing the Effectiveness and Efficiency of a Police Service: The Analytics of Operational Reviews. *Police Practice and Research*, 16(2): 175–87.

Terrorism Act 2000 [online] Available at: www.legislation.gov.uk/ukpga/2000/11/contents (accessed 12 June 2022).

Theft Act 1968 [online] Available at: www.legislation.gov.uk/ukpga/1968/60/contents (accessed 12 June 2022).

Tong, S and Hallenberg, K M (2018) Education and the Police Professionalisation Agenda: A Perspective from England and Wales. In Rogers, C and Frevel, B (eds) *Higher Education and Police: An International View* (pp 17–34). London: Palgrave Macmillan.

Turner, L and Rowe, M (2020) Police Discretion and the Coronavirus Pandemic. [online] Available at: https://bscpolicingnetwork.com/2020/04/21/police-discretion-and-the-coronavirus-pandemic (accessed 12 June 2022).

UK Borders Act 2007 [online] Available at: www.legislation.gov.uk/ukpga/2007/30/contents (accessed 12 June 2022).

UK Government (2018) History of Sir Robert Peel 2nd Baronet. [online] Available at: www.gov.uk/government/history/past-prime-ministers/robert-peel-2nd-baronet (accessed: 21 February 2021).

UK Government (2019) *Policing for the Future.* [online] Available at: https://assets.publish ing.service.gov.uk/government/uploads/system/uploads/attachment_data/file/786316/ CCS207_CCS0219668100-001_HASC_Inquiry_Government_ResponsePolicing_Web_ Accessible.pdf (accessed 12 June 2022).

UK Parliament (2021a) Ten-Year Drugs Strategy. [online] Available at: https://hansard. parliament.uk/Commons/2021-12-06/debates/54065168-8B45-47B1-BEEB-1BA4B 49DB4AF/Ten-YearDrugsStrategy (accessed 12 June 2022).

UK Parliament (2021b) *The Macpherson Report: Twenty-two Years On.* Home Affairs Committee. [online] Available at: https://committees.parliament.uk/work/347/the-macpherson-report-twentytwo-years-on/publications (accessed 12 June 2022).

UK Parliament (2021c) Creating the Nation's Police Force. [online] Available at: www. parliament.uk/about/living-heritage/transformingsociety/laworder/policeprisons/ overview/nationspoliceforce (accessed 12 June 2022).

UK Standing Committee for Quality Assessment & Quality Assurance Agency (UKSCQA & QAA) (2018) *The Revised UK Quality Code for Higher Education.* Gloucester: UK Standing Committee for Quality Assessment & Quality Assurance Agency.

Umphress, E E, Ren, L R, Bingham, J B and Gogus, C I (2009) The Influence of Distributive Justice on Lying and Stealing from a Supervisor. *Journal of Business Ethics*, 86(4): 507–18.

Vagrancy Act 1824 [online] Available at: www.legislation.gov.uk/ukpga/Geo4/5/83/ contents/enacted (accessed 22 June 2022).

Vollmer, A (1933) Police Progress in the Past Twenty-Five Years. *Criminal Law and Criminology*, 24(1): 161–75.

Waddington, P A J (2013) *Professional Police Practice: Scenarios and Dilemmas.* Oxford: Oxford University Press.

Waddington, P A J and Wright, M (2008) Police Powers. In Newburn, T (ed) *Handbook of Policing*. 2nd ed (pp 465–96). Cullompton: Willan Publishing.

Walker, P (2016) Inquest Ruling on Teenager Prompts Family Criticism of Care. *The Guardian*, 29 April. [online] Available at: www.theguardian.com/uk-news/2016/apr/29/jack-susianta-boy-17-drowned-fleeing-police-accidental-death-inquest-rules (accessed 12 June 2022).

Walklate, S (2013) *Victimology: The Victim and the Criminal Justice Process*. Oxford: Routledge.

Wallace, H (2006) Parliamentary Business – Supplementary Letter from Dr Helen Wallace, Director, GeneWatch, UK. [online] Available at: https://publications.parliament.uk/pa/ld200809/ldselect/ldconst/18/8013007.htm (accessed 12 June 2022).

Welsh, L, Skinns, L and Sanders, A (2021) *Sanders and Young Criminal Justice*. 5th ed. Oxford: Oxford University Press.

Westmarland, L (2005) Police Ethics and Integrity: Breaking the Blue Code of Silence. *Policing and Society: An International Journal of Research and Policy*, 15(2): 145–65.

Westmarland, L and Rowe, M (2016) Police Ethics and Integrity: Can a New Code Overturn the Blue Code? *International Journal of Research and Policy*, 28(7): 854–70.

Williams, E, Norman, J and Barrow-Grint, K (2020) Policing Vulnerability: Attrition, Rape and Domestic Abuse. In Pepper, I and McGrath, R (eds) *Introduction to Professional Policing* (pp 129–45). Abingdon: Routledge.

Williams, E, Norman, J and Rowe, M (2019) The Police Education Qualification Framework: A Professional Agenda or Building Professionals? *Police Practice and Research*, 20(3): 259–72.

Williams Jr, M C, Weil, N, Rasich, E A, Ludwig, J, Chang, H and Egrari, S (2021) *Body-Worn Cameras in Policing: Benefits and Costs*. NBER Working Paper No. 28622. [online] Available at: www.nber.org/system/files/working_papers/w28622/w28622.pdf (accessed 12 June 2022).

Williams, P (2015) Peace Preservation Force. *Journal of the Police History Society*, 29: 6–10.

Winsor, T (2014) 2014 PEEL Assessment. [online] Available at: www.justiceinspectorates.gov.uk/hmicfrs/peel-assessments/how-we-inspect/2014-peel-assessment/#force-assessments (accessed 12 June 2022).

Wood, D (2020a) *Towards Ethical Policing*. Bristol: Policy Press.

Wood, D (2020b) Maintaining Professional Standards and Reflective Practice. In Pepper, I and McGrath, R (eds) *An Introduction to Professional Policing: Examining the Evidence Base* (pp 7–23). Abingdon: Routledge.

Woodcock, A (2020) Majority Concerned About 'Heavy Handed' Policing of Lockdown Restrictions, Finds Survey. *Independent*, 4 September. [online] Available at: www.independ ent.co.uk/news/uk/politics/lockdown-restrictions-police-civil-liberties-poll-coronavirus-a9703886.html (accessed 12 June 2022).

World Health Organization Europe (WHO Europe) (2021) Violence and Injuries. [online] Available at: www.euro.who.int/en/health-topics/disease-prevention/violence-and-injuries/violence-and-injuries (accessed 12 June 2022).

INDEX